D0065477

PRAISE FOR *THE EDGE*

"Michael Useem extracts an array of *compelling* lessons from the tangible experiences of ten executives who learned to lead in a new era without letting go of what had worked for them before. *The Edge* provides *the* roadmap for drawing on the past while mastering the future."
> —Ram Charan, author of *Execution* and
> *Rethinking Competitive Advantage*

"Michael Useem stands as one of our seminal leadership observers. Generations of students and executives have been shaped into better leaders through his teaching. He is one of those rare professors who blends academic rigor with practical guidance and who has a gift for bringing ideas to life with vivid analogies from history and adventure. His accumulated years of perspective make him one of the wise men among us."
> —Jim Collins, author of *Good to Great*, *How the Mighty Fall*, and
> *Turning the Flywheel*

"For most CEOs today, one of the most important questions they must answer is how to maintain a competitive edge in turbulent waters. Drawing upon the experiences and lessons of ten major CEOs, Michael Useem once again delivers the goods—fast paced, no-nonsense, penetrating views. One of the nation's best authorities on leadership, Useem is a man with an edge all his own."
> —David Gergen, cofounding director, Center for Public Leadership,
> Harvard Kennedy School of Government

"Wharton's Michael Useem draws on the close-in experience of ten CEOs to help us all understand not only what is still true for leading an enterprise but also what is new as customer markets and security measures transform around us. *The Edge* offers the essential guide for leading in an ever-changing and more uncertain world."
> —Rob Katz, CEO, Vail Resorts, Inc.

"Developing the skills required to grapple with ever-escalating demands—whilst simultaneously doubling down on the traditional but still crucial skills of strategic vision and operational excellence—requires going to the very edge of modern practice. In this engaging and eminently practical book, Mike Useem takes us into the intimate stories of an extraordinarily diverse group of business leaders. Moving beyond platitudes and easy generalization, *The Edge* shows us what post-pandemic leadership looks like on the ground for leaders everywhere."

> —Rebecca M. Henderson, university professor, Harvard Business School, and author of *Reimagining Capitalism in a World on Fire*

"*The Edge* needs to be read by global leaders and those who aspire to be global leaders. The themes that bind these ten individuals together of over-communication, over-collaboration, and over-commitment to employees, customers, partners, and the underserved are the keys to future enlightened world economic success."

> —Stephen K. Klasko, president & CEO, Thomas Jefferson University and Jefferson Health, and distinguished fellow, World Economic Forum

"In a vivid look at how CEOs have led their enterprises through thick and thin, *The Edge* presents actionable guidance on how to lead with both enduring principles *and* emerging precepts, including a learning tour, a flywheel for growth, and a partner at the top. For becoming a complete leader in the years ahead, this is the book to absorb."

> —Indra Nooyi, former chair and chief executive of PepsiCo, Inc., and director of Amazon and the International Cricket Council

"Michael Useem's *The Edge* offers gripping accounts of how company executives lead their firms through challenging times, updating the best leadership principles of the past, and providing a tangible playbook for steering your enterprise into the future."

> —Ron Williams, former chief executive, Aetna, chief executive of RW2 Enterprises, and author of *Learning to Lead*

THE EDGE

THE EDGE

How Ten CEOs Learned to Lead—

And the Lessons for Us All

MICHAEL USEEM

PUBLICAFFAIRS

New York

PublicAffairs
Hachette Book Group
1290 Avenue of the Americas, New York, NY 10104
www.publicaffairsbooks.com
@Public_Affairs

Printed in the United States of America

First Edition: June 2021

Published by PublicAffairs, an imprint of Perseus Books, LLC, a subsidiary of Hachette Book Group, Inc. The PublicAffairs name and logo is a trademark of the Hachette Book Group.

The Hachette Speakers Bureau provides a wide range of authors for speaking events. To find out more, go to www.hachettespeakersbureau.com or call (866) 376-6591.

The publisher is not responsible for websites (or their content) that are not owned by the publisher.

Library of Congress Cataloging-in-Publication Data
Names: Useem, Michael, author.
Title: The edge : how ten CEOs learned to lead—and the lessons for us all / Michael Useem.
Description: First edition. | New York : PublicAffairs, 2021. | Includes bibliographical references and index.
Identifiers: LCCN 2020052501 | ISBN 9781541774117 (hardcover) | ISBN 9781541774100 (epub)
Subjects: LCSH: Leadership. | Chief executive officers. | Success in business. | Organizational effectiveness.
Classification: LCC HD57.7 .U829 2021 | DDC 658.4/092–dc23
LC record available at https://lccn.loc.gov/2020052501

ISBNs: 978-1-5417-7411-7 (hardcover), 978-1-5417-7410-0 (ebook)

LSC-W

Printing 1, 2021

CONTENTS

THE GREATEST CEO
OF THE CENTURY

Just Not This One

The oracle was about to speak. The room quieted as the assembled CEOs, arrayed classroom-style, leaned forward in their seats, not wanting to miss a word. I did the same, even though I was an instructor. This was at the CEO Academy, which had invited Jack Welch, the legend who transformed General Electric, to speak at its annual "war-room" training ground for people newly appointed to their company's top job. Welch had just published his memoir, *Jack: Straight from the Gut*, and had been named by *Fortune* magazine as the "Manager of the Century"—the twentieth century, that is.[1]

Welch rewarded our attention by saying that he had only a single piece of guidance to share. No, it wasn't the word *plastics*, Mr. McGuire's advice to Dustin Hoffman's character in *The Graduate*. It was TSR, total shareholder return. Yet it was an equally memorable suggestion, capturing the mindset that dominated both executive suites and business school teaching at the time, my own school included. Knowing how to increase TSR was the edge every business leader had to have.

Even more striking, however, was the line that formed for the book signing, the first and only time I have ever witnessed chief executives waiting in line for anything. Whatever Welch brought to the corner office, it seemed they all wanted a part of it. The era of the late 1990s through the early 2000s was one of American triumphalism in business as well as international politics. I keenly remember a Davos reception at the World Economic Forum where

Intel CEO Andy Grove and Microsoft CEO Bill Gates strolled in private conversation, cutting through the crowd like prophets parting the waters.

Jack Welch's focus on creating shareholder value had become the coin of the realm, and his leadership at GE over two decades seemed to prove that the currency was solid. In pronouncing Welch the premier manager of his era, *Fortune* highlighted his multiplying of General Electric's "value beyond anyone's expectations," from a market cap of $14 billion when he took charge in 1981, to $410 billion when he stepped down in 2001. In growing GE's worth some thirtyfold, he had made the enterprise the second-most-valuable firm on Earth and at times even the first. As *the* model for judging and developing leadership, TSR had become gospel not only at GE's famed leadership center above the Hudson River in Crotonville, New York, but at universities around the world.[2]

But then, the deluge.

In 2001, Enron and WorldCom went bankrupt, a collapse that brought a twelve-year prison sentence for Enron CEO Jeffrey Skilling, and a thirteen-year sentence for WorldCom CEO Bernard Ebbers. In 2002, only a few short months after Tyco International's CEO, Dennis Kozlowski, was cited by *Business Week* as one of the "Top 25 Managers of the Year," Tyco imploded as well. The company had built a market value of $114 billion, the magazine had explained, exceeding Ford, General Motors, and DaimlerChrysler combined, "thanks to the relentless deal-making and lean operating style" of Kozlowski. The Tyco chief said at the time that he wanted to be remembered as a "combination of what Jack Welch put together at GE and Warren Buffett's practical ideas on how you go about creating return for shareholders."[3]

Kozlowski, however, would go on to serve six years in a New York penitentiary for his criminal actions at the company. The later failures of American International Group, Lehman Brothers, and Merrill Lynch that brought on the global financial crisis of 2008–2009 added further doubt about the prevailing model of leadership. Slavishly pursuing total shareholder return, CEOs had led these companies into taking unwarranted risks and breaking the rules with abandon, cratering not just their own businesses but the world economy as well.

But the damage caused by leadership misdirection did not end there. Thousands of homeowners drowned in debt and lost their houses during the financial crisis. Meanwhile, many of the executives who had brought on the catastrophe, and who then embraced the federal bailout when it saved their skins, complained loudly about regulations that limited their bonuses. One banker demanded a pay package from the Troubled Asset Relief Program that exceeded the combined compensation of all the executives at General Motors, then threatened to decamp to China if the government did not approve (neither happened).

Such moments of wretched excess made it easy to decry the hubris and greed of individual leaders, but I remember a moment at another World Economic Forum, when I was part of a group of business professors and others raking over the calamity for its root cause. Was it the mortgage companies that loaned too much to unqualified borrowers, or the commercial banks that resold the loans, or the insurance companies that guaranteed the loans, or the financial deregulators who permitted the loans?

The atmosphere became uncomfortable when a colleague from another business school, in a tremulous voice, pointed to our own culpability in promoting the primacy of the TSR metric for corporate leadership. Later wrongdoings by those running Volkswagen, Wells Fargo, and Boeing would underscore the point and make clear that it was time for a major shift in what we thought and what we taught. The edge was changing.[4]

Over time, it would become apparent to me that the defining qualities of business leadership in the 1990s would not be the same as the 2000s, that the 2010s would be different still, and that they are certain to evolve even more during the 2020s, especially in the aftermath of the coronavirus pandemic.

Jack Welch's top-down drive for shareholder value had worked well at the end of the twentieth century, but as markets and mindsets morphed in subsequent decades, corporate growth had come to depend less on TSR and more on orchestrating meaningful work. Employees asked if their contributions would improve the lives of customers and communities, not just fatten investors' portfolios. Both shoppers and staffers demanded safe workplaces with sustainable practices and public purposefulness. TSR may have been the metric for meeting owner expectations in the 1980s and 1990s, but its dominance was no longer acceptable to a rising generation of stakeholders who were more diverse, more socially conscious, and more outspoken.

Another shift necessary for the new era was in the training of future executives and entrepreneurs. At Wharton, where I teach, it took one hundred years for leadership to finally join the required-course pantheon of accounting, finance, marketing, operations, and strategy. And when it did, we needed more than just a new offering; we needed new methods to move our leadership theories into management conduct. To get where I needed to go, I needed to think outside the classroom.

One day I loaded students onto a bus for a two-and-a-half-hour drive to the town of Gettysburg, Pennsylvania, where the Union and Confederate armies clashed on July 1–3, 1863, in what proved to be a turning point in the American Civil War. Our purpose was to learn from the historic events on the battlefield, and during our first, early-morning stop, our guide focused us on the failure of a Southern general, Richard S. Ewell, to capture a ridge southeast of the town. Ewell had been promoted to the command of a twenty-one-thousand-soldier army corps just two months earlier, after his superior officer, Thomas "Stonewall" Jackson, had been killed by friendly fire at the battle of Chancellorsville, Virginia.[5]

Though revered in the Confederate Army for his strategic thinking and decision-making, Jackson ultimately came up short by not providing personal guidance to those reporting to him, one of whom would someday replace him. When Richard Ewell's leadership moment came at Gettysburg, he was underprepared for the responsibilities thrust upon him.[6]

On the afternoon of July 1, General Robert E. Lee had sent to General Ewell by courier an order to attack and occupy a ridge southeast of Gettysburg "if practicable." Ewell decided it was not practicable, and his unforced decision allowed the Union Army to form what would prove to be an impregnable defensive line throughout the three-day engagement, culminating in the Confederate Army's defeat after Pickett's charge, a failed infantry assault, on the afternoon of July 3.

Historians have been debating Ewell's decision ever since, and some believe that it might have been possible for Ewell's corps to seize that ridge, an aggressive but feasible action that Stonewall Jackson himself might well have taken. We will never know for sure, but it appears that Ewell's failure to take the high ground that day may have proven a fatal turning point in the Confederate invasion of the North. "While some of the most fateful seconds in American history ticked past," offers one historian, "he waited," allowing the Union Army to entrench on the ridge from which it could not be dislodged over the three days of battle.[7]

Ewell's apparent timidity tangibly reminds us of just how important mentoring can be for developing your successors. Jackson's earlier failure to engage his subordinates in his strategic thinking and decision-making predictably led to an overcautious replacement when the battlefield called for a bolder replacement. It is also true that Lee himself may have erred in not appreciating that Richard Ewell was no Stonewall Jackson.

Wharton now offers optional professional leadership coaching to all its two thousand MBA students, a major expense since many students do want it. Through our McNulty Leadership Program, where I serve as faculty director, we provide personal guidance and development for all takers, and having stood where a battle was lost by an ill-prepared army commander, I have never doubted the value of a coaching program for everyone.

During our trip to Gettysburg that day, we also stood where Union colonel Joshua Lawrence Chamberlain defended his battle line on a hill against an overwhelming assault; where Confederate general George Pickett launched his ill-fated infantry charge; and where President Abraham Lincoln delivered his history-defining address at Gettysburg. At each location we focused on leadership lessons from more than 150 years ago: the importance of determination at the first stop, the importance of purpose at the second, and the authority of words at the third. I had stressed all of these concepts in our classroom in Philadelphia, but here they became more memorable and more tangible, and thus more actionable and more applicable.

I have now walked the Gettysburg battleground with groups of students and managers well more than a hundred times, and it has never failed to vividly transform academic models into practical principles. Over the years, Wharton's leadership program has expanded this learning model into dozens of other learning venues where we can see and test our leadership concepts, from Antarctica and Patagonia to the New York City Fire Department to the Marine Corps Officer Candidates School.[8]

Richard Haass, president of the Council on Foreign Relations, has argued that when it comes to pragmatic engagement with globalism and its dysfunctions, academic theories are "too abstract and too far removed from what is happening to be of value to most of us." In the case of leadership, though, we have found that university theories and research actually are of value—but that we also need to take aspirants and practitioners well beyond them to appreciate what managers and executives require to confront and lead in today's new reality.[9]

WHERE'S THE EDGE?

These experiences have convinced me that the best way to learn about and absorb the leadership essential for the years ahead is to observe leadership's changing nature close up, to see what executives are actually doing. I thus examine in this book the emerging leadership styles of a number of executives to better appreciate what gives them the edge that outsiders, aspirants, and instructors may still not appreciate or see.

How should the higher circles and their decisions be better judged, beyond their firms' market value, at a time of rising concerns about black lives, #MeToo, extreme poverty, growing inequity, a killer pandemic, and climate change? In other words, by what millions of people want, not just what investors demand?

From my time with the executives profiled here, ten fresh leadership principles have emerged that should be seen as essential for the years ahead—alongside a time-honored repertoire from the past. This is the leadership edge, that place or point or period where your past skills are still serving you, but you need to bring new skills on line as well. It can feel like a cliff edge because your comfort zone, the solid ground you navigated to get you where you are, is behind you. What lies beyond the edge is the opposite, an unfamiliar landscape barely coming into focus. Your task is now to acquire the skills you will need in this new territory before your career or your enterprise falters as a result of your personal limitations. This is the particularly hard part: leaping across the breach with the skills you have while also mastering the new capabilities required for landing and pioneering on the other side. Thus, what's required is a mixture of traditional capacities, fresh capabilities, and a learning bridge for combining the two.

I've hardly been alone in my search for a more encompassing set of skills and for a method of acquiring them. Rosabeth Moss Kanter of Harvard Business School has long advocated "advanced leadership," the skills required for confronting and doing something about daunting social and economic challenges that hold back national progress. Her colleague Rebecca Henderson has made the case for an even broader skill set that can build a more sustainable capitalism by rebalancing the power of the market with democratic, accountable government and a strong civil sector. David Rubenstein, co-executive chair of a private equity firm, The Carlyle Group, interviewed a host of leaders from business and

other walks of life, including Jeff Bezos of Amazon, Tim Cook of
Apple, and Indra Nooyi, formerly of PepsiCo, to identify a dozen
enduring or emerging capacities—including humility, integrity,
and persistence—all of which are learnable, even in midlife.[10]

And if those capacities, both established and evolving, have
come to define leadership at its best now, they've been vividly
thrust into the limelight by 2020's coronavirus outbreak, in which
public leadership has been seen at both its worst and its best. The
US president and his lieutenants dithered and denied, allowing
the virulent microbes to establish stubborn beachheads in all fifty
states—hardly a paragon of thinking strategically and acting decisively. They also failed to anticipate or address the heightened
demand for protective equipment and virus testing. State governors and city mayors, by contrast, preemptively instituted their
own safety measures, imposing quarantines, amassing ventilators,
and encouraging mail-in voting. The "federal government did not
take this seriously early enough," stated the governor of Michigan,
Gretchen Whitmer. "Whether you're a Democrat or a Republican
governor, we're who people are looking to at a time when there's
not been a lot of clarity or honest dialogue about the seriousness of
the situation."[11]

Company executives stepped forward too. Amazon stocked
fewer children's toys and consumer electronics to make way for
medical supplies and household essentials; American Express
waived late fees for its personal and business cardholders; Marri-
ott gave lodging to health providers; and Uber offered ten million
free rides and food deliveries to first responders. Other companies,
however, fell short, firing staff who complained about compromised protection, exploiting federal funding intended instead for
small firms, and reopening before local authorities permitted it. In
open defiance of California officials, for instance, Tesla's chief executive, Elon Musk, restarted his California assembly plant while
the state was still locked down, daring officials to arrest him or halt
production.[12]

At the same time, most companies scaled back their operations as customer demand plummeted and security measures prevailed. OpenTable reported that the number of restaurant visits in Washington, DC, cratered by three-quarters from a year earlier. Those especially ravaged, from cruise ship companies and global airlines to Broadway productions and sports teams, shuttered operations, mothballing ships, airplanes, arenas, and theaters, and furloughing millions. Amtrak ridership dropped by more than 90 percent nationwide, and its high-speed Boston-to-Washington service fell by 99 percent. The New Hampshire chapter of the Appalachian Mountain Club, which manages backcountry lodges across the state's peaks, shut nearly everything.[13]

As companies responded to the calamity, fresh leadership directives came to the fore. Consider the chief executive of PriceSmart, a Costco-like chain of forty-five warehouse "clubs" with more than nine thousand employees and three million members across the Caribbean and Latin America. Sherry S. Bahrambeygui had not come to her summit through a traditional path. She had served as stockbroker, investment manager, and litigator for years before taking the company helm in early 2019. "I had zero background" for a retail chain, she confessed, but PriceSmart's financial performance, besting the Standard and Poor's 500 (S&P 500) in her first year, smoothed her arrival.[14]

The company's disclosed risks during Bahrambeygui's first year—work stoppages, political instability, liability claims—seemed predictable, modest, and without a hint of the disaster coming. Then, just a year in, came the company's greatest calamity and the largest leadership challenge of Bahrambeygui's career, one that would require management actions she had never entertained before.

As the coronavirus wreaked havoc in China and then Europe, Bahrambeygui foresaw an "existential moment" coming to the Americas. She shifted into high gear, moving offline work online, arranging laptops for those sheltering at home, and convening a task force that met every morning, seven days a week, with Easter

Sunday the only exception. She asked executives to predesignate replacements, should they be felled by the virus. Personally directing a war room focused on employee safety gave her the leadership credibility, she reported, and managing the crisis engendered a uniting purpose that shareholder value could not.

The stunning effects of the 2020 pandemic thus radically reinforced what's always been requisite for business leadership—such as thinking strategically and acting decisively—but also further called for what's new—such as putting social value over shareholder return. Company responses to COVID-19, for better or worse, have served as a microcosm for company leadership. With the healthy or deadly consequences of company decisions made far sharper during the coronavirus havoc, we can see the best of the new leadership required now—and the worst of leadership that falls short.

If you are a company manager or executive, you have all the more reason now to seek mastery of the entire skill set. If you are a customer, worker, supplier, stockholder, or just a spectator, you have all the more interest in seeing company leaders embrace these skills. In the absence of a silver bullet or pharmacological fix, whether for growing an enterprise or surviving the coronavirus, becoming a complete leader demands a template broader than the past's to meet the challenges of the second quarter of this century.

CHAPTER 1

FINDING YOUR EDGE

Leaders Still Require What They've Always Needed,
but Now Also What's New at the Edge

"Being big does not give you the right to live forever."

Leading a company is a hot seat, whatever the era, and few days come easily to those who occupy that chair. For many, the duties are weighty, the decisions thorny, the demands incessant. And they come with personal risks and recriminations when things go wrong. You are always on the line, especially today, when your decisions can make *the* difference between a firm's prosperity and its poverty. "The bosses always worked in a frying pan," offers a former Disney and Comcast executive, and "now they work in an inferno." Executing well when so much is at stake has thus become one of the great callings of our times.[1]

Working directly with company leaders in a range of industries and countries, I had earlier identified fifteen capacities that are universally expected of company leaders—regardless of time, place, or product. Like mission-critical checkpoints for pilots before takeoff or for physicians before surgery, these capacities include such fundamentals as thinking strategically, communicating persuasively, and acting decisively. Ignoring any one of these foundational abilities can prove disastrous.[2]

But you may have come to management in an earlier era, one without the coronavirus pandemic; without protections against harassment; without protest movements for diversity, inclusion, and Black Lives Matter; without the popular drumbeat for greater investment in community prosperity and less spending on executive perquisites; and without company headlights on climate change and extreme inequality. These and other disruptions are signaling an entirely new era for enterprise leadership.

In addition, powerful institutional investors of publicly traded companies have become far more demanding of their leaders. We might look with nostalgia to the "old days," circa 1950, when individual and family holders owned most of America's biggest companies and simply collected their dividends, rarely challenging those running their firms. Small investors, however, have been replaced by BlackRock, Fidelity, State Street, and Vanguard, institutions with trillions of dollars under management and index funds at their core. For perspective on just how much economic power has been concentrated in such firms, consider that the $5 trillion-plus at each of two largest firms exceeds the GDP of almost all the world's economies.

Exercising their power through ratings, proxies, and media campaigns, professional investors have pressed executives and directors to junk their poison pills, pay with stock options, create "lead directors," and make boards less ceremonial and more consequential. The age of investor capitalism—in which institutional owners calling the shots supplant senior managers exercising complete control—has triumphed.[3]

Yet if institutional investors stop there, they will have provoked a revolution without framing a constitution, overthrown the old order but left the new one rudderless. Thankfully, professional owners in recent years have allied with company directors to finish the job, empowering the latter with a roadmap for coleading their enterprise. Yes, genuine leadership, including a working partnership with the chief executive for setting strategy, building capability, and preventing catastrophe. Boards are becoming more of a high-performance squad, less an assortment of disparate individuals.[4]

Research confirms that boards now depress company value when their directors are not steeped in business leadership. One university study, focused on directors of Fortune 500 companies, asked what happens when several directors hold significant owner-ship stakes in a firm but lack experience in leading a big enterprise. As the number of such "SOLE" directors—those with significant ownership but low expertise—increased on a board, it found, company value decreased. Investors played a role in this, the study also discovered: when SOLE directors stepped down from a board, shareholders drove up the company's share price, judging the firm to be undervalued because those directors had provided less leadership for the company.[5]

Another study of publicly held US firms examined stock prices after the unexpected deaths of nonexecutive directors. Investigators found that when directors had served between seven and eighteen years—enough time to learn the business but not so much that they resisted change—their unexpected death in office led to a share price decline, and for good reason. When companies have more directors in that optimal seven-to-eighteen-year range, they more tightly link their executives' pay to the company's performance, thereby driving better financial results. "Director leadership," to give this historic shift its own term, had risen on the back of investor capitalism's earlier triumph. Debates over investor authority have now been replaced by questions of director strategy.[6]

"WE HAD OUR WORK CUT OUT FOR US"

The demands from such outside forces for expanded company leadership capacities converged in 2018 on America's largest supermarket chain, Kroger Co., headquartered in Cincinnati, Ohio, and selling through more than 2,700 store across thirty-five states. Despite its heft, chief executive Rodney McMullen had been struggling since 2014 to lead the company through a period made difficult by Amazon's move into groceries, by Walmart's move into online sales, and by supermarket delivery becoming increasingly digital. Same-store revenue had flatlined in the industry while internet-driven revenue had been growing annually by some 40 percent.[7]

McMullen's predecessor had hesitated. "Most of us, when we say the digital world, automatically conclude that e-commerce is where everything is going," then-chief executive David Dillon had told investors in 2013, but "I don't draw that same conclusion." New CEO McMullen, however, would draw that same conclusion.[8]

As an instructive warning from shareholders about the unrealized potential of e-commerce, in the wake of Amazon's 2017 acquisition of Whole Foods, investors pushed down Kroger's share price by 15 percent during a single trading day. Another warning sign came from customers: after years of annual growth, Kroger's same-store sales were starting to decline, and the company was feeling the heat from below as well. The discounter Grocery Outlet Holding Corporation had gone public in 2019 with a plan to expand its shelves by 10 percent a year.

Amid these fateful changes, McMullen's experience-based mastery of a world that was fading into history proved a potential millstone. He had risen through the ranks from bagging groceries during his college days to chief financial officer and then CEO. "You are in Cincinnati," warned an institutional holder skeptical of the headquarters' culture, and "you are a conservative bunch of people." The investor questioned whether executives could adopt the "entrepreneurial bent" now required. Still seeking to stimulate store sales when others were already stoking delivery services, Kroger's managers had initially proven cautious. Managers quarreled over whether to accept online payments by Apple Pay or PayPal. In a meeting with a technology provider, the provider stalked out in protest.

Though McMullen was buoyed by same-store growth in his first years as chief executive, it did not last, and he later acknowledged a contributing factor. Under his direction, Kroger had been slow to invest online. "There was no doubt that we were behind," he confessed, and now they had "to get our butts in gear." He sought to reassure shareholders that his investments in everything from new product categories, including apparel, to new operations, including warehouse automation and home delivery, would pay off. "You have to start somewhere, and you have to learn" the additional leadership skills that were now required, he said. He found some traction, turning the firm modestly around from declining sales to a 2 percent uptick in 2019, though still hoped for more. "We had our work cut out for us," he declared, and rethinking his own leadership would be step one.[9]

HOW EXECUTIVES MASTERED
THE NEW WORLD OF LEADERSHIP

Executive coach Marshall Goldsmith captured the imperative of surmounting these new frontiers with the phrase "what got you here won't get you there," also the memorable title of one of his books. Though focused on shedding annoying habits that get in the way of rising responsibility, such as berating associates or withholding information for personal gain, the phrase is also central to our main point here. The factors that led others to select you to manage a team, an office, or even an enterprise, are going to change as markets and methods evolve, pushing you to the edge, and making it vital to continually consider the additional leadership capacities required now. The best capacities of an earlier time thus remain informative but also incomplete for the challenges we face ahead.[10]

Through chronicles of leaders' pathways in real time—drawn from my experience in observing and interviewing them—we will see how they learned to lead in the new ways without abandoning the tried and true. A starting exemplar is John Chambers, who for twenty years was chief executive of Cisco Systems, one of America's largest technology companies.

Chambers had earlier worked for IBM Corporation and Wang Laboratories, where leadership at both fell behind when the company's markets morphed, resulting in deep losses at IBM and the complete ruin of Wang. Personally seared by these leaders' failures to embrace what was becoming new at that time—mini-computers and distributed computing—Chambers reported, in his subsequent years at Cisco, that he conscientiously sought to grasp what was new while not giving up what was still true. Among the former, he recalled, he came to appreciate that in fast-moving industries like high technology, one must preemptively disrupt oneself from time to time to forestall disruption by others. Among the latter, he still followed the enduring principle of remaining tranquil during a crisis in order to orchestrate a disciplined comeback from it. As a result, "my management style evolved at each of the stages," said Chambers, "and I had to reinvent myself at each one."[11]

RISING CORPORATE MORTALITY

In times past, some incumbent organizations had remarkable staying power. Nokia, the Finland-based telecommunications company, was founded in 1865; Brown Brothers Harriman, an American private bank, dates its ancestry to 1818; Germany's Merck, a pharmaceutical and chemical company, goes back to 1668; and Japan's Sumitomo Group traces its origins to 1615. Even Standard Oil, founded in 1870, is still alive one hundred fifty years later through its many offspring, including Exxon Mobile, Chevron, and Marathon. Most companies will fail to outlast a typical human lifespan, but some have stayed on top for decades and a few for centuries. They are, alas, increasingly the exceptions.

The rule of military promotion and college tenure—"up or out"—and business watchwords such as *churn* and *creative destruction* instead rule the day, as indicated by the thirty blue-chip companies the Dow Jones Industrial Average comprises. With General Electric's removal from the index in 2018, a precipitous fall from grace for a company that had stood as America's most valued fewer than two decades earlier, none of the index's original cast remained on its roster.

Or consider the ranks of the Standard and Poor's 500, a roster of the largest publicly traded firms in the US that serves as a benchmark for long-term index investing. Together, the five hundred firms account for about 80 percent of the worth of all publicly traded equities in the US, a total value of more than $25 trillion at the beginning of 2020. Drawing on a seven-year rolling average of company lifespans, the average longevity of companies on the S&P 500 dropped from more than sixty years in the early 1960s to fewer than twenty-five or even twenty years during the past decade. If the current churn continues, and is likely exacerbated by the COVID-19 pandemic in 2020–2021, about half of the S&P 500 on the roster now will disappear within the coming decade.[12]

It should be cautioned that a fraction of the declining survivability metrics is a product of mergers, acquisitions, public listings, privatizations, and evolving criteria for inclusion on the lists. Those considerations aside, however, the long-term trend nonetheless points unequivocally toward shorter company preeminence at the top. Of the Fortune 500 firms in 1955, only sixty still remained in 2017. To make those failure rates more tangible, one analyst created three company subsets, each set off by its inclusion on the Fortune 500 in 1955, in 2017, or in both, displayed in Figure 1.1.[13]

FIGURE 1.1. Companies on the Fortune 500 in 1955 and/or 2017

1955 but not 2017	*2017 but not* 1955	*1955 and* 2017
American Motors	Amazon	Boeing
Brown Shoe	Facebook	Campbell Soup
Studebaker	eBay	Colgate-Palmolive
Collins Radio	Home Depot	Deere
Detroit Steel	Microsoft	General Motors
Zenith Electronics	Google	IBM
National Sugar	Netflix	Kellogg
Refining	Office Depot	Procter & Gamble
	Target	Whirlpool

Source: Perry, 2017.

Here's another way to slice the same data: nine out of ten denizens on the Fortune 500 in 1955 had merged, contracted, or closed by 2017. Projecting this rate into the future, 90 percent of the companies on the current Fortune 500 will not be there in 2077—unless of course their leaders can avert their likely exits. As summed up by an executive at Johnson & Johnson, a fixture of the Fortune 500, "Being big does not give you the right to live forever."

The S&P and Fortune 500's rising turnover in recent years points to the fateful fact that those who run large enterprises find it increasingly more hazardous to do so. And at the heart of these leaders' chances to nonetheless survive will be their ability to identify and embrace the essential leadership capabilities for confronting the emerging moments of truth and sustaining growth through both the good and hard times ahead.[14]

Even more startling than firms' shortened lifespans at the top are self-reported data about executive obsolescence. Three researchers surveyed more than 7,000 executives of medium and large companies in 145 countries in 2018, asking them what fraction of their personal skills became outdated each year. The executives reported that their own obsolescence had risen to 20 percent annually, twice the rate of loss a decade earlier. The inescapable conclusion: a fifth of what you knew last year is no longer relevant this year.[15]

While self-disruption has become more important, though, strategic thinking has remained no less important. In a dogged quest for immortality, some companies have completely reinvented themselves. Wipro, an India-based information technology enterprise with more than 160,000 employees in 2020, began as a cooking-oil producer, and preserved its original name, "Western India Vegetable Products Limited," in its present-day acronym, even though the company no longer has anything to do with cooking oil. Finland's telecom giant Nokia, with 98,000 employees in 2020, began as a pulp maker; Nucor Corporation, America's largest steelmaker with more than 26,000 employees on its payroll in 2020, came from Nuclear Corporation of America Inc., which initially applied radiation to inspect steel products, not make them.

Whatever the successful reconfiguration, each situation required the firm's executives to adopt an additional set of leadership capacities without relinquishing their original template.

By 2020 even IBM, originally International Business Machines, was drawing only a fraction of its revenue from machines. Thomas J. Watson, who joined the company in 1914 and became president in 1915, bestowed its name. *International* was more aspirational, but *business machines* described the company's core products for years, which included clocks, tabulators, bombsights, typewriters, and, eventually, computers. The company prospered on that diet and so did most of Watson's successors, who hired workforces in the hundreds of thousands, but when a later CEO failed to staunch massive losses in the early 1990s, the board hired an outsider to engineer one of the largest turnarounds of the era, forcing a streamlined workforce to focus more on the market, and less on itself.[16]

Two IBM successors later, in 2012 Virginia Rometty, the incoming CEO, pressed still another redirection, this one out of software and hardware and into artificial intelligence, cloud computing, and data analytics. By 2018, she'd raised IBM's revenue from cloud computing and related services, for instance, from 15 percent of total revenue to 35 percent, selling off large parts of the company's hardware business and acquiring Red Hat, Inc., a provider of open-source software for the hybrid cloud market, for $34 billion.

Still, when Rometty stepped down from the corner office in 2020, she had not revived the company's overall fortunes. IBM's annual revenue had fallen from $81 billion in 2002 to $77 billion by 2019, and its market value from $220 billion to $120 billion. For shareholders, the company's financial performance had been woeful, dropping its share price by 25 percent while the S&P 500 index rose by more than 150 percent.

Yet, in my view, IBM's executive leadership had not stalled. Rometty appreciated that, while making mainframes and selling software was no longer enough, her earlier ways of directing the company would no longer suffice. To lead through the wrenching changes required, and to avoid the fate of now-defunct technology companies like Kodak and Wang, she needed to place huge bets on new arenas, and fast, a leadership capacity not always required of her predecessors. "I have trained my life to fly a 747," Rometty explained, and that was "way different than piloting a two-prop engine plane," her metaphor for the speed and agility now required at IBM. Or as a business partner, Apple chief executive Tim Cook, affirmed: "It's not the same IBM." And though Rometty had come up during the mainframe era, the company anointed as her successors Arvind Krishna, who had engineered IBM's acquisition of Red Hat, to serve as CEO, and James Whitehurst, who had run Red Hat, to serve as his number two.[17]

More generally, three-quarters of the CEOs responding to a 2019 survey of large companies reported that they were now looking for greater expertise on their executive team in digital transformation, artificial intelligence, and data science. They were self-critical as well, stressing that they needed to gain greater proficiencies in domains well beyond what had brought them to the apex. As Surya N. Mohapatra, a former chief executive of Quest Diagnostics, put it, "The next CEO, apart from having the qualities like integrity and high values, has to be a subject matter expert" in the new subjects.[18]

A prime example of this kind of transition occurred at Walt Disney Company in 2020. Its long-reigning CEO, Robert Iger, stepped down (one film producer called it "the King abdicates his throne") in favor of a less charismatic and more unexpected successor, Bob Chapek. Iger had been known for his hands-on insistence on perfection. But "comparing Mr. Chapek to Mr. Iger," suggested the New York Times, "may be missing the point." The successor would not be filling his predecessor's shoes so much as presiding over the far more complex enterprise that the company had become.[19]

Over Iger's tenure, Disney had created two streaming services, expanded from two cruise ships to seven, grown from two movie studios to eight, and increased theme-park attendance by

45 million. Given its far greater scale, Disney now called for a top executive who could lead that complexity on an entirely new level. Chapek was characterized by those familiar with his style as making his intent clear but then delegating its execution to his direct reports, defining unambiguous targets and holding his managers accountable. Iger and Chapek "may share the same first name," explained two reporters, "but there are few other similarities."[20]

The greatest leadership dissimilarity of all, however, hit with a vengeance just days after Chapek took the reins on February 25, 2020—in the historical moment that *New York Times* columnist Thomas Friedman described as marking a new divide between eras, "BC" and "AC," before the coronavirus and after the coronavirus. Much of Iger's business model depended on people in close proximity—think four thousand customers on his largest cruise ships and more than four hundred thousand visiting his parks every day but that also made for a perfect storm when the virus raced through. During his fifteen years as chief executive at Disney, Iger had grown the company from a market value of less than $50 billion to more than $275 billion. Now, in Chapek's very first quarter, his profits plunged by 91 percent.

With cruise ships anchored, theme parks shuttered, Broadway shows closed, movie theaters darkened, television ads canceled, and film productions halted, Chapek would have to lead the enterprise with a playbook he, his predecessor, or anyone else could never have imagined. Iger had presided over a "bulletproof business plan," in the apt characterization of one observer, but his successor would preside over just the opposite. The company faced "unrivaled earnings risk for the foreseeable future," warned an equity analyst. Chapek cut his own salary by half and furloughed one hundred thousand employees. "We're doing everything we can to mitigate the impact of the cash burn," he reported, a pledge no doubt inconceivable to his expansive predecessor.

Iger had led well in BC, and now Chapek would have to master the new moves required for leadership in AC, going from growth time to wartime, somehow bringing visitors back to the Magic Kingdom without spreading the virus through it.[21]

Updated leadership for a new era is just as essential for smaller companies, nonprofit firms, and government agencies as it is for the giants like IBM and Disney. Consider Ayla Göksel, the chief executive of the Mother Child Education Foundation, which operates in Turkey and the Middle East on women's empowerment and rural development. Though an experienced social service leader who'd reached more than a million beneficiaries during the past quarter century, she warned in 2019 that her existing leadership template was no longer sufficient: "What worked twenty-five years ago won't necessarily work today. We have to have the bandwidth to explore new areas," including program diversification and distance learning to reach the underserved, empower families, and advocate policies.[22]

Much the same was urged by the former top American military officer General Martin Dempsey, Chairman of the US Joint Chiefs of Staff from 2011 to 2015. "My instinct tells me," he observed, "that the twenty-first century will be a period where we will be asked to apply our military instrument decentralized" without at the same time losing our "ability to aggregate it when necessary." In other words, senior officers will need to master the additional leadership skills required for both disaggregating and then reaggregating the nation's military assets.[23]

College and university administrators are confronting their own moments of truth. With student enrollments languishing and public funding plunging in 2020, the *Chronicle of Higher Education* advised presidents, provosts, and deans to think of themselves as less like a "steward" of their venerable institutions and more as a "change maker" for a species endangered by spiraling operating costs, student indebtedness, and COVID-19. Incumbents and aspirants would need to preserve their rituals and assuage their alumni—the faculty senate and football tailgates will remain important—but also need to innovate like a start-up, tweet carefully, and teach remotely.[24]

HOW DO WE FIND OUT?

In a study of networks among business leaders in New York and London, I asked executives in both cities why they had, in many cases, agreed to serve on the governing boards of publicly traded companies in addition to their own companies'. Such service can be an enormous time-sink—one hundred hours or more annually for each board seat—and thus seemingly not in the narrowly defined self-interest of the executives' home companies, nor within the fiduciary role that the executives had pledged to them. Their answers were unexpected but informative. They had accepted service on additional company boards, they reported, because it was a better way to learn about company practices and executive leadership than any other single activity.[25]

The same point has become evident at the CEO Academy, which I help run. This annual program, with a heritage stretching back two decades, brings together forty to fifty CEOs and heirs apparent for a two-day intensive look at the practical decisions and pragmatic challenges that they face, with presentations ranging from "How Global Business Is Changing" to "How Should CEOs Think About the Tradeoff Between Short-Termism and Going Long?" We bring in a half dozen Wharton faculty to share their research-informed guidance on topics ranging from acquisitions to governance, but we also recruit a number of current or recently retired chief executives, which in past years have included Verizon's Ivan Seidenberg, DuPont's Ellen Kullman and Ed Breen, and ITT's Denise Ramos.[26]

Similarly, for the past eight years William Lauder, executive chair of Estée Lauder Companies, has offered our MBA students an elective course called Decision Making in the Leadership Chair. For each of his seven three-hour class sessions, he hosts the cream of the corner office, ranging from Ford Motor Company executive chair William Clay Ford Jr. to Rockefeller Foundation president Judith Rodin, *New York Times* publisher Arthur Sulzberger Jr., and Focus Brands (owner of Auntie Anne's, Cinnabon, and Jamba) chief operating officer Katrina Cole. The classroom comes to life with their tangible insider accounts of executives who have led major organizations, and the degree of student interest in that content has soared. With just forty-eight openings for the course and admission essays required, they filled the room during its first year, but by 2020, its eighth year, more than 280 of our MBA students applied for acceptance.

Academic research confirms that when it comes to conveying tacit knowledge and complex information, personal exchanges are better conduits than more formal channels. Informally conveyed information is more nuanced, more credible, and more trusted. For instance, a study of company subsidiaries in the US from twenty-seven foreign countries found that the subsidiaries drew more upon local immigrants in the US from their home countries for guidance than the rest of the population. This was especially true for companies that lacked prior experience in the US and were knowledge intensive, such as high-technology firms. A 1 percent increase in immigrants from a home country in a given state thus doubled the likelihood that a company from the home country would have opened a location in that state. If the number of immigrants in California from Korea doubled, for example, that doubled the chance that a Korean company would have set up shop in that state. Moreover, having more local immigrants near the new location improved the company's survival rate. Arguably, this is the result of the firm having better access to tacit local knowledge. And these findings held true for both consumer and industrial subsidiaries, ruling out a potential counterargument that the results may stem from local immigrants being drawn disproportionately to buying from firms headquartered in their home country.[27]

BROADENING THE CEO

These insights and my experience in working with students and managers in classrooms, battlefields, and a range of other leadership venues led me to ask nine company leaders to take a risk. Let me interview you in detail, I asked, and permit me to watch you in action. What new skills did you have to master to lead now—and what traditional skills do you still require from the past? I also arranged for discussions with their direct reports and even their company directors.

I had sought to include a diverse array of executives, and fortunately all those I first approached agreed to the request. I interviewed most repeatedly and observed many recurrently, and from that I sought to extract a set of emergent leadership principles for you to strengthen your own current and future capabilities. To add historical perspective, I also examined the leadership of a tenth individual, the commander of the Continental Army, George Washington.

I wanted to study all the leaders close up as they faced both exhilarating and trying times when their past skill sets still served them well but they also required new capabilities. None displayed the entire range of contemporary leadership callings, but taken together, the actions of the ten as a composite provide a pragmatic roadmap from which everybody can seek to craft their own future leadership.

I have worked to make the emergent principles both instructive and persuasive. *Instructive* meaning that the leadership principles are cognitively understood, and *persuasive* meaning that they are accepted in a way that can lastingly inform and shape one's behavior. Together, instructive and persuasive principles are not only appreciated for their value but also valued for their applicability. Here is a preview of how the ten leaders in this book exemplify leadership at the edge:[28]

- Confronting an economic meltdown that threatened Armageddon, Bill McNabb of Vanguard built a growth engine for a changed market.
- Tricia Griffith of Progressive used a strategy of inclusion to bring out the best from her workforce.

- Mark Turner unplugged from an always-on office to personally grow and understand what was transforming his industry—and then ramped-up WSFS Bank to take the lead in it and prepare his successor for it.
- William Lauder of the Estée Lauder Companies watched traditional sales channels wither, assessed his personal strengths, and recruited a partner to take the company into a radically changing marketplace.
- Denise Ramos broadened her expertise in finance to embrace all her company's functions in a newly constituted ITT Inc., enabling her to serve as a general manager of it and build a fresh identity for it.
- Invested in a promising technology company with an under-performing CEO, Bo Ilsoe of Nokia Growth Partners bet on a new leader whose more meticulous appraisal of the firm's assets and more disciplined execution of its operations allowed for better exploitation of its promising technology.
- Seeing his markets imploding, splitting, or consolidating, Ed Breen faced one crisis after another, but he confronted each with a fresh eye, triaging his firm in one case, dividing and recombining the enterprise in another, and confronting a viral threat in a third.
- Beset by a host of legal and product controversies at Johnson & Johnson, Alex Gorsky harnessed the magnetic power of corporate culture by modernizing the company's credo.
- Jeffrey Lurie, owner of the Philadelphia Eagles, mastered the field and won the Super Bowl by connecting the talent of his staff and players so that they actually worked as a team.
- Given command of the Continental Army, George Washington learned to master the art of command.

We will see in the experience of each leader the value of mastering the new, however complete their own leadership past. That value of drawing on prior tests but at the same time preparing for future trials has been instructively affirmed by America's forty-sixth president, Joseph R. Biden Jr. He had already served in the White House for eight years as vice president, where he had been widely engaged in the country's direction under President Barack Obama, and that experience arguably could have more than prepared him for his own presidential leadership ahead. But he concluded otherwise. "What do you say," asked a television news anchor, "to those who wonder if you're trying to create a third Obama term?" Biden responded: "This is not a third Obama term. We face a totally different world than we faced in the Obama-Biden administration." As we will see in America's first president as well, in a different world a good mix of the true and the new is required from everybody seeking to lead through it.[29]

CHAPTER 2

BUILDING A GROWTH ENGINE WHEN THE CHIPS ARE DOWN

Vanguard Group CEO Bill McNabb
Accelerates His Firm's Flywheel for Expansion

"We realized our world was going to be very different."

The chief executive of Vanguard Group, one of the world's largest investment managers, once arranged for the delivery of a massive flywheel to one of the world's most discerning observers of company leadership, Jim Collins. It was a highly unusual gift, sent by CEO Bill McNabb in gratitude for Collins's personally rendered advice with a flywheel metaphor at its core. The shipper charged more than the original manufacturer.

A flywheel's mechanical value is in its storage of energy, which is the square—the multiplication of a number by itself—of its physical weight and rate of rotation. The greater the weight and the faster the spin, the greater the compounding energy driving the attached device, whether in a farm tractor, a steam engine, or an investment company.

Finding your own flywheel is one of the new callings of company leaders. What spinning device can sustain your momentum, each part reinforcing the next, to instill an unstoppable motion that keeps you moving through both market highs and coronavirus lows? In reviewing McNabb's ten years at the helm of Vanguard, we'll see the adoption, refinement, and acceleration of a flywheel that powered the firm in ways that McNabb's predecessors never imagined. And he had to devise it in the wake of a financial crisis, at a time when what had worked in the past was no longer adequate.

VANGUARD GROUP'S BILL MCNABB

Vanguard Group, created in 1975 by John C. "Jack" Bogle, emerged with the historic rise of institutional investing. In 1950, wealthy individuals and families directly held most of the shares of publicly traded companies in the US, but five decades later, professionals in outsized investment firms had come to manage most. Individuals and families remained in the market, and a kind of investment democracy had triumphed, with stockholdings spreading to millions of middle earners. Yet the exercise of those widespread ownership rights had been increasingly delegated to trained investment managers, leaving it to the experts to decide which companies to buy, hold, or sell. Vanguard was at the center of the run-up, and by century's end it oversaw assets of nearly $600 billion.[1]

Bill McNabb had ridden that wave. Joining Vanguard in 1986— he had no idea what it did before a business school friend advised him to go to work for the company—he started as a "generalized product investment manager," a role for which he had no background or familiarity. But he prospered, and he came to lead multiple divisions and later served on Vanguard's senior team under both Jack Bogle and his successor, John J. "Jack" Brennan.

When Vanguard's board of directors picked McNabb to run the whole show in 2008, he knew he had his work cut out for him. But first he had to get over the shock.

McNabb's first reaction when Brennan called him in was disbelief. "Stop joking," McNabb insisted, "what's the real purpose for our meeting today?" When Brennan assured him that his succession to the top job was indeed the purpose of their conversation, McNabb felt a flutter of butterflies, but he reminded himself that the blunt-spoken Brennan would not have promoted him without having full confidence in him. Still, McNabb wondered, "What am I getting into here?"

McNabb's career progression to a top job in asset management was hardly typical. He had taught Latin to seventh- and eighth-graders and had served on the board of the Philadelphia Zoo, where "Tony the Rhinoceros," he reported, was "my guy, my spirit animal." (Once, at a company event, he added a temporary tattoo of Tony to his arm, neglecting to tell his wife that it would wash off.) Through it all, he had been a devotee of putting team over personal achievement since his college days. "Everything I know about teamwork," he recalled, he learned as a walk-on member of Dartmouth's rowing team, where his six-foot, five-inch frame proved a potent propellant, though only when delivered in total harmony with others.

McNabb and his wife and four children lived near Vanguard headquarters, outside Philadelphia, only several hours' drive from New York City but light years from its trading floors. Though he had worked in the city for three years with JPMorgan Chase after his MBA, he remained something of an outsider. "We don't consider ourselves part of Wall Street," McNabb said of his firm. "We're serving Main Street investors, helping people save for college or a first house."[2]

As McNabb took the helm, Vanguard faced a host of behemoth competitors, including BlackRock, Fidelity, and successful upstarts like E*Trade and iShares, plus challenges from cross-national investing, exchange-traded funds, and price-conscious customers. Vanguard already dominated low-cost index funds that invested in a given set of companies, like the Standard and Poor's 500 largest US publicly traded companies, but for holdings abroad, exchange-traded funds, and online trading, others were offering attractive alternatives that threatened to overtake Vanguard.

McNabb questioned whether he could keep up the momentum that his two preeminent predecessors had generated. Jack Bogle had taken the company from zero to $180 billion in assets, and Jack Brennan had grown it to $1.3 trillion, making Vanguard one of the world's largest investment management firms. Because of that expansion, Jim Norris, managing director of Vanguard's international operations, recalled, "it was easy to think that things can only go down from there." And since the "machine was working," many thought, "why fix it if it was not broken?" Even if a challenge was threatening to break it now, fixing it could be postponed by pride in the past.

Competitors were seeking to match Vanguard's offerings, institutional investing was spreading abroad, and the internet was cutting the costs of transactions. Only by growing in new ways could Vanguard be sustained. It was up to McNabb to define his way forward, and it would have to be a different way. He needed a leadership path that would be right for his moment, no matter what his predecessors had done in their moments.[3]

BECOMING CEO

This need to find a new way was presented to McNabb in dramatic fashion. He was named to the top job on August 3, 2008, and on September 15, Lehman Brothers failed. The next day, American International Group and Merrill Lynch tumbled as well. On September 29, the Dow Jones Industrial Average dropped 778 points, a one-day decline of 7 percent. In just two weeks, Vanguard investors would lose $170 billion. By the end of 2008, nationwide job losses totaled 2.6 million, the highest number in six decades, and the unemployment rate reached 7.2 percent before soaring further to 10 percent in 2009. Home prices dropped 18 percent. The federal government came to the rescue of commercial banks and automakers, but it provided no safety nets for millions of homeowners and small shareholders.

Lehman's failure, said McNabb, was "our Pearl Harbor," and it could have gotten worse. Vanguard has "never endured anything like the markets we've experienced this year," he told his equally shell-shocked lieutenants. "The credit markets are frozen, the global capital markets have fallen sharply, and the economic outlook is grim." Over the next six months, the Dow Jones dropped by more than half from its precrisis high, costing Vanguard's customers some $300 billion.[4]

For McNabb, it was an unhappy welcome to the edge, and the perils intensified as terrified investors headed for the exit. He and his deputies gathered in a war room twice a day to react, retain, and rebuild. There, McNabb applied an enduring leadership prerequisite: resilience under pressure. As described by his managing director for strategy and finance, Glenn Reed, McNabb was "totally composed when we did not know what was coming." He offered a "preternatural calmness" and "never wavered," making him a "perfect fit" at the firm for this moment.

McNabb and his top team soon concluded that their best strategy for client retention began with employee preservation. McNabb sent a reassuring message to all of Vanguard's "crew members" that he would impose no furloughs or layoffs, letting them shift their attention from protecting their own well-being to restoring their clients'. Preserving the ranks proved a contrarian move in the industry, and as a result, reported McNabb, he could not cut his other costs fast enough, slashing contract workers and slicing bonuses in half. But the personnel policies worked. Clients largely stuck with their accounts, and some even added more to their portfolios. It appeared that McNabb would bring Vanguard back from the brink.[5]

But the outward trend lines belied a newly troubling reality. When McNabb instigated a detailed analysis of where Vanguard's recovery was coming from, he was astonished that much of it actually stemmed from its newly introduced exchange-traded funds. ETFs are bundles of securities that can be actively traded on a stock exchange, akin to mutual funds except that they can be priced and swapped during the day rather than just at the end of the day, which was the case with Vanguard's traditional funds. Clients were now flocking to ETFs even though they had been much disparaged in their early days by Vanguard's founder and patron saint, Jack Bogle. ETF assets worldwide would triple from $700 billion in 2008 to $2.3 trillion over the next five years. They were becoming the *new* new thing for investment management, and they were now responsible for much of Vanguard's recovery.[6]

That insight, however, only threw into comparison otherwise dismal news: Vanguard's traditional investment funds, the core of its business, remained stagnant, and the company was badly lagging its key competitors in the ETF business. Barclays Bank, for instance, had been building an ETF portfolio since 2000, launching more than forty such funds, and in 2009 Vanguard archrival BlackRock acquired the business from Barclays for $13.5 billion, instantly giving it a commanding presence in the ETF market. Though Vanguard had been *the* pioneer in index funds, it was now a laggard in exchange-traded funds. They "changed our world," warned McNabb, and "we have to evolve" with it.

THE HEDGEHOG AND THE FLYWHEEL

As the economy slowly improved from the worst damage sustained in 2008 and 2009, McNabb returned to the still-unresolved engine-for-growth question: How would he stimulate Vanguard's expansion in this new era? One thing he knew was that whatever had driven his predecessors' success would not propel his own.

To find the engine that he would need, McNabb turned to Jim Collins, or at least to Collins's celebrated book *Good to Great: Why Some Companies Make the Leap ... And Others Don't*. First published in 2001, it has become one of the most influential guides to company leadership ever published. Collins's new leadership notions have become part of the business canon, including the concepts of "Level 5 leadership," "getting the right people on the bus," and "the hedgehog." McNabb was especially taken with the last.

That curiously named concept draws on a famous essay by philosopher Isaiah Berlin that explored the distinction between foxes, who know many things, and hedgehogs, who know only one.

Having studied in great detail companies that had risen from "good to great" over a decade, Collins found that those "who built the good-to-great companies were, to one degree or another, hedgehogs," while those "who led the comparison companies tended to be foxes, never gaining the clarifying advantage" of a narrow and distinctive focus. The foxes, he explained, were "scattered, diffused, and inconsistent." Refining his insight, Collins traced the hedgehogs' behavior to a combination of three mutually reinforcing factors. These leaders, he found, were riveted on what they were passionate about, what they did extremely well, and what fueled their company's engine.[7]

Since the three components circularly powered one another with increasing strength, Collins likened them to an industrial flywheel whose momentum can sustain an enterprise through thick and thin. Imagine "a massive metal disk mounted horizontally on an axle," Collins wrote, and "imagine that your task is to get the flywheel rotating on the axle as fast and long as possible. Pushing with great effort, you get the flywheel to inch forward, moving almost imperceptibly at first." You "keep pushing, and the flywheel begins to move a bit faster, and with continued great effort, you move it around a second rotation." And then, "at some point—breakthrough! The momentum of the thing kicks in in your favor, hurling the flywheel forward." Each further turn of the wheel "builds upon work done earlier, compounding your investment of effort. A thousand times faster, then ten thousand, then a hundred thousand. The heavy disk flies forward, with almost unstoppable momentum." That, thought McNabb, was exactly what Vanguard needed to accelerate its own momentum under his direction for long-term growth.[8]

McNabb and his senior team were also mindful of another Collins volume, *How the Mighty Fall*, which chronicled why some flourishing companies went from good enough to gone. Whatever the reasons for their decline, McNabb was on notice. Vanguard, too, could end up on a downslope unless its new CEO identified a new set of drivers geared to the post–financial crisis world.[9]

McNabb telephoned Jim Collins at his home office near Boulder, Colorado. "We realized our world was going to be very different,"

McNabb said, and he invited Collins to come and explain hedgehog and flywheel concepts to McNabb's top team at their headquarters near Philadelphia. When Collins demurred, McNabb
flipped the request, asking if Vanguard could bring its top team to
Colorado instead. If the mountain will not come to Mohammed,
then Mohammed must go to the mountain.

Collins assigned his students plenty of homework before coming, inviting detailed responses to a host of questions, including:

1. How is Vanguard's world changing?
2. What ignites your passion about Vanguard?
3. How clear are you on what Vanguard can—and cannot—do
    better than any organization in the world?
4. What is the primary driver of Vanguard's economic engine?
5. What percentage of the key seats on the Vanguard bus are
    filled with the right people?
6. What has Vanguard failed to do that you know must be
    done?
7. What are you most afraid of for Vanguard in the next five
    to ten years?

For three days in September 2009, just a year after Lehman's
failure, McNabb and his team worked with Collins to answer the
questions and to identify the key features at Vanguard that would,
in circular reinforcement, keep their company growing—and
which features would keep their hedgehog, the top team, pushing for growth faster and faster, accelerating its flywheel. Collins
also challenged the team to respond to an obvious but still-unasked
question: If Vanguard was as superior as they believed from the
firm's performance to date, why had all asset holders not yet come
to the company for management of their monies?

Collins pressed the Vanguard leaders to identify the five or six
most important drivers of performance, and then to connect them
in a circle so that the first enhanced the second, the second the

third, and so on around the circle. The last driver would strengthen the first, then the first the second again, and then around the circle once more to further propel each driver, making a kind of perpetual motion machine. While McNabb and his team worked nonstop to build it over their three days in Boulder, Jim Collins, an extreme rock climber, relaxed on the nearby cliffs.

Vanguard's first version of their new flywheel, displayed in Figure 2.1, arranged its reinforcing factors in a clockwise sequence, with each chevron propelling the next.

The initial drivers of the flywheel were the firm's undisputed strengths—low-cost mutual funds and long-term outperformance. Combined with high-quality service, the team concluded, Vanguard

FIGURE 2.1. Vanguard's Flywheel, 2009.

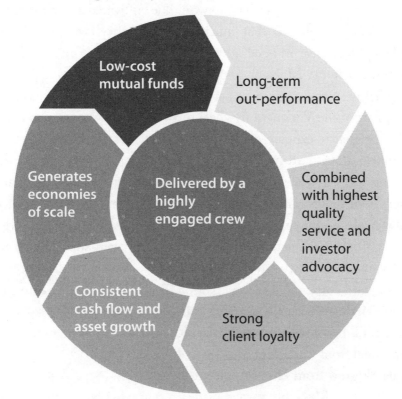

Source: Courtesy of William F. McNabb III.

could use its strengths to generate more client loyalty, which would lead to asset growth and economies of scale. With growth and scale, Vanguard could in turn further lower the cost of its funds, making it even easier for the firm to outperform its peers. And so the cycle would continue.

Vanguard placed its employees, the "crew," at the core of its strategy deliberately. McNabb believed that a highly engaged and collaborative workforce was essential for the flywheel's acceleration.

As an auxiliary roadmap, the Vanguard team identified ten actions that the crew would have to prioritize to keep the wheel spinning and the hedgehog pushing. The company would, for instance, have to more fully master exchange-traded funds, international expansion, and retirement savings. It also would have to ensure that employees saw the company as a preferred place to work, and that the next generation's leadership would be cultivated among them.

McNabb believed that much of the flywheel was already in place. More clear minded now about how the parts connected, on returning home McNabb and his team broadcast its components explicitly so that crew members could each deliberately accelerate the part of the Vanguard flywheel for which they were responsible.

Vanguard's expense ratio—its cost to clients for managing their money, a standard metric for the "economies of scale" driver on Vanguard's flywheel—declined over the next five years by a quarter, from 0.205 percent to 0.148 percent. "Client loyalty," another flywheel component, reached its highest level ever: annual fund redemptions as a fraction of assets under management dropped to 11 percent, just two-fifths of the industry average of 25 percent. Vanguard consequently drew half of all new cash coming into the entire industry over the next five years, and it even wrestled some of the ETF business away from BlackRock. The latter's market share declined from 47 percent in 2009 to 40 percent in 2013, while Vanguard's grew from 12 to 19 percent.

Even so, McNabb warned his team that what had carried them through the past four years would not necessarily get them through the next four. They returned to Collins's turf in 2013. There, Vanguard's inner circle reported to him that the components of the flywheel and their reinforcing actions were working, but now Collins pressed for greater clarity on which components and actions were most critical for sustaining company growth—and thus deserved greatest management attention. "You guys are off to a decent start," offered Collins in faint praise, pressing McNabb and his team to further flesh out their specific actions, including greater mastery of the ETF universe and stronger cultivation of the next generation of company leaders.

With even greater clarity on the priorities for the flywheel components and the specific contributions of each component, the company further accelerated its hold on the industry. Over the next several years, Vanguard upped its ETF market share from 20 to 24 percent; reduced its expense ratio from 14 to 12 basis points, and captured a stunning 92 percent of the net cash flow into the industry. It expanded its assets under management by 14 percent annually, for a total of $4 trillion by 2017, more than the GDP of most major economies, including those of Brazil, Russia, and Germany.

THE FLYWHEEL 2.0

Despite the unequivocal signs that McNabb's flywheel had driven his sought-after growth, he returned to Colorado yet again in 2017. Vanguard's market had morphed still more, and McNabb's leadership in it would thus have to continue to evolve. Ultra-low-cost providers chipped away from below, client expectations demanded ever more, and the company's success—doubling its assets over the past several years—challenged its further scalability.

This time, the guru in Boulder began not with congratulations but "condolences," hardly what McNabb had expected to hear. "You won," Collins explained, but that came with a new hazard: taking your eyes off the flywheel and the hedgehog and their own evolving requirements. McNabb and his leadership team had seemingly mastered the market of the past five years, but Collins wondered if they were still motivating the hedgehog at the center. Was each chevron of the flywheel optimal? And had they created the next generation of leadership the company would need?

Prior Vanguard CEO Jack Brennan had warned repeatedly about complacency, one of the deadliest of company sins, and Collins raised the same concern. He pressed the executive team to identify what they should stop doing that detracted from the new flywheel and its executors. "I think it's a really good start," he counseled, but you should still be looking at how to take yourself from "good to great." Some companies get there, but others die along the way.

With Collins's new questioning of Vanguard's client experience and company scalability, McNabb and his team revised their flywheel yet again. They concluded that the earlier focus on "low-cost mutual" funds should now shift to the "best-performing mutual funds and ETFs," and that "quality service and investor advocacy" should instead be directed at "trusted advice" and "world-class client experience." The updated, 2.0 version of the flywheel, McNabb concluded, should enable him and his lieutenants to even better drive the clockwise flow.

McNabb's analysis also led him to conclude, like so many contemporary enterprises, that though Vanguard's past growth had come largely from American customers, future growth would have to come from international clients. The managing director of Vanguard's nascent international operation, Jim Norris, who had attended both off-site meetings with Jim Collins, returned to his London office determined to identify how the flywheel could better support the firm's global ambitions. The company had built a vibrant business in Australia, with $35 billion in managed assets, but otherwise had achieved little global traction, with a scant $25 billion in assets elsewhere. Its global operations were, in Norris's word, still a "sidecar," a weak appendage to the firm without a strategy or flywheel of its own, while entering a period of global expansion in asset management that would more than double in the decade ahead.[10]

Drawing on the circular elements of the flywheel, Norris teased out what McNabb had sought from each of his executives. He gave special attention to the flywheel's center, a "highly engaged crew" and building a "talent factory" for the production of more qualified managers, on the premise that the international operation had sufficient cash but insufficient leadership. In the years ahead, Norris increased operations from five countries to twelve, the international workforce from 300 to 1,300, and assets under management from $65 billion to $382 billion. In 2017, after Beijing ended foreign-ownership restrictions on local asset managers, he added a China operation employing 20 people on the mainland by 2019. No longer a sidecar, the international division had become an integral part of the flywheel of the firm, and indicative of the operation's centrality to the firm, by 2019 five of Vanguard's executive team of twelve had risen to the top through its international division.[11]

For the many offices of the company to appreciate the power of the flywheel metaphor, McNabb and his direct reports repeatedly referenced the model to company employees. "We talked about the flywheel at every opportunity," recalled Glenn Reed, the managing director for strategy and finance. McNabb cited it again and again at Vanguard's general gatherings, and Reed and other executives did so with their own teams.

FIGURE 2.2. Vanguard's International Assets Under Management, 2008–2019.

Year End	Number of Employees	Assets Under Management	Number of Countries
2008	330	$65 B	5
2019	1,318	$382 B	12

Source: Vanguard Group, 2020.

TORQUING THE COMPANY FLYWHEEL

Though central to McNabb's revised leadership of the company, the hedgehog and flywheel should not be viewed in isolation from more traditional leadership directives. Most companies place a premium on engaged employees, for instance, even if they fall short in engaging them. Vanguard just took it further, both defining the flywheel as "driven by a highly engaged crew" at its center and actually making it real. "We had to put our people first," reported McNabb, and to drive that change he focused on the ratio of "engaged" to "disengaged" employees, as measured by standard questions on an annual survey. In 2009, the engagement ratio stood at 2.9 to 1, he had moved that up to 6.9 to 1 by 2013, and he set 17 to 1 as an aspirational target. He rotated managers around, assigning a former bond trader to head the London office, and reassigning a former head of Australian operations as his human relations officer. McNabb also refreshed his top tier. By the time he stepped down, just two members of his 2009 leadership team remained in place, Jim Norris and Mortimer J. "Tim" Buckley, who would replace McNabb as CEO at the end of 2017.

McNabb also pressed his top team to face existential questions rarely explicit in any company: "Why do we exist?" and "How do we know if we are successful?" In response to the first question, his team concluded the company would have to:

- take a stand for all investors,
- treat investors fairly, and
- give investors the best chance for success.

And for the second question, they concluded that knowing that they were successful would come down to:

- strong employee engagement,
- high performance among investments,
- client loyalty, and
- achieving all this at half the current price to investor.

The answers and the expanded leadership model driving them worked. Jack Bogle had started the company in 1975 with fewer than three dozen employees and just $1.8 billion under management at the end of his first year. By 2017, Vanguard was drawing in a third of a trillion dollars annually. When Bill McNabb stepped down as board chair at the end of 2018, the company employed more than 17,000 people, serviced 25 million customers with a redemption rate just a third of its competitors', and managed $5 trillion in assets. And at least $2 trillion of that, estimated McNabb, came from his decision to behave like a hedgehog with a flywheel.

STOKING THE ENGINE

McNabb had given explicit attention to what is sometimes underappreciated when executives map out their strategy and intent: Who will actually drive and deliver a new idea or plan, transforming concept into action, and bring company strategy into business reality? One seeming solution is simply to take it for granted that execution will follow instruction. And, of course, this assumption is not entirely incorrect given the forceful levers of pay and promotion, or conversely, demotion and dismissal.

But McNabb decided that those levers were not fully sufficient. He believed that torquing his flywheel depended on the quality of the human engine at its center, and that he could not take that level of skill and engagement for granted. In this he was supported by research from experts such as the University of Southern California's Edward E. Lawler III, and Stanford University's Jeffrey Pfeffer, who have long argued that finding better talent and managing it well makes for stronger performance, whatever the company strategy.[12]

To meet his own standards, McNabb determined that Vanguard would have to become a "talent factory," creating a pipeline for the upward movement of its most capable people. To be sure of placing executives in positions where their abilities were best suited for the acceleration, McNabb initiated a detailed evaluation of the members of the senior team, giving greater attention to the hedgehog capabilities of each. Before bringing executives into his inner circle, he also asked directors to weigh in on who among the candidates would be best for powering the flywheel.

In a hard-hitting appraisal, McNabb concluded that some of his senior managers were B- or even C+, and he imposed a policy of pressing for all his managers to reach A+. He tightened Vanguard's hiring from the most competitive MBA programs, created his own MBA program within the company, and provided scholarships for rising managers to attend selective outside programs. In one of Wharton's own offerings, the Wharton MBA Program for Executives, a two-year degree with coursework every other weekend, 7 of the 120 students from across the country enrolled in the class of 2021 came from Vanguard. *Chief Learning Officer* magazine named a program in Vanguard's own "university" as best in the US, ahead even of those at the giant consulting firms of Deloitte, KPMG, and PwC, where employment ranks were ten or twenty times Vanguard's.[13]

When McNabb began to consider whether the company should build a business in financial planning and advice, the talent question loomed large. Previously, Vanguard had been more of a "product" company, through which customers could shop for funds but received little guidance on which to choose. McNabb and the board initially invested $100 million in a build-out of the business beginning in 2014, and within three years it employed 475 financial planners and had attracted another $70 billion in assets from 90,000 clients.

DEVISING YOUR OWN FLYWHEEL

Comprehending what's grown their enterprise in recent years is an essential first step for any newly appointed company leader, but past success merely adds to the imperative of leading one's own path forward to sustain and improve the company. We know from behavioral economics that individuals can be more complacent when they have positive markers close behind them. Despite the global financial crisis of 2008–2009, McNabb came into office with strong tailwinds from his prior CEOs, but he knew that what had worked well for others in the past was unlikely to work well for him in the future.[14]

Yet appreciating the limits of past experience is only the first step for devising one's own means for going forward. McNabb's proactive search for what was new as well as what was still true is one instructive model.

Sitting with an outside oracle, even if that meant transporting his entire upper tier some 1,500 miles to do it, was a gutsy move, but the value of outside advice obviously depended on the match between the outsider's ideas and the company's leadership. When McNabb read Collins's *Good to Great*, the concepts of the hedgehog and the flywheel resonated with him, but he still didn't know how exactly those concepts could work together—in detail—or how his company could optimize the drivers for each. For that, he needed face time with the source, and more than once.

Other business leaders have embraced comparable concepts for similar purposes, perhaps most notably at Amazon. Chief executive Jeff Bezos applied the flywheel concept to reducing costs and speeding delivery across the operating units flying the Amazon pennant. Lowered prices bolstered customers, which in turn attracted third-party sellers, and that increased revenue, yielding greater economies of scale, thereby further lowering costs, as Figure 2.3 illustrates.

The flywheel's power at Amazon depends in part on its wide, preexisting familiarity. It is said that job candidates know that they're expected to speak its language. Like McNabb, Bezos also customized his application of the model, spinning it faster to stimulate same-day delivery and to pump out new products ranging from cloud services and machine learning to grocery products and a virtual assistant.[15]

In 2014 Amazon created Alexa, the assistant that allows customers to ask for Bob Marley music or storm warnings. Alexa became one more driver of the company's flywheel, and in 2020 Amazon added medical advice to her digital capability. When customers

FIGURE 2.3. Amazon's Flywheel.

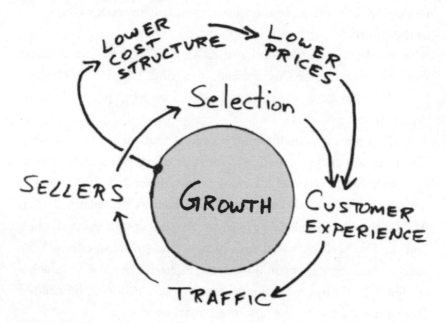

Source: Courtesy of Amazon.com.

asked, "Alexa, what do I do if I think I have COVID-19?" she queried their symptoms and followed up with customized guidance from the Centers for Disease Control. Or if you wanted to donate during the pandemic, you could just tell her to arrange it: "Alexa, make a donation to Feeding America COVID-19 Response Fund." She even closed her artificial dialogue with the moment's commonplace, "Stay safe!"[16]

For incumbents and newcomers alike, the common theme is to think new thoughts in new ways without giving up proven ways. Although Bill McNabb feared at the outset that he had no inherited roadmap to get to great, he devised his own way, and now his successor, Tim Buckley, has been designing his own roadmap for the 2020s, though he has also retained much of the tried and true. During their respective calamities of the financial crisis and the coronavirus, McNabb and Buckley each demonstrated cautious optimism. McNabb advised his investors to remain "long-term, balanced, and diversified"; Buckley urged his investors to take a "big breath," "don't panic," and "stay diversified." All the same, McNabb counseled his successor to indulge in "no nostalgia." Just as Jack Brennan had urged McNabb to "think differently" from him, McNabb in turn told Buckley, "Don't think like me."

CHAPTER 3

INCLUSION AS
LEADERSHIP IMPERATIVE

*Progressive Corporation CEO Tricia Griffith
Insists on Being Directive but Not the Big Boss*

Bring "your whole self to work every day,
and you'll be successful."

They were driving home from a weekend trip when they hit a
deer that had darted across the highway. Stunned, Tricia Griffith and her son pulled off to survey the damage. It was significant,
and she instantly wondered how she would report a claim from a
remote roadside on a Sunday evening. Who would she call, what
did she need to report, and could she even get through at that hour?

Many of us have gone through a similar experience and are able
to empathize with Griffith's feeling of disorientation. Accidents
can cause great distress, and it's hard enough to know what to do
even when your head is clear. In this case, though, the driver happened to be the chief executive of Progressive, one of the largest
auto insurance companies in America. She, if anybody, ought to
have had the playbook at her fingertips.

Griffith's own moment by the side of a busy roadway late at night
brought home to her just how lost and helpless the feeling could
be, and how much her customers would want someone they could
rely on for guidance and reassurance with absolute confidence. The
experience reinforced her sense that everyone on her team ought
to understand Progressive's practices from the outside in and then

turn them inside out, to give customers what they needed even before they knew they wanted it. To accomplish this, every player had to be all-in and fully engaged. To get them there, she realized, she would need to continue leading from above, but also find ways to make herself accessible to each of her employees and foster a shared ethos throughout the workplace.

MIDDLE AMERICAN

In 1988, fresh out of Illinois State University, Susan Patricia Griffith joined the Progressive Corporation, a provider of auto and property insurance for millions. She started in Indianapolis as a claims representative trainee for auto damage, and then rotated rapidly up the ranks through a host of other functions, from sales and audit to customer relationships and loss reporting, and finally to the C-suite two decades later.

Progressive CEO Glenn Renwick named Tricia Griffith chief operating officer for the firm's personal lines in 2015, and the board elevated her to the CEO position in 2016. *Fortune* named her "Businessperson of the Year" two years later, and the headline for its list of the year's best executive, atop the five hundred largest American corporations, enticed readers to "MEET THE CEO OF THE INSURANCE COMPANY GROWING FASTER THAN APPLE."[1]

The company expanded more than 20 percent annually in recent years, adding 8,400 new employees in 2019 alone. Its net new premiums had jumped by 50 percent during the previous three years, pushing it to overtake Allstate as America's third-largest auto insurer after State Farm and Geico, and catapulting it onto the *Fortune* 100.

Griffith may not be your typical chief executive—only thirty-three women held the top post among the Fortune 500 in 2019—but her distinctive style and the firm's rapid growth could become a model for company leadership everywhere. No matter their gender, industry, or home country, leaders would do well to emulate her appealing amalgam of direction, presence, and inclusion that lets her personally engage and guide the frontlines without having to compel much of anybody.

OUT AND ABOUT

A mother of six children, Griffith has been getting up at five o'clock in the morning to exercise for years. She also keeps moving once she gets to the office. She described herself as being frequently "out and about," trying to be visible, and said she asks her direct reports to do the same. The head of a company of forty thousand people, she stops to greet and swap the latest with just about everybody she encounters, some at their desks and others in the hallways. "I never take the elevator," she says.

During one event for new employees, a woman recruited from an archrival admitted that during twelve years at her old company, she had never met her boss's boss, let alone the chief executive. On first meeting Griffith, the newcomer's intimidation was evident, but the CEO soon had her talking. "People feel like I'm the girl next door," Griffith said, making it a lot easier to travel the frontlines.

At another welcome for fresh hires, rather than boldly striding to the front as a deferential hush descended on the hundreds waiting to see "the big boss," Griffith worked the room the way a politician might, sharing handshakes and greetings along her path, brushing past no one. And then, with no stage, riser, or lectern, when she spoke she appeared both personal and professional.

Griffith began her welcome with a reference to her own college, Illinois State University, located coincidentally in the same town as archrival State Farm Insurance. It's not the Ivy League, but it's solid—a *U.S. News and World Report* rated ISU 197th among 399 national universities in 2019—and its midranking was partly her point. Like so many in the room, Griffith's credentials reflect middle America, and she stands with the newcomers, not above them.

Her first job at Progressive, near the bottom of the pyramid as a claims representative trainee, crawling under cars and talking with injured customers, was hardly a prestigious, fast-track entry point. At the time, the company itself was such an unknown quantity that when Griffith told her mother that she was going to join Progressive, her mother responded, "Oh, the soup company?"

During her newcomer speech, Griffith also revealed that she was fork-lift certified, a curious but instructive factoid. The US Occupational Safety and Health Administration requires a training course for anyone operating machines with a pronged device to lift and move heavy loads in warehouses, factories, and shipping depots. Although now at the top of the white-blouse world, her blue-collar working days were still part of her persona, which was also true of many in the room.

INCLUSION

For Griffith, though, being a "people person" is not just a matter of personal presentation—it's how she runs Progressive. Since insurance policies are so intangible, she explained, customers look especially to employee behavior as an embodiment of the company's character, and in her own experience, a degree of humility with a take-charge attitude were among the qualities most expected.

Doing well by her customers, she found, carried them back again and again, a source of pride throughout her years at the company. She sees this same kind of customer commitment from each new employee as essential now for the company's continued growth, and new employees are more likely to "bring their whole selves" to work if they have seen Griffith's whole self at work, she explained. She believes that when followers know something personal and appealing about the leader, they are more ready to stay the course with her. But that leadership presence has to be actively projected. "I'm a greeter," she said, with a disciplined gregariousness that dates back to her six years as chief human resources officer, where she had learned to engage and relax with others, whatever their stature in the company.

When she applied for that HR job in 2002, she recalled, "all I knew then about HR was raising six kids." She "probably couldn't do that," she'd thought, "You don't have the experience." But undaunted, she asked to do it, and the chief executive decided to give her a shot. She took the HR assignment as a way to master a new arena, and it proved a personal "game changer," she reported, showing her that human factors and work culture are key for company results.

Now as chief executive, Griffith makes it a point to eat in the employee lunch room on Fridays, where she often asks a table with five or six employees if she can join them. Though some may feel intimidated or "put on the spot," soon they're all taking animatedly about their plans for the weekend. Text messages fly: "I'm having lunch with the CEO!"

What does that have to do with company strategy? Little. But does it contribute to employee engagement with the strategy? A lot. Griffith says that her approach was sparked by an employee who admitted, "I hate Monday mornings." When asked to explain, he confessed that he felt like he had to lie when, inevitably, someone asked about his weekend. He was gay but not yet out, and he said he never felt comfortable sharing that he had gone on a date with a man. Now, encouraged by the culture of the company, he was out and free to live his life in the open.

When Griffith talked with others, she realized how common it was for anyone who did not fit the "straight, white, male" stereotype of corporate America to experience similar silencing. To combat the insidious impact, Griffith worked to send a company-wide message, personally joining company panels on "being a woman" and "coming-out day," and she asked the same of her direct reports. She herself had suffered from the "good ol' boy" ethos of anti-inclusion in her early days. Back then, she found herself avoiding talk about her family and just "tried to be one of the guys." Since

"I didn't want to be seen necessarily as a female," she confided, it "didn't actually allow me to fully be myself."[2]

Now she was herself, and she encouraged all to be the same. When Griffith met with a group of company recruiters, for instance, she quickly reminded them of their value to the company, honoring all in the room. "You are hiring thousands of employees this year," she said, and your work is exacting since you recruit only one applicant in fifty. "We would not be growing if you did not get your job done." Her human resource executive reported that teary eyes could be seen in response to the heartfelt compliments. When an employee congratulated her for being named to a list of the most powerful women in business, she instantly returned the compliment: "I am on the list because of you."[3]

DIRECTION

Projecting herself and her inclusiveness were the first half of Griffith's newcomer agenda. The other half was conveying the company's purpose and strategy to the new arrivals in ways they would personally embrace and never forget. Though always inclusive, she was always directive as well.

The company needed fresh hires, she explained to the newcomers in her speech. There was plenty of room for growth at Progressive, driven by new financial technologies and disruptive opportunities, and she wanted that growth now from them. Her goal was for the new blood to help Progressive become American consumers' first choice for auto insurance, overtaking State Farm and Geico.

In addition, the company had recently stumbled on a new business niche with Lyft for insuring the company itself, its ride-sharing drivers, and their vehicles and passengers. She wondered out loud what other emerging prospects might be ready for Progressive's plucking. She then emphasized that, to seize the right levers for getting that new business, all employees would have to internalize and embody the business basics of mission, strategy, and performance.[4]

Progressive hires just a fraction of those considered, Griffith explained in her speech to the newly recruited, and as a result it has "the best talent in the industry," which gives the company its competitive advantage. The bottom line, as she laid it out, was that "shareholders want a return on their investment, and we will give it to them." But, she added, while "CEOs work to generate profits and return value to shareholders, the best-run companies do more," which is "the most promising way to build long-term value." (Griffith had signed the Business Roundtable's pledge in 2019, in which corporations committed to building what will benefit all stakeholders, not just stockholders.) When employees see their boss pressing for not only investor gains but also customer services, she reasoned, they are more willing to devote an extra hour to resolving a claim. "When you have great employees, who love to come to work, that equals happy shareholders."[5]

To this end, Griffith added, product pricing and company branding will be critical as well. "Flo," for instance, the fictional character promoting Progressive for more than a decade played by an actress/comedian, had turned into an iconic voice for the company, exuding enthusiasm and sincerity, if sometimes quirky in expression, that worked. All these factors, Griffith explained, were now pulling together to accelerate the company's growth. It had taken the company eighty years to reach annual revenue of $20 billion, but just the last two to add $10 billion more.

And for executing on the company's vision and strategy, Griffith urged her new frontliners to see their own calling through the eyes of customers, especially when faced with a personal setback that had been or should have been insured. This was the moment when she and her colleagues could make the biggest difference and would be most acutely judged.

Griffith further anchored her leadership concepts when she spoke to another audience by recalling a change in company operations that she had instituted while serving as Progressive's chief operating officer. She came to believe, she reported, that her sales agents did not sufficiently appreciate the nuances of their customers' needs. "I realized that the people who were answering the phones to take sales calls and to service our customers," she remembered, "really didn't understand the different types of customers" and thus could not service each in a personally nuanced way.

Griffith found that dividing customers among their usual sub-categories, such as "preferred," provided little actionable guidance; accordingly, she created more granular personas to represent the variety of individuals. "Sam," for instance, stood for the inconsistently insured; "Diane" owned an automobile and could be a homeowner one day; and "the Robinsons," by contrast, already had an auto, a house, and Progressive insurance, a kind of "holy grail" since they were likely to stay with the company for years. As a result, Griffith found, her sales representatives "now knew what we're trying to get at" and could refine their approach. She soon noticed that competitors were moving to create their own equivalents.[6]

BUT NOT BEING THE BIG BOSS

As should be obvious by now, Griffith sought to be the antithesis of the typical "big boss." That is the familiar but fading model—at least in the US—typified by Jack Welch in his heyday, when the one on the top rung is *the* one, always authoritative, never wrong, the decider in chief. But that model still persists elsewhere.

The CEO of a Chinese company, for instance, told me that it was "no mystery" why his employees were willing to follow his lead. It stemmed, he baldly explained, from their "absolute admiration" of his "capabilities in always making the right decision and seizing the business opportunity at every critical moment." He had made all the major calls, he said, and so far they had always been "right."[7]

Griffith came to the top job with a perspective that differed by 180 degrees. She never exhibited the bounding ambition that appears to fuel the rise of some executives. When asked by Progressive's previous chief executive, Glenn Renwick, if she might consider his job one day, she at first demurred. "What I should have said," she recalled, "was absolutely, I'm in one hundred percent." But in keeping with her character, she instead responded, "I need to think about it, I need to pray about it, I need to talk to my family." Two of her six children still lived at home. A week later she reported back to Renwick that she actually would "love to compete for the job."

She quickly became one of a few inside contenders. But when the company scheduled Griffith to meet with the governing board for one final vetting, it was the same day that one of her sons was to play in the state championship football game. She could not attend both, and she texted the chief executive that her son's moment would have to take precedence, even if it weakened her professional prospects. She worried that the directors would wonder if she truly wanted the job, but in the end, her concerns were misplaced. One of the other candidates yielded their timeslot, and Griffith secured her facetime with the board. The board liked what it saw, elevating her along with her inclusive, people-first philosophy to the top.[8]

Once in the job, collaboration and engagement were Griffith's distinctive capabilities, not omniscience. "I'm an advocate of getting our team together" for top decisions, she explained, thinking "about the enterprise, not just their sole position." Sometimes this "greater good" approach resulted in one executive giving up a large part of her or his budget to allow another to get through a quarter. No rocket science here, just plenty of partnership in which her voice, the most important one in the room, was not the only one. At other times, this collective eye on the long term could mean that a given division would take a hit in the near term, as deemed necessary for the top team. As Griffith put it, company "management comes from hierarchy but leadership comes from everywhere." She could tell all forty thousand employees what to do, but things would go so much better for the company if they knew what to do without having to be told, guided of course by the purpose and intent she had set forward for them.

This collaborative approach to decision-making was exemplified when the former chief executive of eBay and Hewlett-Packard,

Meg Whitman, came to pitch a streaming service start-up, Quibi, or "Quick Bites." Cofounded by Whitman and Jeffrey Katzenberg, who had run Disney Studios and DreamWorks Animation, Quibi was scheduled to be launched in 2020, offering high-end ($100,000-per-minute-of-production time) videos for mobile devices, but in formats of under ten minutes. They wanted Progressive to come in as an advertiser, and for the meeting, Griffith brought in an insurance executive, two of the executive's direct reports, and her chief marketing officer. When it came time to decide, Griffith took a poll—and it was for real. As Griffith explained, "I was only one of the votes." Ultimately, the company joined General Mills, Procter & Gamble, and Walmart as an early sponsor, though Quibi failed to gain viewer traction and closed within a year.

Far from seeking "absolute admiration" in her personal interactions, Griffith is free with stories and quips that convey personal vulnerability, believing that admissions of human frailty and concessions of weakness actually elevate her stature. "Oh my gosh, she's real," exclaimed one employee. Another told chief human resource officer Lori Niederst, "It must be fun working with the chief executive since she's not on a pedestal." Yet the down-to-earth persona does not mean that she fails to exert her authority.

"It's different being number one from being number two," Griffith explained. "I have got to make the calls. We have forty thousand employees and twenty million customers," and she knows that she is *it* when it comes to final decisions. In the interpersonal space, though, she wields that authority with a gentle touch.

In one case, Griffith had to chide another of her direct reports for not fully appreciating the negative effects of an announcement she'd made. But Griffith delivered the admonitions with a soft brush to avoid defensiveness. "It never feels like feedback, it's just part of the dialogue," the recipient said. And yet, as Niederst observed, "She's given me more direct feedback that anybody in my entire career," and as a result "you always want to exceed her expectations."

With Griffith's having worked in an array of the company's functions, beginning in claims, her guidance often comes very granularly, as if she were an immediate supervisor. Having filled so many jobs herself, she appears to appreciate what it's like to be in the recipient's shoes.

When it comes to "managing up," Griffith acknowledges that running a board is very different from running a line of insurance, but it requires the same willingness to engage with others, to build personal relations, and to draw everyone into choices on the company's future. Not surprisingly, this dovetails with her board's desire to take an active role with her in defining strategy and setting dividends, not just monitoring her actions and leaving the bossing to her. And they remain in sync in other ways. A board meeting was scheduled on the same evening that another of Griffith's children was going to be honored as a member of his high school lacrosse team. She was to walk her son across the playing field for just a few minutes. The board insisted that she take the time to be a mom, and she did.

Griffith works to sustain "street credibility," she explained, to communicate that she respects the work of everyone and welcomes the approach of all, resulting in a voluminous flow of personal notes from subordinates. She invites employees to walk into her office, and at Halloween, she and her direct reports join the ranks in costume at office parties across the company. Griffith, aka Captain Marvel, appears in Figure 3.1 during a "Halloween at Progressive" event along with Black Panther, Black Widow, Dr. Strange, Hawkeye, Iron Man, Spiderman, Winter Soldier, Santa Claus, and Elf. She participates in celebrations in a half dozen company buildings, greeting thousands in costumes and setting the tenor that work can be fun even in the room with the CEO, or in this case, especially with the CEO. She posts photos, including the one below, on the company's internal website to remind Progressive employees nationwide that their chief executive is not a remote figure in a high castle.

FIGURE 3.1. Tricia Griffith and Progressive employees on Halloween.

Source: Photo by Brian Lavy, Progressive Insurance. Courtesy of Progressive Insurance.

PERSONAL ENGAGEMENT AND PROFESSIONAL COMMAND

While not unique, Griffith's personal, accessible, and inclusive temperament is emblematic of an increasingly important leadership template that gives work an appealing ambiance with an enduring purpose, making a company a more attractive place to devote a large part of one's life. By 2018, Progressive stood in the 96th percentile for employee engagement among companies according to a Gallup survey, and by 2019, more than 90 percent of its employees reported that they were "made to feel welcome" when they joined the company and that it was "a great place to work."

But Griffith's approach to improving life for all Progressive employees is more than good cheer and open exchanges. She includes everybody in an annual "gainsharing" program, in which each employee receives a cash bonus based on the company's performance. In 2018, for instance, she granted all employees at least a 15 percent personal bonus based on the firm's financial results. Progressive employees reported that they were more personally committed to the firm and more likely to stay with the firm at a rate double that of workers across the country.[9]

When the coronavirus hit Progressive in 2020, Griffith converted the gainsharing ethos into a "lose-sharing" equivalent. Though Progressive's underwriting revenue had risen by 30 percent during the first three months of 2020, and auto accidents in March dropped by almost half, its net income had declined by nearly $700 million, largely because of investment losses when the stock market plummeted. Despite the red ink, Griffith opted against layoffs or even furloughs. She advanced employees a portion of their annual bonuses in April, expanded paid time off for those unable to work, and covered copays for telemedicine visits and COVID-19 treatments. Combined with reduced premiums for insurance customers, roadside assistance for first responders, and fee waivers for hard-pressed customers, the chief executive assembled an aid package worth $1 billion for its employees and other stakeholders.[10]

The inclusive ethos at Progressive is a product of changing times and new sensibilities, with younger employees drawn to Griffith's style of more accessibility and less officiousness, an appeal that she recognized and drew upon. She serves as the responsible authority without the onus of being the autocratic or imperious boss. "I can never be a bigwig," she said, and asks her employees to view her as both their chief executive and a person just like them. "It is important," she explained, "to share who you are both inside and outside of work." Bring "your whole self to work every day, and you'll be successful."[11]

CHAPTER 4

STAYING AHEAD OF THE GAME IN AN ALWAYS-ON/24-7 WORLD

WSFS Bank CEO Mark Turner Unplugged from His Office to Rethink the Company's Strategy and Plan His Own Succession

> "I went away as a leader of people, and
> I came back as a leader of *leaders*."

WSFS Bank's chief executive Mark Turner joined Michael Duke at a coffee shop in Bentonville, Arkansas, in 2016 hoping to learn about Walmart's turnaround. Although Duke, who had recently stepped down as Walmart's CEO, acknowledged that he was late to the digital party, he had helped transform the giant retailer from internet laggard to online competitor. Turner wanted to see if Walmart's come-from-behind experience could inform his own decisions as he grappled with the challenges of the new digital environment in banking.

Turner's stop in Bentonville was part of a highly unusual and rigorous effort to get a grip on the changes roiling his marketplace. Turner had completely unplugged from the home office, just as Bill Gates used to fully disconnect from Microsoft headquarters for a semiannual retreat to the woods. This kind of personal learning journey can be used by virtually any manager to get a better grasp of the changes sweeping an industry, whether new technologies, social movements, or awareness of racial inequalities.

In Bentonville, Turner quickly noted that Walmart's online comeback had not been at the expense of its vast retail network. In 2016, the company maintained 11,000 stores that drew 250 million weekly visits, and in 2020, its physical presence was still much the same. Customers, Turner realized, still appreciated being able to see and interact with merchandise firsthand.

Whatever the internet was adding to the retailing mix, brick-and-mortar still had a big role to play, and Walmart remained committed to its physical presence in communities across the United States. Still, the company had plunged headlong into online orders and digital delivery, including a $3 billion purchase of Jet.com to accelerate its move onto the digital stage.

Although WSFS was firmly anchored in branch banking, Turner believed there was a still an underdeveloped channel that, if he didn't strengthen it soon, would yield its opportunity to someone else and thus undermine his business. His visit to Walmart flipped the switch on a light bulb, enabling him to see more of what he ought to be doing back at his Wilmington headquarters.

WSFS BANK'S MARK TURNER

WSFS Bank served 150,000 customers in Delaware and Pennsylvania in 2016, when its chief executive, Mark A. Turner, concluded that he had to better understand what they would want in the years ahead, how they would want it, and how his bank could best provide it. He had been in the head job for nine years, and he was on top of the game—the bank consistently outperformed other banks and even the S&P 500. While total shareholder return, a combination of share-value growth and dividend payments, was up during the past seven years by 155 percent for the S&P 500 and 174 percent for the Nasdaq Bank Index, WSFS far outpaced both indices, its total shareholder return rising by 314 percent.[1]

But Turner also appreciated that he was having to learn a new game, and his successor in turn would have to become a master of a still-different game, as new technologies and new mindsets were upending traditional banking practices. Turner's solution: a three-month "leading practices tour," a professional sabbatical during which he would have virtually no contact with his own firm and instead travel the country to see a diverse array of companies up close. They would include not only established technologists like Apple and Google but also newer tech firms like Lending Club and Plaid, and even retail firms like Wawa, Inc., a chain of convenience stores on the East Coast.

From the financial services company Northern Trust, for instance, he learned how vital it was to have an explicit "do now" agenda along with "do not," "do next," and "do beyond" options. From DaVita, a national provider of kidney dialysis, he brought back the idea of a "paid-time-off gift bank," allowing employees to donate their unused paid time off to fellow associates in times of distress or illness, as would later prove invaluable when the coronavirus forced bank employees home for family care. From Becton, Dickinson and Company, a medical technology company, he appreciated the value of customizing WSFS's leadership and coaching programs around its specific values and operating principles. From ChristianaCare Hospital System and Twilio, a cloud communication company, Turner learned that telehealth could serve as a model for "telefinancial health," allowing customers to "put a personal banker on the phone," and that soon evolved into a mobile app, myWSFS.

WSFS had long prided itself on customer service. Headquartered in Wilmington, Delaware, and originally named the Wilmington Savings Fund Society, its initials were repurposed to represent its well-known motto, "We Stand for Service." It had been serving the region since 1832, making it one of the nation's oldest banks continuously operating under the same name. It offered a full menu, including retail banking, commercial banking, and wealth management. If customers needed a checking account, savings account, home mortgage, or property loan, it was ready to

serve. While large financial institutions like Citi and Chase operated nationally and internationally, regional banks like WSFS
provided many of the same services to local customers within one
or several states, and community banks concentrated on consumer
and commercial lending in even more local markets.

WSFS was also a pioneer, issuing the nation's first debit card
in the 1970s and spearheading the expansion of ATMs nationally.
By 2018, it serviced more than 400 ATMs of its own and managed
cash for some 26,000 ATMs across the country.

Turner joined WSFS in 1996 and became chief financial officer
in 1998. Four years later, chief executive Marvin "Skip" Schoenhals
asked Turner about his personal aspirations. Turner candidly responded that he had his sights on becoming chief executive in due
course but was not yet fully prepared. CEO Schoenhals concurred,
but viewing Turner as a "special talent," he accelerated Turner's
readiness, exposing him to more of the bank's varied operations.
But Schoenhals also decided to move up his own exit several years
earlier than planned.[2]

In preparation for the top job, Turner mastered the diverse services and functions of the bank by personally performing as many
of them as possible. He thus became WSFS's chief technology officer, then head of retail banking, and finally chief operating officer.
But it was not all goal oriented. "I enjoyed making a difference in
the company and the community," he said.

Turner gained technical mastery of the company's services
and functions, but it took him a while to broaden his perspective
and realize the importance of getting all those services and functions working effortlessly together. In a meeting with the CEO
and other officers while he was still CFO, he deliberately with-
held a crucial piece of data from the discussion because doing so
was better for him personally though not better for the company's
decision-making.

A few hours later, Turner called chief executive Skip Schoenhals.
"I held it back selfishly," he confessed, and the CEO's response

came as a thunderbolt: "That was the most important thing that you have ever done," Schoenhals said of the admission. Just thirty-five years of age, Turner turned from seeing his relations with his colleagues as win-lose and began to fashion them into win-win. If his colleagues prospered, he and the bank would too. "This was a leadership moment that really mattered," Turner recalled. It became a personal turning point and an operating principle that his boss deemed a prerequisite for company leadership. Placing the firm ahead of yourself is what Jim Collins has called "Level 5 leadership."[3]

Turner's commitment to the principle of the greater good was demonstrated dramatically in 2008 when he saw one of his competitors, TD Bank, struggling to consolidate its purchase of Commerce Bank. Its direct-deposit platform malfunctioned on the day the integration closed, with TD deposit records temporarily reporting incorrect balances to its panicked customers. Turner and his colleagues at WSFS saw customer lines snaking out of a TD branch and across the street. Reports of panicked customers storming other branches came in as well.

Turner heard that TD's customers were berating their tellers with the unequivocal demand "I want my money!" He was also told that an opportunistic competitor had posted a sign nearby: A Problem with TD? Come to Us. Taking a very different tack, Turner commissioned his colleagues to walk over to the TD branch to personally reassure customers that their deposits were safe and retrievable. He asked his own employees to assist TD directly, some working there for several days until the glitch was resolved. Later, the market manager for TD called Turner to thank him for his improvised intervention. The world was changing—it was late September 2008, the height of the financial panic—and smashmouth competition was giving way to a greater sense of "we're all in this together."

CEO Schoenhals admitted that he himself "was too much an individualist" for the collaborative sensibilities that had emerged under him. He still acted as the "big boss," but he could also see that his successor "had a special genius for the team." And that social skill was becoming vital as the bank's increasing complexity called for a flatter decision-making structure with more leaders within, able to make decisions and take actions on their own within a broad agenda coming from the top.

When "I started," said Schoenhals, "I could keep my arms around the whole bank," but over time, it simply grew too large and complex. Turner would have to lead in a new way, relinquishing more responsibility to others. In doing so, he also better positioned his bank to weather the COVID-19 crisis several years later, when thousands of urgent actions had to be taken throughout the ranks.

Not that Turner did not try to maintain tight control at first. "I grew up as a hierarchical micromanager," he explained. Much of the big-boss mindset, still hovered; "Mom and Dad" would instruct, others were to salute. Both big and less big questions found their way up to him, but then, in 2008, just a year and a half after Turner took the helm of the bank, Lehman Brothers collapsed. WSFS Bank's distressed assets mushroomed, imperiling its capital requirements and even its reputation. Disposing of the non-performing assets now called for high-wire decisions on what and when to sell, and how to price.

Turner's instincts pointed toward a "war room" with him the commanding general. But the crisis had thrown up hundreds of urgent decisions on the assets' value, and, in his own words, "it would have broken me" had he tried to wrestle with them all himself. But the bank had to come up with answers. The federal regulator, then the Office of the Comptroller of the Currency, wanted to know the real value of WSFS's many loans, including nonperforming assets, by finding a buyer willing to acquire each. "Prove It" was its mantra.

For this Turner turned to his executive vice president for commercial banking, Rodger Levenson, who oversaw the unit where the distressed assets were centered. "You guys just do it," Turner instructed, then added, "by the end of the quarter." Delegating can be dangerous when the recipient is less able than the delegator, but Turner had by then become confident in his vice president. "We were in new territory, but I knew Rodger could do it better than me since he had a background in commercial banking; it was his bailiwick." Turner then focused on righting the bank's troubled finances, where the CEO was himself more steeped. Led by Levenson, the bank managed to dispose of much of its distressed portfolio by quarter's end, some for as little as twenty or thirty cents on the dollar, a significant loss, but one that successfully moved the distressed loans off the bank's books.

For Turner, as for Tricia Griffith at Progressive, the necessity of delegation became a new virtue. This inversion of such a fundamental tenet of a leader's template—directing significant decisions personally if they were to be made well and timely—came to him from the crisis of 2008. "I realized that I could not do everything," though that carried the caveat that he had to be comfortable with those around him who would do the hands on execution. Turner concluded that he no longer needed to wrap his arms around the enterprise, and "delegation became a principle" as he gave more and more of the operations to Levenson, liberating himself from the daily details that were increasingly beyond his bandwidth. He had to become a leader of leaders.

Now, "very few decisions had to get to me," Turner recalled. To take one mundane example: whenever the company moved into a new headquarters building in the past, all decisions down to the floor carpet and wall trim came up to the CEO. Now Turner simply instructed others, "Here's the budget, figure it out." He elevated it to a personal operating principle: give direct reports two or three strategic goals annually, "then let them run" with them.

THE LEADING PRACTICES LEARNING TOUR

Learning to lead is a lifelong endeavor, requiring an ever-broader understanding with ever-rising responsibilities. Learning to lead in his run-up to CEO and then as CEO, Turner realized that the techniques he had absorbed and that worked well for him would not fully serve his successor. "Every ten to fifteen years," he said, "the company needs to reinvent itself." He would become the catalyst.

Turner had become aware, for instance, that "millennials," those who reached young adulthood in the early twenty-first century, anchored in new technologies and distinct mentalities, were customers with distinct demands. The wanted more mobile apps and didn't need as many branch tellers. They also made employees with different values, concerned as much for company purpose as for corporate profits. Artificial intelligence, mobile banking, and customer analytics were also altering the equation. "I could have taken these on, but it would have been hard for me to lead the change," he admitted. Yet seeing them coming, he sought a successor who could direct the new WSFS the way he might not. To groom the right person, he wanted a better understanding of what that person would need to know, and what he could do to prepare him or her for it.

Radical times required radical action, and Turner decided on an unprecedented step—a three-month learning sabbatical away from running his enterprise. Imagine your boss's reaction if you sought a quarter year's absence with full salary and benefits, handing all your obligations to those left behind. Undaunted, Turner made the case that if the company were to have the right direction and right leadership during the coming decade, he needed to take the leave. "We have been around for one hundred eighty-four years," he argued, and the company required an executive temperament now that scarcely resembled that of even a decade earlier. And as he entered his tenth year, he confessed that "unless you shake things up after ten to fifteen years, you may become arrogant or complacent."

Turner's absence would also help his executives and directors determine whether or not his likely successor, Rodger Levenson, was ready to take on the top job he would be filling temporarily. Unlike an academic sabbatical, a time for professors to reflect and recharge, Turner intended his learning tour to be of tangible value for the bank's leadership, uncovering practices he and his likely successor could apply immediately, and testing the probable successor while at it.

The board embraced the plan, confident that the top team Turner had built was now ready for a trial run. As nonexecutive director Jennifer "JJ" Davis explained, "It allowed the board to test the organization without Mark," at a time when he had topped out much of his strategic agenda. Both he and the board were ready to see if his team was indeed "ready for what's next."

"What are the disrupters" of financial services? the directors asked. "What's coming next?" The sabbatical not only gave the board a tangible chance "to know and work" with the heir apparent, but to appraise one another on the extent to which each was able to rejuvenate and refresh, a vital ability for those with responsibilities at any level.

"Everybody has to be a leader of leaders," Turner argued, and that included the discernment to pick fellow leaders. In the recruitment of a new chief financial officer, for instance, the strongest prospect emerged from a pool of more than five hundred candidates considered by an executive search firm. Before the recruit received the nod, though, WSFS's ten most-senior managers interviewed him, as did two of the company's directors and all of those who would be reporting to him. Though Turner served as *the* company leader, he expected all of his senior managers and even his directors to help lead the enterprise as well, in this instance by helping to identify and recruit the right person to spearhead the financial function.

As for their choice to be the next CEO, Rodger Levenson had spent more than a decade at the bank, rotating through a host of diverse responsibilities, including chief commercial banking officer, chief corporate development officer, chief financial officer, and chief operating officer. Levenson came with all the requisite skills for running the bank now, but would he be equipped to lead it in the decade ahead? Turner had taken his bank from a market value on the NASDAQ exchange of $100 million to $1.9 billion. Would Levenson be able to magnify it nineteen times, too, taking it from $1.9 billion to $36 billion?

Those were the issues that prompted Turner to embark on his leading practices tour—to learn what his successor would need to know to lead the company into the future. Of particular interest to him were innovative strategies, digital service delivery, millennial thinking, and workforce engagement. Turner reached out to 115 companies and organizations around the country to ask for time with their top management. To ensure he learned from a diverse array, he went wide, from Bank of America and Berkshire Hathaway to Facebook and FedEx. Expecting a dozen to respond, he received forty-nine invitations despite the time burden it would impose on his hosts. An excerpt from his request to the companies appears in Figure 4.1.

FIGURE 4.1. Request of WSFS CEO Mark Turner to Visit 115 Companies and Organizations.

May 6, 2016

The Board of WSFS Financial Corp. and I, as President and CEO, **are undertaking a thorough exploration of dynamic practices in all industries around innovative strategies, the evolving economy, and the emerging workforce.**

As a result, I am excited to be embarking on a **"CEO Leading-Practices Tour."** For nine concentrated weeks starting this summer 2016, I will be visiting with leading companies nationwide and attending leading professional development experiences in the following areas:

- Developing innovative strategies, cultures, and workforces;
- Evaluating the on-demand and sharing economy and working business models;
- Creating integrated multi-channel delivery (including digital delivery) of B2B and B2C services;

- Capturing and effectively using "big data";
- Engaging Millennials as Associates (employees) and as Customers; and
- Building Associate wellbeing as a means to workforce fulfillment, loyalty, and productivity.

I am asking for your help to identify advanced conferences (including symposiums, forums, etc.) as well as progressive host companies for the Tour. Ideally each host company visit would be a few hours to a full day in length, and each conference would be 1 to 3 days in length. In every case I will document the experience, and I will ultimately synthesize the cumulative learnings for the WSFS team and for broader education and implementation.

My bio is attached. You can learn more about WSFS (NASDAQ: WSFS) at www.wsfsbank.com. If you **are willing to participate as either a host company or a referrer to a host company or professional development experience, please email me directly at: mturner@wsfs bank.com.**

Anyone participating will receive a detailed and comprehensive document of the leading practices from the entire Study Tour, as well as a follow-up meeting, if so desired.

My sincere appreciation for your help.

Very Truly Yours,
Mark Turner
President, CEO and Director
WSFS Financial Corp & WSFS Bank

Source: Company records. WSFS Bank is a subsidiary of WSFS Financial Corporation.

Source: Courtesy of Mark A. Turner.

During the twelve weeks of the learning tour, Turner logged 44,180 miles. During his three days in Bentonville, Arkansas, he learned from Walmart how "clicks and mortar" could work together. He met for four hours with the former longtime CFO of Apple in California. From these and his many other stops, Turner concluded that WSFS required a leadership program taught by his own executives, partnerships with fintech providers, and a cohesive multichannel system for engaging customers.

The most important thing he learned, the "ah-ha" moment, was the realization that while fintech certainly would become more important, it "would *not* take over traditional banking." Furthermore, the combination of bricks and bytes would add value only if the choice of technology were aligned with the company's strategy. In the words of outside director JJ Davis, "the tech disruption was real," but not overwhelming. Customers wanted 24-7 banking services, but they still demanded face-to-face consultation when they confronted larger questions.

The tour proved no vacation for Turner. Each stop required detailed preparation, and each depended on his driving the dialogue throughout, sometimes in meetings that stretched on for days. The first challenge was to explain why he was there and what he wanted. Then he had to lead every facet of the engagement. That often entailed two or three meetings a day when he had to be "on" at all times, forever preparing, being curious, taking notes, and adjusting to the local style and culture.

The travel, Turner confessed, was especially hard. In his own words: "planes, trains, taxis, Ubers, check-in lines and security lines; soulless hotel rooms, bad beds, packing and unpacking; last-minute travel and meeting changes, crossing time zones, quick (bad) food, little exercise, not seeing family much." He was "constantly in the position of being needy, being the stranger, trying to quickly make meaningful personal and conceptual connections and relationships; and synthesizing then blogging my learnings into something worthwhile for me and WSFS." It resulted in "tension, headaches, poor sleep, back pain, indigestion, loneliness—and mental, emotional and physical exhaustion." He compared the experience to serving as a war correspondent, fortunately "without the fear of death," and said the learning tour required several months of recovery. "I was beat-up physically and emotionally."

The learning value, however, more than made up for the personal wear and tear. During his time with former Walmart CEO Mike Duke, he met as well with the company's current chief financial officer, chief operating officer, and even its "chief heritage officer." Turner learned that they had radically underestimated the market disruption of the smartphone, seeing it as more a tool of the wealthy than of the modest-means customers who frequented Walmart. Turner also learned that Duke had even decided to step down in favor of a successor who better understood the web. Turner was again reminded that "every CEO has their right place in time," and like Schoenhals, Duke modeled executive wisdom and selflessness.

The sabbatical was also a time during which Turner detached himself from his own company. It required iron self-discipline on his part to keep from checking in even just now and then, and for his lieutenants back home to keep from contacting him. During Turner's three months on leave, a time in which the executives in Wilmington completed and integrated three acquisitions, he received only a single call from the office. "The bank may miss me," he said, "but it will not miss a beat." In effect, he said, "I learned that they could do what I used to do, and I am now a 'guest' in my own organization." Though still in charge, Turner forced himself to let others take a stronger role. You show yourself as a leader, he said, when you do not have to get involved in everything. "Be quiet in your own meetings," he advised, and "other leaders will step up." He had in effect taken his leading-leaders agenda to its logical extreme, preparing others to lead so well that he could pull back his own presence, even absent himself for three months. "I went away as a leader of people," he said, "and I came back as a leader of leaders."

In 2018, drawing on his learning tour insights into the continuing importance of both physical commerce and e-commerce in banking, Turner engineered the acquisition of yet another bank that brought both tech and traditional banking to WSFS, sharply expanding its footprint. WSFS paid $1.5 billion for Beneficial Bancorp, which held $5.3 billion in assets and had sixty-one locations in Pennsylvania and New Jersey. The acquisition nearly doubled WSFS's $7.1 billion in assets, bringing the combined total to more than $12 billion.

The newly integrated organization closed a quarter of the combined branches, and started creating a more consistent experience for customers across the digital channels that were becoming increasingly important. WSFS found that 80 percent of its customers were now interacting with the bank via the web, and more than 60 percent had opened an account or applied for a loan online. Turner and his team eventually would calculate that more than $60 million per year was saved by the merger and the consolidation of thirty branch offices while still preserving ninety branches. The economies of scale allowed them to modernize their technology for customer interaction, risk management, data analytics, and workflow, a "tech transformation" of both back-office and customer-facing functions.

Turner later reported that without his direct knowledge of Walmart's belated push into digital sales, and how financial technologies were opening up in banking, he never would have fully appreciated the value of acquiring Beneficial. For years Walmart had been the country's behemoth retailer, but many of its offerings were being usurped by Amazon. Turner was now forewarned against the same for WSFS, fearing that new fintech equivalents could soon cut into his business unless he built up his own financial technologies. "What if we got five years behind?" he worried.

Prior to the Beneficial acquisition, creating a new deposit account at WSFS online took as long as twenty minutes, an eon for digital natives. Turner used the cash savings from the merger to acquire a fintech product that cut the process to less than five minutes. Another expensive application: a mobile app with a click-to-chat button that immediately brought a customer face to face with a WSFS specialist. Cycle times were shortening as well, Turner recognized, and he knew that he had to be more flexible and agile than his predecessor, and his successor even more so. *American Banker*, the industry's publication, in naming Turner as the "Community Banker of the Year" in 2018, warned, "Other banks take notice."[4]

Turner's vehicle for transmitting his new insights to Levenson and the company was a weekly "log" of what he had learned on the road, delivered to all 1,200 employees. Referring to all that was going on in fintech development, he cautioned that while "that all seems overwhelming and ominous, we need to be careful not to be too reactive. Much of that is start-up venture ideas, which will go the way of most start-up venture ideas." His conclusion was that rather "than revolutionary and disruptive, the space is becoming more evolutionary and collaborative, with the fintech world becoming, it seems, a giant R&D arm of the traditional financial service marketplace." That said, "we still must pay heed. While companies and platforms may go away, there are still disruptive technologies happening in our space, and we must make sure we are paying attention."

PREPARING THE SUCCESSOR FOR WHAT LIES AHEAD

Turner had instructed his direct reports that he was not to be contacted for three months unless he somehow held the only key for a challenge at home. In the meantime, heir apparent Rodger Levenson would run staff meetings, board meetings, investor meetings, and everything else. Both the board and Levenson's subordinates gave him high marks in Turner's absence. Turner anticipated that, as a result, January 1, 2019, when Levenson would take over, would be "just another day." The learning tour had both instructed and updated Turner on what company leadership would be required of him in his own time remaining—and what leadership would be required of his successor in the time ahead.

The transition from Mark Turner to Rodger Levenson in 2019 came with the same continuities Skip Schoenhals passed to Mark Turner more than a decade earlier. A culture of focusing on what the company's customers wanted in banking remained. But it also came with new stipulations. "To run a company in a landscape of

demographic and technological changes," reported Levenson, "you
have to have a capacity to see well beyond what it took" in the past.

That would prove prescient in 2020 as WSFS faced the rav-
ages of the coronavirus; protest movements for diversity, inclusion,
and social justice; and a shift to online everything. As COVID-19
exploded in March and April 2020, mobile banking registrations
doubled, and mobile traffic rose by 85 percent. That mindset in turn
facilitated the bank's lending through the Coronavirus Aid, Relief,
and Economic Security (CARES) Act and its Paycheck Protection
Program for small businesses. WSFS disbursed loans totaling $965
million to firms in its market, protecting some 100,000 jobs

"What we're seeing," said an analyst at Wells Fargo Securities,
"is the greatest acceleration of digital banking in history." Millennial
depositors expected simple touch points with the bank and instant
confirmations of their transactions. "People want their experience
with their bank to be like when they're shopping on Amazon or
using Uber" before the pandemic, explained Levenson. Younger
employees brought comparable expectations for the workplace. As
a result, he created a "Chief Customer and Associate Experience
Officer" who would report directly to him as chief executive; he also
appointed a chief digital officer. And the faster cycles of change in
financial technologies led him to invest more in the bank's own research and development. "How do you meld digital and branch delivery of its services?" he wondered. It shouldn't take, for instance,
more than five clicks to open a new banking account, and the bank
still required far more. And "we have to do it ourselves."[5]

Levenson also believed he had to devote more time to working
with outside constituencies, including technology firms, government regulators, and large customers. With more complexity both
inside and out, he decided to rely more on experienced executives
who could keep up with the accelerating rate of change. As the
two companies—WSFS and Beneficial—merged their operations,
Levenson added managers who could oversee more divisions and
expand the use of digital banking and emerging technologies.

WHAT'S NEW

In the two WSFS successions we've been discussing, each of the departing CEOs explicitly recognized that what had brought him to the fore was not sufficient to ensure success going forward. When the baton was passed from Schoenhals, Turner accepted that his predecessor's model of dominant leadership was an artifact of the past, and that he would have to preside over a more lateral world, requiring collaboration as much as command.

Following his own dictum, he recognized that the time had come for him to pass the reins to a new leader to avoid "becoming complacent, becoming arrogant, losing energy, or becoming irrelevant." Even though his successor was actually a couple years older, he would bring "a different view and a different vision." You still "have to understand all the functions," Turner explained, but the successor would also require an expanded skill set, knowing more about financial technologies, millennial sensibilities, flatter hierarchies, and lockdown practices.

In 2020, as COVID-19 bore down, monthly snapshot deposits at WSFS rose from 30,000 during the year's first two months to 40,000 in the next two months. Teller transactions declined from 452,000 in January 2020 to 266,700 by April. An app that allowed customers to "pick your banker" for online service increased its usage volume fivefold. At the same time, WSFS kept sixty of its ninety branches open for customers who still relied on them. The bank also gave hard-hit employees and customers financial breaks amidst the crisis, again costing cash but cementing the bank's reputation.[6]

Turner's quarter-year learning tour required more time than most executives could ever allow, but the concept can take on other, more affordable incarnations. Bill Gates's time away every six months was a mere "think week." Even so, after arriving by helicopter or seaplane, Gates made his cabin off-limits to all except for a caretaker who delivered two meals a day. Completely unplugged from Microsoft management, a metaphorical Don't

Bother Me sign on the door, he poured over a host of employee proposals for innovations and investments, sometimes a hundred or more—a kind of overstuffed suggestion box. Like Turner, Gates later summarized his insights for executives back home, and while most ideas went nowhere, among the diamonds were proposals to create more secure software, delve into video games, and build what would become for a while the world's most widely used web browser, Internet Explorer.[7]

WHAT'S STILL TRUE

All three chief executives of WSFS Bank reported that in other leadership fundamentals nothing had changed at all. Vision, strategy, and execution were still vital; so too was a culture of customer focus, employee engagement, and community service. Mark Turner had circulated a personal leadership statement early in his tenure: "I am a leader who believes in service, purpose, and strategy" and also in "values, self-awareness, open communication, learning, winning, and personal well-being and an integrated life." He was driven, he reported, by a calling to "make a positive difference every day in the lives of others," including employees, customers, community, the needy, and the bank's owners.

Though differing in diction, Turner's predecessor had championed much the same set of values, and his successor did the same.

The shared principles constituted a template at the bank that had been and still remained invaluable for its leaders, but at the same time each executive added his own, distinctive signature. "Like Skip, I had my place and time," Turner reckoned. "I got us from there to here, and now it is time for Rodger to take us further." And together they did. An industry publication in 2021 identified the nation's best performing banks over the past twenty years for shareholder value. WSFS ranked fourth of 584.[8]

CHAPTER 5

RECRUITING A PARTNER TO LEAD CHANGE BEFORE YOU HAVE TO

The Estée Lauder Companies
Executive Chairman William P. Lauder
Partners with President and CEO Fabrizio Freda
to Build the Global Leader in Prestige Beauty

"I felt we needed to change the culture to better
balance art with science and intuition with data."

W hen Estée and Joseph Lauder cofounded their company in
1946, they targeted their first products for premium department stores where shoppers expected quality merchandise and a unique shopping experience. For the next six decades, that selling strategy worked wonderfully through emporiums like Saks Fifth Avenue, Harrods, and Lane Crawford, catapulting their company into one of the world's premier prestige beauty companies.

The Estée Lauder Companies' sustained success propelled the company to expand into over 150 countries and territories and four categories of skin care, makeup, fragrance, and hair care. Newer channels, including travel and online retail, specialty-multi stores like Sephora and Ulta, and freestanding retail stores, emerged and grew into a significant portion of the business.

Before these trends were evident to most of his peers, the founders' grandson, chief executive William P. Lauder, had identified the opportunity inherent in rapidly growing alternative channels. The company's department-store sales still dominated, but Lauder foresaw the necessity to evolve and diversify the company's distribution options, and to drive the organizational and cultural change necessary to position the company for a sustainable future.

Yet Lauder concluded he could not lead that redirection on his own, and he decided to bring in a partner who could help identify the essential changes and then execute them ahead of the coming demand. Every leader has to drive change based on the specific needs of the moment. We have seen how Bill McNabb turned to the concept of the flywheel, Mark Turner went on the road for three months, and Tricia Griffith got off the pedestal. Lauder's tack centered on partnering with a comrade-in-arms.

ESTÉE LAUDER COMPANIES' WILLIAM LAUDER

William P. Lauder had come into the firm in 1986 as a marketing director for one of its better-known brands, Clinique. He went on to hold a range of senior positions, including president of Clinique, founder of the Origins brand, and creator of the company's online division and its freestanding stores. In 2004, he succeeded Fred Langhammer, the first person serving as chief executive who was not part of the Lauder family, taking the helm of one of the world's largest providers of prestige skin care, makeup, fragrance, and hair care products, including marquee brands such as Bobbi Brown, Clinique, MAC, Origins, Jo Malone London, La Mer, Aveda, and the company's namesake, Estée Lauder.

Growing up the son of Leonard Lauder, who had served as chief executive from 1982 to 1999, William had enjoyed a head start on the business, working summers there since age thirteen. But it was when he later served as a special assistant to the special assistant in the federal government, as he described it, that he really began to appreciate the skill set that he would one day require to lead the enterprise.

Lauder reported to an official who reported to the US Treasury Secretary, Donald Regan, a former CEO of Merrill Lynch. When he first met America's chief financial officer, arriving even two minutes early didn't seem prompt enough. Regan barked, "If you're not in control of your calendar, *you're not in control.*" The advice was obvious enough but it also proved enduringly instructive, Lauder offered. To "this day it has helped shape how I manage myself, and my philosophy on motivating people."[1]

I saw it myself when I met Lauder one morning, but I also saw another side of his time discipline, and that was to make himself completely available when it was important to do so. We were comparing calendars over breakfast near the campus of the University of Pennsylvania, trying to find a mutually open time for a future meeting. I thought I was busy, but I was stunned to learn of his own nearly wall-to-wall commitments stretching out months ahead. Still, he found extra time that morning when I asked him if he might want to accompany me to a nine o'clock course with sixty-five first-year MBA students.[2]

Our topic was managing people at work, and midway through the class I asked Lauder, then comfortably seated in the back row of my tiered classroom, if he would step to the front to tell the class how he managed the thousands who worked for him at Estée Lauder. It was a matter, he told the students, of first appreciating and then bringing out the best in each person working for him rather than trying to impose a standard leadership model on all of them. Coming from an experienced denizen of top management, the point hit home with me and the students. Academic research had amply confirmed the idea, but now it was coming directly from a successful executive who had included it among his first principles for leading a corporation.

For those aspiring to lead an enterprise, like many of my MBA students that morning, few moments are more instructive than watching executives like Lauder who were already doing so. By hearing how he led, they learned of battle-tested ideas about how they could one day lead themselves. And since these ideas were rooted in the tangible experiences of an individual with a proven leadership record, they came with exceptional authority. Executive leadership is largely exercised behind closed doors, invisible to almost everybody outside the corner suite or boardroom. Learning from the personal experience of those who live there and are willing to candidly share their wisdom can thus be invaluable, and that day they learned about how Lauder prioritized his time to bring out the best from everyone.

When Lauder became chief executive of his family's company in 2004, presiding over more than twenty-five separate brands, he acknowledged that managing himself across them was everything. "My job," he vowed, "is to ruthlessly manage my time." The same for his direct reports, and when he saw any waste it, he called them on it. "Time is their greatest resource, and when it's gone, it's lost forever." Coming from his meeting with the US Treasury secretary, it was the best advice, Lauder would later say, he had ever received for his own leadership of the company.[3]

Five years after that morning, however, Lauder foresaw and feared a tidal wave of change heading for his industry, requiring still more skills. New competitors, new markets, and new channels—including an ever-growing e-commerce business with an attendant trove of data—would require established players like his company to embrace new capabilities and ways of working. He concluded that he needed an ally to help him lead the company into that future. He remained confident of his own capacities, but he also recognized that he needed a complement, and the surest way to acquire it was through partnership with an additional company executive.

Lauder sought a compatriot who brought fresh ideas from outside the insular beauty industry. He was looking for a partner with the insight to help him change what had long been a successful strategy at the company. "I knew I couldn't bring that outsider's view, having grown up in our industry," Lauder explained, and "most of the executives I'd worked with didn't have it for the same reason." They remained confident, even too confident, in their long-standing ways of creating and selling their products. Resistance resulted. "My name being what it is," he explained, "oftentimes there were executives who heard what I said" and just "didn't do it." It was time for a "fresh perspective."[4]

The particulars: Some managers still prioritized growth in sales instead of earnings, pumping cash into unprofitable areas while starving more lucrative ideas. Matrix reporting left it unclear whether brand leaders, regions, or affiliates held the ultimate decision rights. Brands built their own bunkers and competed against one another; cash was more to be spent than managed; procurement varied from country to country; costs were rising faster than revenues; distribution facilities had duplicated; and marketing had been starved or misallocated, as when half the company's US advertising budget went to fragrances at a time when they constituted just a fifth of company sales. What was missing at the company was an encompassing, enterprise-wide mindset, and Lauder concluded he would have to look outside for a partner who could help establish one, a controversial proposition for a tight-knit family-controlled company, but one he felt was right in light of what he saw on the inside.[5]

WHAT NEEDED ALTERING—AND WHAT HELD IT BACK

An array of market forces was pressing William Lauder to transform the company. Geographically, the major markets for prestige beauty were evolving rapidly, with demand for high-end cosmetics increasing in China and India, and among visitors to the US from those markets. The company estimated that Chinese travelers spent at least as much on its products abroad as at home. Brazilian tourists were responsible for more than half of the sales volume in the MAC store in New York's Times Square.

A second force was the long-term decline of sales through upscale department stores in North America, the dominant distribution channel since the firm's founding. A third was the accelerating shift from brick-and-mortar to online buying. Less than 4 percent of company sales came from e-commerce transactions in 2011; by 2017, that had reached 11 percent, then 15 percent by 2019, a high double-digit annual growth rate.[6]

The new market trends also spelled enormous potential for the company, Lauder concluded, but understanding them would require more careful analysis and evidence-based choices at the top. When it came to decision-making, Estée Lauder Companies' approach had too often been "ready, fire, aim," based on too much personal instinct and too little data analysis. Come up with an idea, try it, and make it work, or if it didn't work, try something else. "I felt we needed to change the culture to better balance art with science and intuition with data," Lauder explained.

Established methods had served the company for decades, but they were not well positioned to serve it in the future since other companies were embracing data analytics and nonintuitive thinking. If others could make more-grounded forecasts of what customers wanted and better understand where they wanted to buy it, ELC faced tougher going. It increasingly depended on Lauder to adopt and impose those methods if the company were to stay competitive with other providers.

Still, the company was performing well, and Lauder found little appetite for the changes he envisioned. "What brought us there was forty years of tremendously good instincts and an obsession with flawless execution. What we were lacking," he explained, "as we were getting bigger, more global, and more sophisticated in the diversity of our consumers and channels, was any verification of our instincts." Complacency had become an insidious byproduct of past success, and for that, Lauder argued, the best time to press company change was before it was forced.

At the same time, many company decision-makers were "reluctant to embrace the change," Lauder found, "because they didn't necessarily see the need for it since we were doing well. What they didn't recognize was the leadership principle I was trying to espouse: when things are good, that's when you can take the risk to change. If you're at the point where you're being forced by your circumstances to change, it's already too late."

It "became increasingly clear to me," Lauder continued, that "we needed an outsider's perspective" one that could "sharpen our consumer insight." And at the same time, an outsider who would "bring greater discipline and analytical rigor to decisions." Not many on the inside were ready to do so, but going to the outside was not a direction he could take on his own. He explained his thinking to the board, and it authorized him to bring in a chief operating officer.

Even so, the decision to reach outside for new talent did not negate the leadership principles that Lauder had long applied at ELC. "Think about what you *don't* want to change," he enjoined himself, "as well as what you do." When asked to identify the "fundamentals of leadership" that had not morphed during his stint as chief executive, he ticked off: the ability to articulate the company's mission and inspire others to execute it; an urge to explore new ideas and markets; adaptability, boldness, and courage; and a readiness to manage all the firm's stakeholders. Lauder now added an ability to foresee and capitalize on changes in the market, requiring agility, resilience, and "fewer preconceived notions of how things should be done."

RECRUITING AN EXECUTIVE WHO COULD

For a global search, Lauder reached out through a well-known executive search firm, Heidrick & Struggles, and after a competitive winnowing, he interviewed the finalists. One candidate stood above the rest, a rising Procter & Gamble executive, Fabrizio Freda, and they quickly established personal rapport. The initial meeting had been scheduled for one hour, but "two hours later someone finally knocked on the door," Lauder recalled, and "said, 'You guys have to go.'"

After graduating with a degree in business and economics from Italy's University of Naples in 1981, Freda had joined Procter & Gamble for four years in Italy, and worked the next two in strategy and marketing with Gucci, the Italian luxury and leather fashion house. He returned to P&G for two decades, steadily progressing up the ranks of one of the largest consumer-products companies in the world.

Freda had risen within that empire to run its $1.7 billion Pringles business. Along the way, he had also acquired a credential essential to Lauder's search. "I really have no patience for what is not working," Freda explained. For his handling of troubled operations at Procter & Gamble, he had become known as a "turnaround guy," and now for the Estée Lauder Companies he might become the perfect "makeover man."[7]

Believing that Freda had the right skills for the role, Lauder's task was to convince Freda that the New York–headquartered company was the right fit for him. Freda had been working in Geneva and living in Rome. Could his family get comfortable with the idea of leaving Europe and living in New York City? "We spent a fair amount of time talking about that," explained Lauder, "because you couldn't be a leader like we would expect if you had to be commuting back and forth to Rome."

There were other questions, too. Was the company ready again for nonfamily leadership that had only once been tapped before, and then only briefly? By the same token, was Freda ready for independent leadership in a family-dominated company? Private control remained total and out of sync with an era when most S&P 500 companies had long since lost their dynastic identity. The Lauder family still held about 48 percent of the firm's shares and 89 percent of its voting power.

Freda came to New York during the courtship to meet the Lauder family and to see company executives and directors up close. Each side passing their initial vetting, board chair Leonard Lauder asked Freda to invite his wife, Mary-Ann Freda, a Belgian native residing in Italy, to come for a visit. Like his son, Leonard Lauder insisted that Freda's family be behind his decision to take the helm in New York; otherwise, a relationship was unlikely to last. Mary-Ann Freda suggested that they meet instead in London, a kind of midway point. That worked, and when Freda's wife arrived at her London hotel room, she found a gift of a hundred white roses, a personal welcome to both the company and the Lauder family.

In 2008, with his wife now fully onboard, Fabrizio Freda agreed to join Estée Lauder Companies as chief operating officer with a promise that he would be elevated to chief executive within eighteen months. It did not take that long for Lauder and the board to see that Freda was a perfect fit for the company. They decided to accelerate his promotion to CEO, and in 2009, William Lauder stepped down from that role and up to replace his father as executive chairman. With new titles, the partnership would continue.

During his first six months as COO, Freda benefited from Lauder's advice to go on an internal "listening tour," not as long as Mark Turner's—few are—but still invaluable. He spent his time hearing from an array of company managers and sales partners. "Before you jump to solutions, try to just listen and learn." Only then was it "time to create." In the meantime, the world outside the company seemed to be going off a cliff. AIG, Lehman Brothers, and Merrill Lynch had just failed, and the world's economies were in reverse. For the first time in its history, ELC's annual sales declined, along with just about everyone else's.[8]

Despite the global financial crisis, the pair saw an opportunity to fast-track the more affirmative changes Freda had been brought on to lead. "I faced one of the most daunting recessions this world has ever seen," Freda recalled, but he also found that it had better prepared his employees for the adjustments he would make upon becoming CEO the next year. "We had to change some aspects of the business quickly" while "preserving others," said Freda, and the recession "gave us the impetus to move more aggressively." Everyone "could see how dramatically the world was changing around us." He used the moment to accelerate what in his view had to be embraced, including evidence-based decision-making and new technologies, if the company were to rebound stronger and remain a leader in a shifting market.

The beauty industry had already been facing other disruptions before the 2008 economic collapse, and they added their own impetus. ELC had grown up selling prestige beauty products mainly through luxury but also some midtier department stores in the US, UK, and Asia, and through perfumeries in Europe. Beauty was always on the first floor in the department stores, what shoppers would first encounter, and trained consultants helped them identify the fragrance or cream that worked best for them. Now the online retail revolution was gathering its own momentum, driven by millennial shoppers.

Lauder and Freda believed their agenda should still include selling through the well-established channels, premier department stores above all, but also accelerating the company's presence in the exploding digital channels and fast-growing global markets. "My goal" with Freda, Lauder reported, "was to position the Estée Lauder Companies" to "be a leader in China, to be at the digital forefront, and to take advantage of new technology to make us more efficient." Just fourteen months after Freda joined, at a time when the company was booking annual sales of $7.3 billion, Lauder and his board promoted their chief operating officer to chief executive officer.

Freda would now be responsible for bringing in more than $600 million a month—*and* radically expanding it. He pressed for moving from a model of "continuous improvement," to a faster and more aggressive growth agenda. Given the pain and urgency of the plummeting economy at the time, "the risk of inaction was far greater than the risk of speed," he explained. To that end, he revised the company's architecture, setting up regional divisions and brand clusters to reduce internal competition, foster shared learning, and optimize operating costs. He sought multiple engines of growth through data analytics, and they pointed to prestige cosmetics, online selling, travel retail, and expanding operations in China and India. "If you anticipate change," he explained, "you can direct it."

From his listening tour, Freda also concluded that aligning everybody in the new direction would require a more energizing vision for where he and Lauder sought to take the company. After many employees' input, testing, and refinement, they positioned ELC to be "the global leader in prestige beauty" as a "well-diversified, brand-building powerhouse of unrivaled creativity and innovation." This meant that they would treat some popular product lines as stand-alone enterprises known as "hero franchises," make investments in innovation more strategic, and focus managers more on anticipating future customer desires even if buyers could not articulate them now. "In a volatile world, you need to not only be following trends," explained Freda, "you need to *create* them."

Capitalizing on the trends required a detailed understanding of them, and for that, said Freda, "data is the new oil, the new fuel of growth." The company collected reams of information on consumer behavior, and its leaders now asked managers to wring fresh ideas from it by "connecting the dots." The "ability to process data and combine it with creativity," explained Freda, "is what's key."[9]

As a case in point, ELC had sought to introduce a new product into Japan, and evidence pointed toward the particular appeal of "makeup primers"—a cream, gel, or powder base that smooths and sustains makeup application. More data helped point the company toward a particularly popular formulation, and the fact that first-time users tended to be roughly twenty-five years of age. Further research revealed that 80 percent of purchasers in Japan turned to a single website that posted ratings and reviews of the country's top products, and if your primer was not among the top ten, it was not even mentioned on the site. Moreover, reaching the top three products in sales was particularly important in Japan since the concentration of sales among the top three prestige products was extreme: more than 90 percent, in comparison with the US, where the top fifty prestige products accounted for 90 percent of its market.

The team thus concluded: if you were going to launch a new primer in Japan, whatever your instincts, the data revealed that you had to target the particular formulation on twenty-five-year-olds and introduce it so aggressively that it became a top three best-seller within two months. "Just launching a primer in Japan," Freda warned, "you will have been doing nothing" to gain traction "without all this information." He turned such data-driven insights into a management mantra. "The first thing I want to hear from you is the consumer understanding. I really want you to show me that you have understood what the consumer wants."

In another case, Freda learned that in the US, prestige brands were increasingly being sold through specialty-multi channels like Sephora, providers of beauty products from a host of makers. The specialty-multi format subverted the department store model that had made ELC successful for decades, eliminating branded counters and employing store staff in place of brand-trained beauty advisors. Furthermore, ELC already had full distribution through department stores, so adding new distribution such as specialty-multi stores would have diluted the company's efficiency. But Freda saw the need to balance efficiency with the opportunity to learn in this new channel, especially as younger US consumers started to prefer it to department stores.

To sharpen and focus the company direction, Freda instituted a planning cycle that included creating a three-year strategy informed by a ten-year compass that foresaw longer-term trends. This strategic discipline would then be reflected in the company's one-year plan, with a supporting compensation structure. To diversify the company's engines of growth, Freda drew on the longer-term agendas to identify areas offering the highest return on investment.

More recently, Freda has thrown his weight behind greater efficiencies within ELC's functions. Among other things, this has resulted in the consolidation of select shared services for the company's legal, financial, and talent functions in North and South America. ELC housed the new services center in Panama at half the cost and with greater effectiveness, prevailing despite the company's US-centered DNA. To allow the company breathing room for this and other far-reaching changes, Freda worked with Lauder to continue to recruit longer-term investors whose interests were more aligned with the company's value of "patient capital." He also instituted a reverse mentoring program, in which the company matched young employees with top executives; by 2020, the program had grown to six hundred younger mentors advising three hundred executives in thirty countries. Company veterans learned of the power of emerging social media platforms, and of the new "omni-channel" shopping experiences through visiting stores with their millennial mentors.

At the same time, Freda sought to sustain a set of core values that the Lauder family had already instilled in its enterprise. "The art of leadership is making choices and distinguishing what you want to protect from what you need to change," and to that end, he held sacrosanct ELC's long-standing beliefs in brand-led prestige beauty, high-touch service, and family values. Those he would not change. When Freda arrived in 2008, the Lauder family had spent over sixty years building the company, and Freda's mission, as he understood it, was to ensure it would be around for another sixty.

Freda's agenda to further globalize the company before the market forced it to change proved prescient. In fiscal year 2010, Freda's first full year as chief executive, 56 percent of ELC's revenue came from Africa, Asia, and Europe. By fiscal year 2019, 68 percent derived from those regions (Figure 5.1). In dollar terms, revenue was up modestly in the Americas, but it had more than doubled elsewhere.

The same was true for the agenda of moving beyond department stores. That channel had always dominated, and in Freda's first full year as CEO, it still did, accounting for 57 percent of the company's

FIGURE 5.1. Net Sales of the Estée Lauder Companies by Region, Fiscal Years 2011–2019.

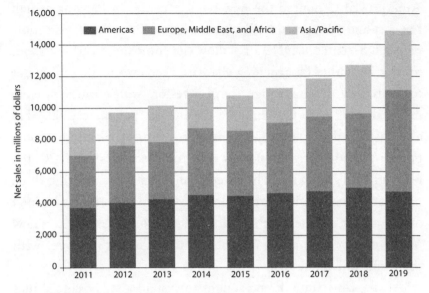

Source: The Estée Lauder Companies, 2019.

sales. But just five years later that had declined to 50 percent, and then to 39 percent by 2018, as Figure 5.2 shows. At the same time, online sales had grown from 3 to 13 percent, still a modest fraction, but the two trend lines were likely to cross within a decade.[10]

When Freda first came on board, a modest flow of the company's sales came through its own 737 freestanding stores. A decade later, ELC had doubled the number of its own stores to over 1,500 worldwide, and their combined sales had more than tripled, from $393 million to $1,543 million (Figure 5.3).[11]

Freda's push for innovation bore out in metrics, too: by fiscal year 2019, 30 percent of ELC's annual sales came from products newly launched within the previous twelve months, up from 8 percent in fiscal year 2009. When he began, ELC had 50 employees located in China, but that grew to 5,000 a decade later. Freda also doubled the company's revenue, from $7.3 billion when he started to $14.9 billion by fiscal year 2019, and grew its market value tenfold, from

FIGURE 5.2. Distribution of the Estée Lauder Companies Sales by Channel, Fiscal Years 2009–2018.

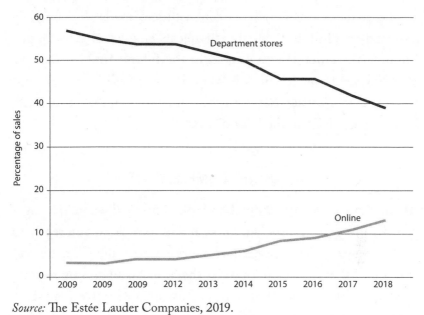

Source: The Estée Lauder Companies, 2019.

FIGURE 5.3. Number of Freestanding Retail Stores of the Estée Lauder Companies, Fiscal Years 2009–2018.

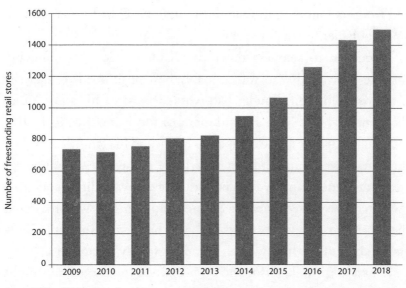

Source: The Estée Lauder Companies, 2019.

$6.4 billion at the beginning of fiscal year 2010 to $66.3 billion by the end of fiscal year 2019.

The changes Freda and Lauder instituted made the company more agile and resilient by diversifying its engines of growth, positioning the enterprise to expand in the future. In 2018 *Barron's* included Freda on its annual "World's Best CEOs" roster, and the *Harvard Business Review* listed him among the "100 Best-Performing CEOs in the World" in 2019.[12]

A PARTNER COMPLEMENTS

As chief executive until 2009, Lauder had decided where the company had to go to prosper and how it had to operate differently to get there—more analytically and more strategically—but he had also found that he couldn't take it there on his own. His recruitment of a seasoned performer from Procter & Gamble may seem inspired in retrospect, given the value delivered under Freda's leadership in the years since, but it was far less obvious in prospect. Lauder's grandparents had founded the company. His father had built ELC over decades, the Lauder family name was on the door, and from its founding in 1946 until 2008, ELC had never allowed a new outsider to reach the apex.[13]

Moreover, in stepping down as CEO, Lauder was removing the one individual who was arguably best positioned to lead the enterprise—himself. Lauder had worked most of his adult life at the company; he'd been a board member for over a decade, he had spent half a decade at the company's helm, and his family controlled the enterprise. Learning from experience is the best schooling for company leaders, and by then nobody knew how to direct and grow the enterprise better than this quintessential insider who mastered the ropes by rising up its ranks and now had five years in the leadership chair under his own belt—and his family behind him.

If handing the keys for the corner office to an outsider might thus seem surprising, even perilous, it's important to remember the risks of not doing so and staying too long. "Growing up, at summer camp in Maine we had one rule: always leave the campsite in better shape than you found it," Lauder said. "I apply that same principle to my leadership" at the company. "My goal is to have an effective tenure here, to not overstay my welcome, and to leave the company in better shape than I found it so that those who come to lead after me can build on our success."

Lauder continued, "My advice to leaders is to not let ego keep you in a position past the point when it's time to step aside." The "moment I recognize that somebody else can do a better job than me, the smartest thing I can do is bring them on. I want to do the right thing for the company. If I do the right thing for the company, it's the right thing for me." In this case, it was not to completely step aside but instead to recruit another executive to jointly run the enterprise.

To that end, William Lauder recruited a partner who could transform ELC's business, a change agent who shared the family's vision but who also brought a capacity to redirect the enterprise and lead with a complementary skill set that had become essential, even if the executive neither had the family pedigree nor was a longtime employee. At the same time, Lauder had sought a partner who would "respect the history and culture of the company" while adding "a new strain of DNA into the company, rather than eliminating something in the process." One of Lauder's points of pride was that Freda has been able to enact his strategy relying, for the most part, on the team that Lauder himself had assembled. Though Lauder and Freda carried distinct titles, they were joined at the hip.

Lauder has continued as executive chair for a decade, updating his own modus operandi to incorporate an appreciation for younger employees' concern about corporate citizenship and environmental sustainability. As a result, he has had to become as persuasive in communicating his company's values as its business agenda. He championed family leave, tuition reimbursement, permission to fail, "productive paranoia," talent management, and leadership development. Though now partnering with Freda, Lauder still brought his own, complementary leadership skill set to the operations.

Meanwhile, Freda played to his own strengths—data-driven decision-making and focusing on emergent channels and global sales. During his decade as chief executive, he has stressed continual change, not just continuous improvement; empowering local managers ("leadership from every chair"); collaboration ("the future of leadership is great partnerships rather than lonely leaders"); and focusing on what managers do well instead of remediating what they do less well. "I believe in leveraging people's strengths," Freda explained, "rather than improvements in their areas of weakness. I really focus 90 percent of my energy in understanding what people are really excellent at," and "making their strengths even more and more unique."

The dual leadership model at ELC remains anomalous, and it is reasonable to wonder how William Lauder and Fabrizio Freda have managed to defy the odds, an issue of concern to managers everywhere who seek to partner with others rather than just presiding over—or reporting—to them. The two worked at drawing boundaries between their duties, but they also worked at reaching major decisions as a united front. "We resolve all disagreements in private," explained Lauder, to be "unified in public." If an executive came first to Lauder to express a disagreement about a policy of Freda's, for instance, Lauder would simply say, "You know what? He and I already discussed it and I happen to agree with it. Let me tell you why. . . ." In the words of one close-up observer, they had become inseparable contrasts, the company's "yin and yang."[14]

It is a managed partnership, explained Lauder, "where you have teams that work together, not with the same skill set, but with different skill sets, so that each executive can respect the expertise of the other and work better as a team." Constituting one of those teams, Lauder and Freda share adjacent offices in their Manhattan headquarters, and they pair for major moments, such as their strategy sessions for brands, regions, and functions, sitting side by side at the table. As a result, explained Lauder, "it's not one of us making the decision for the other to execute. Instead we say, 'Here's the issue; here's the solution that we think is right,' and together we're going to implement it."

The lessons of Lauder and Freda's partnership apply far beyond the C-suite. Leaders at every level can understand that the best time to lead change is before you have to, that teams perform best when each member is playing to their strengths, and that, in the face of resistance, a partner who shares your vision and brings a complementary skill set can be an invaluable ally.

But finding the right partner for the job and maintaining a good partnership takes work. Lauder and Freda did so by establishing clear lanes of authority, presenting a unified front, and taking advantage of crisis to institute the sweeping changes they agreed were necessary. Mutual respect and shared values helped their relationship flourish in the ensuing years, resulting in strong growth to date and strong potential for the future.

The experience of the Estée Lauder Companies over a decade points to another pathway to acquiring what is new, and that is to recruit a trusted partner, a seasoned executive whose core values are shared with the existing leader while possessing a complementary leadership skill set. Together, Lauder and Freda were better equipped to identify opportunities and drive emerging market trends. Freda's position as a company outsider enabled him to refocus resistant managers on needed change, like investments in new channels and enhanced analytical capabilities, readying the company for the uncomfortable but necessary shifts ahead. Lauder's station as a company insider enabled him at the same time to sustain a host of enduring leadership principles that had brought the company to prominence.

One of the major channels to which William Lauder and Fabrizio Freda had pivoted proved a lifeline in fiscal year 2020. With many physical locations devoid of traffic or shuttered altogether because of the coronavirus, online became the beauty industry's sole fully functioning channel. During the first six months of fiscal year 2020, the Estée Lauder Companies delivered the best half-year performance in its public history. In constant currency, net sales rose 14 percent, adjusted earnings per share climbed 21 percent, and the company was on track to deliver a third fiscal year of double-digit sales and adjusted EPS growth.

In the second half of fiscal year 2020, as the COVID-19 pandemic took hold, the management team shifted its focus to navigating through a time of unprecedented complexity and change. Despite extensive temporary store closures worldwide in the second half of the year, sales fell only 20 percent and the enterprise remained profitable as it reduced spending and pivoted online. For the full fiscal year, net sales dropped by 3 percent in constant currency and the company's adjusted net earnings were $1.5 billion compared with $1.9 billion the prior year.

The diverse portfolio of channels and geographies, built by Lauder and Freda, helped the firm steer through the global shutdown. ELC sales in China, for instance, rebounded to double-digit growth by the end of the year, with online sales up nearly 100 percent. As the company prepared to celebrate its seventy-fifth anniversary in 2021, the partnership between William Lauder and Fabrizio Freda had positioned it to not only withstand the crisis but also remain a global leader in prestige beauty. Estée and Joseph Lauder had bet their future on American department stores decades earlier, but new channels and geographies, built by their inheritors, had become vital as well.[15]

CHAPTER 6

COMPLETING AN INCOMPLETE RÉSUMÉ TO THINK LIKE A CHIEF

ITT CEO Denise Ramos Thinks Like a CEO
Before Becoming CEO, Serves as a Turnaround CEO,
and Then Drafts a Dissimilar Successor

"She was CEO before she was *the* CEO."

We all start our working life somewhere, and among large firms it is a long climb to the top, with many rungs to be ascended. It is the specialist—whether in engineering, finance, or marketing—who is first invited on to that ladder. Most of our graduating MBA students as a result get their feet on the first company rungs because of their expertise in strategy, finance, or another forte. And only much later, when fast-tracking functional specialists or divisional directors emerge as generalists, appreciating most of their company's roles and operations, do they have a shot at the high tower where all functions and divisions merge into one.

This was Denise Ramos's pathway. She studied finance, then rose through the financial ranks at energy, food, and furniture companies, ever upward but always with the same core function, culminating in her service as chief financial officer for the near-legendary ITT Corporation. Yet all along the way, Ramos also learned to think beyond her specific sphere, appreciating that counting the cash was essential but not enough to know how to allocate it well. She came to consider how her firm's functions and divisions could work together, even if that bigger picture was not yet her official remit.

In 2011, when ITT split itself into three new companies, its governing board concluded that Ramos was ready to fully run one of the spin-offs. Hers was still an incomplete résumé, but the directors believed that she could expand her range of expertise in the top job because she was already thinking much like a chief executive.

When the moment came for Ramos to test her wings as the generalist in chief, the person responsible for every aspect of every decision, however, the spin-off the governing board assigned her was a mess. It carried asbestos liabilities, bumpy operations, and cobbled divisions. Though officially named ITT Inc., around the water cooler it was known as "Remain Co." So, in addition to the challenges of quickly rounding out her skill set beyond reporting year-end financial results, and on top of becoming proficient in ensuring that her workforce had the wherewithal to build and sell worldwide the desalination systems, shock absorbers, and water pumps that generated those results, Ramos faced the challenge of revamping the entire company.

THE DISASSEMBLY OF ITT

In its day, the International Telephone and Telegraph Corporation had been the stuff of fable, burnished by one of the highest profile chief executives of the era, Harold Geneen. The company was so diversified that he was reported to have had more than a dozen briefcases at the ready on a credenza behind his desk, each set to go with him for a visit with any one of his operating divisions, which ranged from carpets to insurance to hotels to rental cars.

To lead such a scattered portfolio, you had to appreciate not only how to run each of the separate silos, but also how to knit them all together for a shared destiny. During Geneen's reign from 1959 to 1977, he expanded the conglomerate many times over through more than 350 acquisitions and generous rewards for himself and his subordinates. He became the best-paid executive in the country, and he retained other executives, in the phrasing of one veteran, with "their limousines." At its height, his sprawling conglomerate operated in half the countries of the world, its muscle on a par with some of their governments'. To borrow the audacious title of the era's classic account, the company was known as "The Sovereign State of ITT."[1]

Decades later, Jack Welch's "sovereign state" of General Electric had a similar scope, with him reigning over power turbines, television programs, and toaster ovens, which required fluency in management at the top, within, and among a host of very different operations. To succeed there, you had to lead by uplifting the talent of each of the divisions, rotating the best performers among the divisions, and forcing out the underperformers from all the divisions.[2]

But that conglomerate era ran out of steam as investors and analysts drew weary of the diversified portfolios whose complexity they could not comprehend—and even more importantly, whose earnings they could not predict. Their skepticism was reinforced by mounting evidence that diversified firms in the US were simply less efficient than "pure plays," companies that had limited themselves to a single market. With the benefit of hindsight, we can see why. How could executives know how to manufacture, distribute, and sell everything the ITT empire offered at one point—from plywood to Wonder Bread? How could equity analysts know how to appraise companies that both made steel and produced petroleum, such as USX (later U.S. Steel)? How could a plausible rationale be constructed for merging CBS and Coca-Cola, as the chief of the first proposed to the second at one point?

Disillusionment with conglomerates led ITT officials to spin off division after division, and then in 1995, to separate the still massive, global empire into three independent and far more focused enterprises.

THE NEW ITT'S DENISE RAMOS

Ramos studied economics at Purdue, then business at the University of Chicago, completing her MBA at age twenty-two with a major in finance. "I always enjoyed numbers and how they related

to the operations of the business," she recalled, and "that really informed how I thought."

Her first job out of school was a good match for her early credentials, and an excellent place for executive development. At Atlantic Richfield Co. (ARCO), a prominent energy supplier, she
joined a finance team built by a CFO who believed that their work
should be of direct value at both the corporate and divisional level.
As a result, he rotated its members, including Ramos, every other
year among accounting, treasury, and other finance functions to
strengthen their understanding of the whole function. Her boss
was in the business of building breadth, a mentoring essential for
any manager seeking larger and more diverse responsibilities.

Ramos spent twenty years with ARCO. After it merged with
British Petroleum in 2000, she went in an entirely different direction and joined the finance function of Yum! Brands, home of
KFC, Pizza Hut, and Taco Bell. Over the next four years, Ramos
worked to broaden her horizons. "I really wanted to challenge myself to see what I could do that was both different and interesting,"
she recalled, and she did, moving up to chief of finance for the US
division of KFC.

The next step in her diversified career was as chief financial officer at Furniture Brands International, where she learned vital lessons in how to identify and protect competitive advantage, even if
from the firm's eventual failure. When the chief executive moved
some of the company's production offshore, he did not seek to
strengthen the company's other advantages, such as marketing, to
make up for the loss of their manufacturing edge in the US. Years
after Ramos had moved on, the firm filed for bankruptcy.

That such a setback would have great instructional value is not
unusual. Cisco CEO John Chambers weathered an early career catastrophe with the once-high-flying start-up Wang Laboratories.
Chambers saw its annual earnings suddenly flip from $2 billion
to a loss of $700 million when the firm failed to foresee that per-
sonal computers would kill their mini-computer business. Wang's
shortsightedness left thirty-seven thousand employees, including

Chambers, on the street. Later, as a CEO, Chambers always reminded himself that, no matter how successful Cisco appeared, he had to anticipate that new technologies could abruptly destroy whatever advantage it had. In the same fashion, witnessing Furniture Brands' struggle compellingly affirmed for Ramos the primacy of thinking strategically.[3]

Having diversified and enhanced her upper-tier credentials, when ITT came looking for a new chief financial officer in 2007, Ramos said yes. But this was not an auspicious moment for anyone in business. Lehman Brothers buckled fourteen months later, bringing on the great financial crisis of 2008–2009, and killing much of the demand for ITT's engineering and manufacturing products.

What saved ITT for the moment was that more than half of its sales went to defense contractors, which were less pummeled by the meltdown. Military contracting was still a steady business, but hardly the stuff of expansion, and the company could not easily make up for the loss of revenue during the crisis. Ramos estimated that the market came to undervalue the firm by at least a quarter.

In light of that underappreciation, ITT executives and directors decided in 2011 to break their company into three new standalones: one focused on ITT's water technologies, Xylem Inc.; one concentrated on defense contracting, Exelis Inc.; and one taking everything "else," to be known simply as ITT Inc. Investors and analysts loved the first, accepted the second, and questioned the third.

Each new entity required its own top tier, and the board asked Ramos to take charge of the "else," the industrial engineering and manufacturing group. She had long been comfortable with equations, datasets, and calculations—the world of quantitative analysis—with areas of expertise perfectly suited to a manufacturer of parts and components for the aerospace, energy, and transportation markets—but the new job came with plenty of other challenges. Even with rental-car and carpet-making divisions and the like long gone, the pieces of the former ITT left to her still had little in common, and the parent had strapped them with plenty of liability. Ramos would have to streamline, connect, and build the pieces into a coherent freestanding enterprise. Among her first duties was to educate customers and investors on what exactly her ITT spin-off consisted of, as opposed to the other two.

BECOMING A GENERAL MANAGER

Ramos initially doubted that she had the complete leadership skill set necessary. True, she had fast-tracked up to the C-suite of pre-breakup ITT, but she had never carried direct profit and loss responsibility for an operation.

On the other hand, Ramos was an expert at playing bridge, a game that had taught her to think about everybody's bids and plays at the table, not just her own, a mindset that should help her now do the same at ITT. Still, she worried that sizing up others' hands at a table was hardly the same as playing her own hand at the company.

But the spin-off board chair, Frank MacInnis, had deemed Ramos prepared. He'd always been impressed when she'd reported as CFO to the old ITT board, on which MacInnis had served. "I realized," he said, "it was the kind of report that one would expect from a CEO," meaning that, while she did not yet have to make the final calls, she grasped their complexity.

She had come in as a broad and deep long-term planner, MacInnis recalled, and she often seemed more on top of operating detail than even the CEO. She would report the firm's cash position at the moment, a CFO's stock-in-trade, but then she would preemptively identify what ought to be done with the cash, in effect moving from company finance to business strategy, the province of the top executive. "She was CEO," MacInnis summed up, "before she was *the* CEO."

To Ramos, this broader awareness came naturally. In a finance role, she explained, you do not have all the pieces that have to come together, but as chief executive it's required "that you give time to connect all the dots." Once at the summit of the entire enterprise, she knew she would have to be much more focused on the company's strategy, its values, and its culture. And in contrast to her functional behind-the-scenes background, she had come to recognize that she was now the face of the company.

MacInnis told Ramos that he and his fellow directors had picked her because she had already learned to appreciate the imperatives of the corner office. "You had always spoken as if you were running the company," he explained. Thus, the board believed that she would think and judge holistically even if she had served in only one function, bringing her disparate stovepipes together when reaching major decisions.

MacInnis, who had been on the ITT board for a decade before the company split, had served for sixteen years as chief executive of EMCOR Group, a Fortune 500 engineering and construction company, and he would be at Ramos's side as needed to help fill any gaps in her experience or skill set. Ramos still thought long and hard about the offer. She was in her mid-fifties, a time when career choices are increasingly fateful. She recognized that she brought little direct familiarity with how to run manufacturing lines or market industrial equipment. "I knew this was my weak spot," she confessed. It was too late to acquire that experience now, but to tighten her strategic fit with the company's imperatives, she vowed to bring in operating veterans to complement her own skill set. The support of those who had confidence in her helped her overcome any lingering self-doubts.

One of her most fateful hires, Luca Savi, came from a subsidiary of the Italian-headquartered automaker Fiat Group. Starting in ITT's motion technology business, an area that included brakes and shock absorbers for the automotive and rail markets, Savi soon came to oversee much of ITT's manufacturing.

A SHOCK AT THE TOP

Adding to the challenges that Ramos faced in her first months as CEO, morale was terrible, dampened by the uncertainties of the

breakup and the orphan stature of the "else." Doubts about job security and career pathways prevailed; even solvency was questioned.
She also knew that with ITT's divisions cobbled together, there
was no shared history or distinct identity—we "did not know who
we were." Still, she was stunned to read the results of a survey that
showed the scale of worker discontent.

As an immediate step to turning things around, she launched
workshops across the company's ten thousand employees; pressed
for a more people-focused, less numbers-driven culture; urged
managers to better balance work and family life; and corralled her
top team for a brainstorm on how to foster a shared destiny. The
focus had to be, she said, "to create an entity that people identified
with," hardly a concern for a chief of finance, but now the province
of the chief executive.

As if trying to figure out the personality of this new, smaller
ITT were not a big enough challenge, Ramos also had to master
the many nuances of her new, more elevated role at the company.
"People pay attention to everything you say, you are the face of the
company, and I had to listen very carefully to everybody on my
team." When "they have a problem, I have a problem, and I had
to hear it in detail." She also came to better appreciate that no two
of her new executives were the same. Each required customized
direction. At the same time, she learned that it was best to have
people in her inner circle who were different from one another, and
different from her.

Another challenge, more in keeping with her past experience,
was managing $750 million in asbestos liabilities. This huge sum,
imposed on her new company at the moment of its creation,
stemmed from worker exposure to the carcinogen years earlier.
With the directors' backing, Ramos worked down the liabilities
while at the same time pressing for growth, dealing with the obligations without sacrificing the company's seed corn.

Getting there, however, Ramos also faced a possible crisis in
the energy side of the business. ITT sold gas regulators and sump
pumps to energy producers, and when the price of oil plummeted

from $112 a barrel to below $30, leading customers simply stopped spending, which cost the company more than $400 million in revenue. Recovery from the oil losses proved more L- than V-shaped, a sharp decline followed by a slow, prolonged comeback.

In the meantime, Ramos moved a manufacturing facility for the Connection and Control Technologies division from California to Mexico, and the executive in charge of the move did not manage it well. It took another three years of crisis management by Ramos before the relocated facility was up to speed.

In all, Ramos spent five years working to establish ITT's mission, reputation, identity, and brand, as well as its work habits, employee moods, and cultural values. She pulled divisions together, moved operations from one country to another, and streamlined the work force. Despite these activities drawing on skills that she had not exercised during her path to the top, her restructuring of the company consumed her middle years in the corner office, as seen in Figure 6.1.

FIGURE 6.1. ITT Restructuring Costs, 2011–2018.

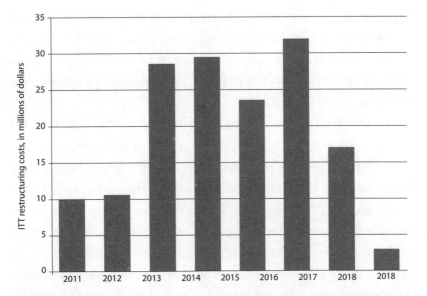

Source: Gordon Haskett Research Advisors, from company data, 2018. Data for 2018 is through September.

A NEW EXECUTIVE FOR
WHAT THE COMPANY NEEDED NOW

Denise Ramos had been very clear about the limitations of her experience, and the dangers of a mismatch, when she was considering stepping up to become CEO. She had never wanted to project anything that was inauthentic or to adopt practices that were not true to herself. If "you bring in something not you," she warned, "people see it," and that would irreparably damage others' confidence in her. Conversely, she believed that a company itself should not alter its imperatives to fit an executive who arrived with the wrong blend of leadership skills.

After seven years at the helm, as Ramos prepared to bring in a successor, she therefore knew she or he would require a very different leadership blend. Her leadership had been devoted to getting an orphan on its feet, but now, with company liabilities resolved, operations regularized, and growth anticipated, her successor would have to take it to adulthood. This meant leading an orderly expansion, which implied that the skill set required for her successor would not be the same as what she'd brought to the job. And just as her résumé had been incomplete at the moment of promotion, so might her successor's, though inevitably for different reasons. What remained the same was that he or she would need to continue enhancing and expanding their leadership templates once they were in the corner office.

On the day the board designated Ramos as the ITT CEO, a nonexecutive director told her that her first task presented yet another skill set to master, cultivating prospective successors. That long-term goal, bringing the future into the present, came from the board again in 2015 when the chair, Frank MacInnis, asked her to give the directors at least a two-year advance notice on her exit or retirement, as well as her thoughts on what they should look for in the next CEO. Three candidates had emerged, but one had become the front-runner in her mind—Luca Savi. She elevated him to executive vice president in 2016, chief operating officer in 2017, and president in 2018, allowing her and the directors a close-up look at his managerial capabilities. Given that he was directing all three of the company's operating divisions by then, he understood more than most how the company cohered and ran.

It was evident to Ramos and the directors that Savi knew well how to develop, make, and sell engineering products in a competitive field. They found that he often viewed his own decisions through the eyes of his industrial customers, an outside-in attitude that made for responsive decisions. Still, like Ramos, Savi came with an incomplete résumé. He had run a business, he had constructed plants in Mexico and China, and he appreciated international markets at a time when more than two-thirds of the firm's revenue came from abroad. But he had never worked with directors or investors. He knew how to optimize manufacturing lines and meet customer specifications, but he had little experience in setting the tone at the top required for inspiring the rank and file.

Still, what Savi did know was what, in the eyes of Ramos and the directors, the company needed most at that moment—how to scale up. China was a vast opportunity for growth, and ITT already supplied automakers and other industries there. Savi had moved to China to be near a production facility that was part of the company's growing motion-technology business.

By that time the board had decided that ITT needed to become a more operational company, explained board chair Frank MacInnis, and less transformative than it had been. Research and development, for example, was inventing exotic materials from its work with aerospace customers, and now was the time to distribute that capability across all its operations, including auto parts. "Luca is a wonderful operator," concluded MacInnis, and "we want him to keep an operational approach." And that approach had been paying dividends: his numbers had consistently exceeded those of his inside competitors.

Savi also foresaw artificial intelligence and digital technologies transforming how the company made products and what products they made. The company, for instance, had created a

sensor-enabled brake pad that increased vehicle stopping efficiency by 10 to 15 percent. It weighed less, improved safety, and
bolstered fuel efficiency. With that technology rapidly coming to
life under Savi's oversight, ITT promised to be among the first to
market with it.

Still, as chief executive Savi would also have to be the public face
of the firm at a time when many publicly traded companies had
come to dread an attack by activist investors, those aggressive asset
managers who take a position in a company and demand new direction, pressing for seats on the board or even a new CEO. Fend-
ing off or negotiating with an activist required leadership of a very
different kind, a combination of strategic thinking and political
savvy. More generally, the largest institutional investors, including
BlackRock, Fidelity, and Vanguard, were insisting that companies
strengthen their governance, focus on long-term value, and disclose
as much as possible. And that pressure required also a capacity at
the top to engage with the company's premier owners, persuasively
communicate the company's strategy and prospects to them, and
manage their expectations of the firm's performance.

During her own time at the helm, from 2011 to 2018, Ramos
had worked intensively with her investors and analysts to convey
the firm's plans and results. "I was looking at this all the time," she
said, and she made a point to talk directly with the analysts after
her quarterly earnings calls to help them better understand the results and the business model. This required credibility, patience,
and active listening, again among the required skills she'd learned
to flesh out her full leadership repertoire.

But Ramos's successor had little experience with the equity market, and for that reason the board chair, who himself had under-
gone a bruising fight with an activist at another company, stepped
forward to coach the upcoming CEO. MacInnis helped prepare
Savi to respond to an activist challenge if one should come along,
and to be prepared even if such a threat never materialized. Success
in this domain required personal familiarity with the company's

shareholders and analysts, a capacity to guide their hopes, and an ability to convey both the CEO's credibility and the firm's strategy. The skill set would also include greater resilience and fortitude in case an unwanted hedge fund stepped forward.

MY SUCCESSOR IS "VERY DIFFERENT FROM ME"

Under Ramos's leadership, ITT had navigated through a precipitous drop in oil prices, reduced asbestos claims against it, and created a shared purpose and separate identity as a maker of engineered products for a range of private manufacturers and even public agencies.

The company's annual revenue in 2018, the last year of Ramos's leadership, exceeded $2.7 billion, up from $1.9 billion the year before she became chief executive. From the first day of Ramos's service to the last, the value of the S&P 500 index rose 123 percent. The value of the new ITT had risen by 161 percent.

"We believe outgoing CEO Denise Ramos," wrote one equity analyst near the end of her term, "can take much deserved credit for defying the skeptics." Compared to the operating units allocated in 2011 to the two other spin-offs, Exelis and Xylem, the operations assigned the new ITT came with parental neglect, and investors had wondered if the "heavy lifting" required for their revival could be achieved by anyone—least of all someone with limited experience beyond finance. But the analyst concluded that she had very much succeeded, "leaving ITT in a very healthy position."[4]

The incomplete leadership résumé with which Ramos had arrived at the top didn't stand in the way of creating value. She had already learned to think well beyond the finance function, and then she learned as well to pull all her divisions into a functioning whole.

"You have to fit what the company wants at the moment," Ramos observed. She came in as her new enterprise was taking form, requiring a readiness to cajole, invent, and improvise; restructure and regularize; and explain the "Remain Co." strategy and even its very existence to skeptical customers and owners. Now, as she exited, her successor would have to be more operational, optimizing ITT's manufacturing and sales in a period that seemed to promise far greater stability.

This meant that Savi's leadership would focus more on innovation than consolidation. Savi would be the key that fit a very different lock than the one Ramos sought to open in her time. Same company name but very different challenges, and for leading that, Ramos said, "Luca is very different from me."[5]

CHAPTER 7

DOUBLING DOWN ON THE RIGHT TALENT

Nokia Growth Partners' Bo Ilsoe
Bets on a Replacement for a Tech Start-Up

"From the brink of bankruptcy to a billion-dollar exit."

Heptagon Micro Optics, a Singapore-based start-up, had pioneered a technology for the miniature but high-resolution cameras that were fast becoming a staple of smartphones worldwide. It was a promising technology for a market that looked like it had a limitless upside. But did Heptagon also have the company leadership that could transform that technical prospect into a profitable reality?

Heptagon had been founded in Finland in 1993 based on research at the University of Helsinki, and although the company was bringing in $12 million in revenue by 2008, that was not nearly enough to cover its burgeoning research, development, and operating costs. Heptagon had instead come to rely on repeated cash infusions from venture capital firms whose partners were willing to place big but risky bets.[1]

With the company facing long odds even in favorable market conditions, Heptagon's negative cashflow became especially perilous when the global economy swooned in 2008–2009. Orders for its optical components ground to a halt as retailers drew down their existing inventories, and the firm required another infusion of VC funding if it were to survive the downturn. Most of the investors who had already bet on Heptagon for a decade were none too happy about this. Foremost among them was Nokia Growth Partners (NGP), a venture capital firm based in Silicon Valley that focused on mobile technology, communications, and the internet. Its stake in Heptagon was $6 million, one of its largest commitments to date, and now its partners wondered if they should double down or try to sell Heptagon to a competitor even though selling would require still more of their money and could prove a bridge to nowhere. Their only other option was to simply throw in the towel to avoid good money chasing after bad.

The biggest uncertainty about hanging in and trying to find a new pathway to profitability was whether they had the right CEO leading the charge. Heptagon's technology was ready, and the market seemed ready, so the question was: Could another executive succeed where the current leader had not?

It is a different question from those we have encountered so far, where we've seen executives on the edge work to round out their template, retaining the leadership capacities that took them to the top but then adding what was still missing, either personally or through a partner or successor. For Bill McNabb at Vanguard Group, that was a matter of identifying and turning the right flywheel for growth. For Tricia Griffith at Progressive Corporation, it entailed learning to be directive as the CEO but also engaged with her frontlines. For Mark Turner at WSFS Bank, it called for a learning tour to appreciate how he could better lead at a time when digital technologies were transforming his industry. For William Lauder at Estée Lauder Companies, it entailed pairing with a partner to jointly direct the enterprise in ways he could not alone. And for Denise Ramos at ITT, it involved expanding her mastery of the financial function to embrace general management of all functions and operations, and then finding the right successor to follow on. At Heptagon, it was a far more existential challenge—to fundamentally revive a company on the verge of extinction.

NOKIA GROWTH PARTNERS' BO ILSOE

Heptagon manufactured the miniature high-resolution camera optics—"wafer-level lenses," in industry parlance—that smartphone customers savored as handheld devices increasingly became *the* omnibus personal platform, bundling quality photography with digital voice and internet access. The company had been founded by a Helsinki student, Jyrki Saarinen, and in 2000 a professional investor stepped in. By 2008, Heptagon was offering a superior lens about one-quarter the size of a contact lens that was already found in millions of smartphones, and enjoying a head start with the intellectual property and process know-how for making those lenses en masse. Taiwanese competitors were using an alternative technology called injection molding, but Heptagon still held large-scale advantages in both yield and price.

Yet Heptagon's success to date masked an underlying weakness. It was selling to giant smartphone makers that held the negotiating power to grind prices down to wafer-thin margins, now just a fraction of a dollar per lens. And its management was struggling. Ramping up new operations and products always took time, and the company was in the middle of scaling up a new yet unproven manufacturing line in Singapore.

Larger players such as Largan, Sunny Optical, and Tessera—each billion-dollar-plus public companies with ready access to capital—seemed poised to crush this small and undercapitalized upstart. The dilemma for NGP was: Should it stay with the same top person, working to round out his leadership repertoire, or had the time come to recruit a replacement who possessed the requisite skill set in full?

NGP had launched in 2005 with a $100 million commitment from Nokia, the Finnish telecommunications giant. One of NGP's first private-equity investments was Heptagon, and though still owning less than 15 percent of the start-up, NGP had the deciding voice given its close ties to Nokia, Heptagon's largest customer, which at the time commanded 40 percent of the global phone market.

When the financial crisis hit in 2008, however, Heptagon's sales dropped to zero. Yes, zero. The company was hemorrhaging more than $1 million per month, and by year's end it was broke.

As Nokia Growth Partners came to play the deciding role at this sink-or-swim moment, its partner Bo Ilsoe took center stage. With a master's degree in electronics engineering from Denmark's Aalborg University, Ilsoe began his career designing satellites for the European Space Agency. After a dozen years at Nokia, helping to build the first digital mobile network, he moved to a venture capital firm affiliated with Temasek Holdings, a sovereign wealth fund owned by the Government of Singapore. Just before the global financial crisis of 2008–2009, Temasek's assets had topped $135 billion.

In October 2008, Ilsoe moved to NGP, tiny by comparison with Temasek, managing funds of just $250 million. As his first assignment, he inherited oversight of Heptagon. Described by his company as "a technologist at heart" who believed "in the positive transformative effects technology has on society," he remained an optimist, despite the collapse of the global economy. Described by himself as "passionately curious," he had developed that quality as a thirteen-year-old during time spent in Greenland when his father had been captain of a merchant ship there. But he also knew just how high the stakes were. Heptagon's immediate survival depended on his funding go-ahead, and Ilsoe's own reputation depended on that funding's outcome. He was fond of Albert Einstein's famous dictum, "Make everything as simple as possible, but not simpler," and he came to believe the company's revival depended above all, and most simply, on its chief executive's capabilities.

THE OPTIONS

As NGP partners met to reach their decision in December 2008, Ilsoe circulated a memo outlining the three alternatives before him and his partners. He was careful to describe the pros and cons of each and expressed no preference of his own, allowing everyone to weigh in. The decision would be collective, but the partners had placed their own wealth at risk individually. They would meticulously and critically weigh the options.

Option 1—Double Down: Ilsoe's analysis indicated that Heptagon needed a minimum of $10 to $15 million in new cash to return to solid footing. NGP could not provide all of it, but fortunately, as is often the custom in venture capital, other firms also had money in Heptagon. One of these other investors proposed that all holders pledge $1 million each—and that each commitment would be contingent upon a commitment by all.

This idea went nowhere, and with Heptagon already burning $1 million a month, it became apparent that to revive it NGP would have to sink a far larger amount of its own capital and then still recruit new investors for the balance. And given the global financial crisis and its attendant deflation, Heptagon's value would have to be priced well below what it was during the last round of fundraising, which would completely wipe out the ownership stakes of existing investors who did not participate in the new round of financing.

Additionally, even if Ilsoe could corral the new funders, there was still no assurance that Heptagon would succeed. He believed that a later sale of a more mature Heptagon under more favorable market conditions could fetch a price in the $75-to-$150 million range. At the lower end, NGP would break even, and at the upper end, it would gain twice its original investment. Unfortunately, where the price would settle depended on uncertain assumptions about Heptagon's comeback. Demand for its products would have to rebound, yields would have to improve, and the company would have to reach a far larger scale. And underlying it all was the question of whether existing management could actually deliver. Adding to the risk, the global financial crisis made the prospect of an executive change seem daunting at best, not to be entertained unless absolutely necessary. As much as NGP may have wished to save Heptagon and sustain its relationship with Nokia, the cost of doubling down but then failing with even more capital at stake seemed financially dangerous and reputationally risky.

Option 2—Sell the Company: A Japanese lens manufacturer had approached Heptagon to buy the business. It was still completing its due diligence, but it had expressed an interest in offering up to $40 million if its appraisal went well. Even so, Ilsoe worried that the offer could fall to as little as $15 million if the Japanese firm's findings proved unfavorable, or if the company simply took advantage of the depressed market to press for a lower price. The low end of the range would result in NGP partners losing 50 percent of their investment; the high end would allow them at least to recoup their own capital, but nothing more. Time was no ally, as NGP and other investors would have to cover Heptagon's ongoing losses— perhaps as much as $5 million—until a sale was consummated.

Option 3—Shut Down the Business: An old adage in the venture capital industry is that it's not the failures that kill an investment fund but the living dead. The temptation to put good money after bad is high, but experienced investors know that often the best option is to end losses and simply shut down a business that nobody can turn around. Moreover, if Heptagon's challenges were truly insurmountable, further funding would only increase the reputational damage associated with Nokia, since, as Heptagon's premier customer, more of its handsets would become reliant on the company's optical components. Most of NGP's coinvestors were prepared to write off Heptagon, and perhaps its partners ought to heed their collective judgment.

THE DECISION POINT

Forecasting in detail the upside gains and downsize hazards of each of the three options would be essential for NGP in deciding which to pursue. Ilsoe had to better understand why Heptagon had flipped from a winner in the second quarter of 2008 to a loser only six months later. The global financial crisis was obviously a huge factor, but not the only one. Two others, Ilsoe concluded, both a matter of executive leadership, or the lack thereof, were also responsible.

The first issue in the start-up's leadership concerned its failure to streamline production, resulting in rising material costs and declining financial margins as the company grew. Manufacturing wafer lenses entailed a complex process with long lead times, which tied up working capital and created special challenges in serving tight-deadline, high-volume accounts. And Heptagon's cycle times were lengthening—rather than shortening—further tying up assets as the company had to pay out more before it could sell anything. It appeared that company managers had failed to understand and master their own manufacturing methods.

The second leadership factor was the top team's inadequate financial adjustments to its operational shortcomings in facing the 2008–2009 crisis. Early warnings, including the rise of undercollateralized subprime home mortgages, and the collapse of investment bank Bear Stearns in March 2008 (followed by the bank's fire sale to JPMorgan Chase for $2 per share), had not been fully incorporated into Heptagon's risk planning. Digging down to appreciate potential threats to a firm's business model, especially during a period with ominous signals, like the first several months in 2020, when the coronavirus was establishing a beachhead in the United States, is a prerequisite for any top team's risk management, but that was missing at the time among Heptagon's executives. As a result, Heptagon was running out of cash when that could have been prevented.

Bo Ilsoe warned his partners that without additional funding, Heptagon would go bankrupt by early February 2009. The company lost $1.5 million in December and customers were unlikely to replenish their inventories until at least January. However, based on discussions with Nokia and other handset vendors, Ilsoe believed that lens demand would return at some point in the first half of 2009. He also concluded that Heptagon's technology was still groundbreaking, if only company leadership could somehow ramp up its manufacturing yields and efficiently expand its scale. Smartphones and their cameras were not going away, and if anything, their markets could soon revive and even explode.

Of the three options, Bo Ilsoe and his partners decided that doubling down offered the best investment prospect if they could further tip the odds in their favor. The first step was thus to attract a new investor with industry experience and a footprint in Asia, especially in Singapore, where Heptagon's manufacturing operations were now located. GGV Capital stepped forward, and with it on board, NGP managed to attract still other investors, including Singapore's Temasek.

Since Heptagon's lack of leadership had played such a significant role in the firm languishing, rather than its technology or strategy—both of which seemed sound—Ilsoe concluded that he should change the top executive as well.

RECRUITING NEW LEADERSHIP

The additional cash infusion staved off Heptagon's immediate threat of bankruptcy and allowed time for the market to rebound. By the end of 2009, sales had recovered and reached nearly $10 million in the fourth quarter. But Heptagon sales plateaued again in early 2010, failing to achieve management's expectations. Moreover, operations continued to suffer as wafer fabrication yields were well below a profitable level even as sales targets were met. By mid-2010, Ilsoe and the other investors agreed that it was time to change out the CEO.

The incumbent, an electrical engineer by training, had worked in consumer and industrial electronics and in semiconductor manufacturing. He had led functions as varied as operations, sales, and R&D, and he thus brought much of the expertise required for running Heptagon. But alas, not a complete package. He came with little experience in actually managing manufacturing, and even less in the challenges of scaling it up. In starting the new manufacturing facility in Singapore in 2008, for instance, he had overseen the installation of nonstandard equipment, good for the moment but later proving a barrier to rapid expansion. Nor was he sufficiently attentive to the details of the manufacturing equipment to foresee emergent snafus. And, as judged by NGP partners, he was not entirely on top of production, not always being clear, for instance, where his products were in the pipeline, or able to implement support systems or enterprise resource planning software.

Once Ilsoe concluded that the CEO did not possess the complete skill set to run, let alone expand the company, he prioritized three additional criteria for recruiting a successor. The new CEO would need to be familiar with 1) the Asian region, where Heptagon had located its manufacturing; 2) managing production in detail; and 3) the steps required for scaling up the enterprise. On top of the foundational qualities of leadership—thinking strategically, acting decisively, and communicating persuasively—these skills would be part of the whole package required for the CEO's replacement.

By pure coincidence, someone with all these qualifications had just pitched his own company to Nokia Growth Partners. Christian Tang-Jespersen asked NGP to consider an investment in his semiconductor start-up, Singapore-based Hymite, and though Ilsoe was not interested in the company itself, he and his partners took interest in Tang-Jespersen. With a law degree from the University of Copenhagen, Tang-Jespersen had practiced corporate law but was more drawn to high-growth technology companies, including a maker of headsets in Shanghai. He radiated energy, candor, and a "take-no-prisoners" attitude—all now seen as essential for facilitating Heptagon's manufacturing in Asia, ensuring in detail that its production would work and ramping up would follow.

Ilsoe called one of the investors in Hymite to verify his own impressions, and the investor confirmed that Tang-Jespersen brought all the requisite capabilities, including an ability to draw others to work with him. Tang-Jespersen also displayed, in contrast to his predecessor, a willingness to heed what his investors counseled from the boardroom. Company leadership, Ilsoe believed, required an ability to lead not only down with subordinates but also up with investors, listening to their guidance, keeping them in the picture, and otherwise viewing them as active partners rather than distant relations. It proved a propitious moment to approach Tang-Jespersen. He had sold Hymite in 2010 to one of the world's largest semiconductor foundries, Taiwan Semiconductor Manufacturing Company (TSMC), and he was moving his family back to Copenhagen when Ilsoe offered him the helm of Heptagon.[2]

Also recruited for his familiarity with the high-tech production challenges that had flummoxed his precursor, Tang-Jespersen took charge in 2010 and pressed to move Heptagon back into the black—a tall order, since it was still deeply in the red, with an $18 million loss on an annual run rate of $25 million. At first, Tang-Jespersen reported, he "could not figure why such a unique technology, verified by Nokia, could not be more in demand," but he soon traced it back to an undermanagement of the company's intellectual property and manufacturing assets. He found unprofitable products in production, underperformers in high office, and low morale in the ranks—all avoidable if the firm had been better led.

Tang-Jespersen terminated a product already under development that had been burning cash but was unlikely to ever prove profitable. He replaced more than half of Heptagon's top team, including its sales vice president, chief financial officer, and chief operating officer. To catalyze candor over complacency, he reported a costly mistake of his own at a general staff meeting: after an exhausting trip, he had too quickly submitted a proposal to another company that contained a huge, irreversible error, ultimately costing the company more than $3 million.

All told, Heptagon's new leadership brought an exacting scalpel to repairing the company, a reminder that within the skill set of the complete leader is disciplined execution. And in bringing what his predecessor had not, Tang-Jespersen affirmed what Ilsoe had earlier concluded: Heptagon had developed a competitive technology, smartphone makers had an accelerating need for it, and the missing link was neither engineering nor strategy but simply the person who could pull all the parts together.

The company returned to profitability two years later, and Tang-Jespersen set aside $10 million of the firm's $185 million annual revenue for bulge bonuses, giving all of his employees an eye-popping one-time equivalent of twice their annual salary, addressing still another shortcoming—a badly demoralized workforce. He unsnarled the company's supply chain, whose quality and delivery had become too variable, and he brought assembly of the optical lens completely in-house, where he could control the precision required for quality assurance and product performance. He moved Heptagon from "being a pure-tech company" to "a product-focused company," in his own words, and "that really changed us."

Still, it was far from smooth sailing. The day Tang-Jespersen came on the job, Heptagon's most valuable engineer said that he was submitting his resignation. Four days later, the chief financial officer told the new CEO that the company should now file for bankruptcy. Rejecting both, Tang-Jespersen concluded that the company would get past the immediate setbacks and return to profitability within two years if he could focus it on its unique capabilities rather than competing in spaces that were already crowded. "We found ourselves in a situation where we were making market-leading technology," he recalled, "but not market-leading products." To that end, he informed his direct reports that the firm was facing a "catastrophe" and that they would have to place more trust in their subordinates and tackle their hidden problems. The company would only prosper, he argued, with more candor from the ranks. He insisted that everybody transcend their parochial interests by, for instance, returning an operation's unspent cash to the company. He empowered employees, permitting them to work at home and decide on their own holidays. "We had gone from deep despair," he recalled, "rebuilding technology, rebuilding the team, rebuilding the whole company" and "going from focusing on the technology to focus on the product."[3]

Because the directors had been repeatedly burned by unexpected shortfalls, the new CEO also worked to restore the governing board's trust in top management. He invited his lieutenants to directly inform his board what was not working, and to better appreciate their complaints, he brought more specialists onto the board. In short, he sought to make the board a partner, drawing upon its guidance in a way his predecessor had not. Leading up, he thought, was as important as leading down.

Tang-Jespersen also pressed for swifter decision-making and shorter cycle times. When one of his largest customers told him that it would not contract with the company for a new phone lens, the chief executive said he would fly out the next day to change the customer's mind. The customer warned that it did not believe that Heptagon could make the new component while still honoring a prior commitment, but Tang-Jespersen contended that his company could indeed do both. He and his top team fleshed out a detailed proposal complete with engineering drawings the same day, promising to deliver a lens at half the requested size, far better for the tight dimensions of the mobile phone. The customer acquiesced, and Heptagon became the premier provider of the camera components for what would become one of the most successful technology products of the era. Heptagon's fast, proactive, and candid leadership at the top came to be a selling point with other handset producers as well. Again, the proprietary technology had been assembled, the market was ready, and it was finally up to Ilsoe as the primary investor to ensure that he had the right leader in place to unsnag a host of managerial problems and align the engineering, production, and marketing of the product.

Heptagon had lost more than $1 million per month in late 2008; by mid-2012, it was *earning* more than seven times that amount. The company expanded its production from wafer-level optics to a suite of optical components for all sensing functions on a smartphone. A major maker became its largest customer in 2012, lifting Heptagon sales by a factor of twenty, to $280 million, generating $80 million in profit. Four years later, its four thousand employees were shipping nearly a million units per day, with more than two billion units in all. This, all from a near-bankrupt enterprise that Ilsoe had revived not by himself, but through the insertion of a new CEO with the skill set necessary for growing the enterprise.

But once again, leadership requirements were ever changing. What worked for NGP and Heptagon under new leadership in 2012 would be challenged again in 2016, when Heptagon won its largest customer's account for optical components in its next generation of mobile sets. This would require Heptagon to invest a further $250 million in its production facilities, though by then it held enough cash to finance the improvements on its own. And the company would prove a far more attractive target for international acquisition, eventually selling for $2 billion in 2016 to Austrian circuit and sensor maker AMS AG. NGP exited, its holding now valued at over $1 billion, more than five times its investment, a reminder that the big decisions—in this case whether to double down, sell abroad, or close out—and the right leadership to execute them can create great downstream value. Over the three years after the 2016 acquisition of Heptagon, AMS itself more than tripled its employment roster and annual revenue.

NEW LEADERSHIP DID WHAT
FORMER LEADERSHIP HAD NOT

The leadership that the prior chief executive of Heptagon brought to the office proved insufficient to steer the company forward as it scaled up in a fast-expanding and highly competitive industry. The prior CEO came with credible credentials, including working experience in industrial electronics and semiconductor manufacturing. He also came as a cross-functional manager, with working experience in research, development, operations, and sales. But he, alas, had not come with a full package.

The former CEO had not ever been fully responsible for a manufacturing line, nor did he have experience in rapidly scaling up production when demand soared. His installation of nonstandard equipment, for instance, had made sense at the time but subsequently made rapid expansion difficult. Nor was he always on top of his operations, slowing response time when bottlenecks emerged. Though enterprise resource planning was becoming standard at the time, he failed to introduce it here.

The possibility of a turnaround had not been entirely evident to Nokia Growth Partners going in—other investors were bailing and NGP itself considered exiting—but doubling down proved prescient once NGP installed Christian Tang-Jespersen. Same company, same challenges, same strategy—but new talent at the helm, taking it "from the brink of bankruptcy" in NGP's own words to "a billion-dollar exit and the world's largest micro-optics supplier."

In opting to double down on Heptagon, Nokia Growth Partners bet they could find a new CEO who would come with the qualities needed for what the company required for growth. It was a calculated gamble on a brink-of-failure company, but one that paid off, confirming the central point of this book: that the leadership that led a company to the present may not be the leadership required for the next stage, and that the challenge can be addressed either by working with an adaptable incumbent or by bringing in a more capable replacement.

CHAPTER 8

TRIAGE OR TRANSFORMATION

Edward D. Breen, CEO Extraordinaire,
Leads Through One Crisis After
Another Though Leadership for No Two Is Alike

"When you're in a crisis, you stay focused
on what is going to fix the crisis."

The headhunter had his work cut out for him.

How do you find a willing replacement for a chief executive who's not only been indicted on eleven felony charges but completely corrupted the management of a Fortune 500 company?

That was the legacy of Dennis Kozlowski, head of Tyco International, who was indicted on June 4, 2002, for conspiring with art dealers to evade more than $1 million in sales tax on six paintings by Monet, Renoir, and other artists valued at more than $13 million. The detailed criminal charges against him read "like an outline for a crime thriller," said two reporters.[1]

But some of his more colorful misuses of company money seemed more out of the Roman satires of Plautus or Juvenal. The $2 million, orgy-themed birthday celebration he threw for his wife (with Tyco picking up half the tab) was held on the Italian island of Sardinia. Seventy-five guests were able to enjoy an ice sculpture of Michelangelo's *David*, a performance by singer Jimmy Buffett, servers in togas and fig wreaths, and Roman gladiators guarding the entry. A waiter poured vodka into the ice sculpture's back that dribbled into a crystal glass from the statue's you-know-what.

Tyco was vast and as unruly as its chief. A haphazard conglomeration without much unifying rationale, it sold products that ranged from electronics and plastics to fiber optics and fire protection. It was overdue for dismemberment, but with Kozlowski slated for jail, it had already been decapitated.

Edward Breen was chief operating officer of Motorola Inc., headquartered near Chicago, when the headhunter came hunting. Would Breen consider becoming chief executive of the damaged behemoth? Tyco's 240,000 employees needed new leadership, they needed it now, and he was *it*.

Breen was only forty-one when he had become chief executive of General Instrument, a $17 billion enterprise. When Motorola acquired the company in 2002, he came to serve as number two at the parent, where he was widely viewed at its next CEO. But he couldn't resist the challenge of trying to straighten out Tyco. He would go on to serve as number one at Tyco, then DuPont, then DowDuPont, and finally a new, restructured DuPont twice. Through it all, his leadership fundamentals changed very little. His tenure at each of his stops was rooted in the same sense of a leader's responsibilities that he'd developed in his early days at General Instrument:

1. Define company culture.
2. Set business strategy.
3. Manage enterprise's risk.
4. Work through the top team.

Still, Breen's later redirection of DuPont would not be the same as his redirection of Tyco. The times were different, the predicaments were different, and his leadership would thus have to be different. Would the integrity crisis at Tyco or a business realignment at DuPont require triage or transformation? Would the 2020 pandemic require still other leadership at the new DuPont? While the fundamentals were unvarying, Breen would have to apply them differently and add to them creatively as the new calamities erupted.

EDWARD BREEN'S TRIAGE OF TYCO INTERNATIONAL

Tyco International planned to announce Breen's appointment as chief executive after the stock market closed on July 25, 2002. But as he sat in his Motorola office that afternoon with an eye on a monitor before the final bell, he wondered if he would be leading anything.

Earlier, there was the urgent appeal from Tyco's interim CEO, John Fort. "Ed, you better get out here right away." We "need you here now. We've got monumental problems. We have no credibility!"

Now there was a CNBC ticker running across the bottom of the screen declaring that Tyco planned to file for bankruptcy by the end of day. "Oh, this is good!" Breen mused ironically. What had he gotten himself into?

To an outsider, taking the helm at Tyco might have seemed a suicide mission. But Breen loved big-company tests like this. If Tyco could be fixed, it would only confirm that almost anything could be turned around by a resolute executive determined to make the right moves.

Prosecutors, regulators, and journalists were already circling the company when Breen first arrived at Tyco's New York headquarters on Monday, July 29, 2002. "If you can think of an agency," Breen reported, "it was investigating us." Robert Morgenthau, the New York district attorney, informed Breen that he planned to charge the still-serving chief financial officer, Mark Swartz, by the end of the week.[2]

A jury later convicted CEO Kozlowski and CFO Swartz of massive corruption. Kozlowski had illicitly given tax-free Trump Tower condos and Florida residences to executives. He'd spent thousands of company dollars on home amenities from French impressionists to ridiculously expensive shower curtains and umbrella stands. In all, the CEO and his CFO had stolen several hundred million dollars from the company, and for that they received state sentences of eight to twenty-five years. In the succinct words of NBC News, they had tumbled from "the boardroom to the cell block."[3]

Tyco would not in fact declare bankruptcy, though it came close. Prosecutors threatened indictment of the company itself, massive debt was coming due, and employee morale had plunged. Despite it all, Breen managed to pull the firm back from the brink and restore its operating verve in one of the most wrenching and far-reaching corporate remakes of the era.

Tyco's comeback stood in sharp contrast to the fate of two other scandalized companies of the moment, Enron and World-Com. Executives of both had criminally misstated their companies' earnings, and as was also the case with Tyco, each's CEO and CFO would serve years in prison. Enron filed for bankruptcy in December 2002, then the largest corporate failure ever, and that record was itself eclipsed just seven months later by WorldCom's own insolvency.

Breen instead cleaned house. "I went in with two thoughts," he explained. "I needed to replace the board and I needed to replace most of the senior management." He fired the chief financial officer in the second week, the general counsel in the third, and the chief human resources officer in the fourth. "I don't know if you're all rotten or not," he explained, "but you at least knew something was going on and didn't raise your hand. You were in the treasury department or the HR department, and you knew!" He forced out 290 of the 300 top executives and purged the entire board within a year.

"When you're in a crisis," Breen explained, "you stay focused on what is going to fix the crisis." You "have got to save the company first!" That had never been one of his explicit leadership principles before Tyco, because the need had never arisen. But now Breen brought it to the fore, as he worked to rebuild management, restore confidence, and compile cash.[4]

Among his early actions were personal calls to the chief executives of his major customers, including all the premier automakers. Some warned they could not work with such a disreputable firm, others reported that they had lost confidence that Tyco could deliver on its commitments. The CEO of Nokia shared those doubts and summed up starkly: "Ed, we can't do business with you because you're an unethical organization." "I can fix this," Breen responded, but he silently warned himself, "If I don't fix this in the next few months, we're toast." It was in fact a matter of just months, as Tyco faced a deadline for repayment of $4 billion in debt early in the new year. Yes, Breen managed to meet that target, and with lenders repaid, prosecutors at bay, customers reassured, directors replaced, and a fresh inner circle, he shifted his leadership of Tyco from triage to transformation.

Kozlowski had followed the Jack Welch playbook in gathering hundreds of disparate firms into a sprawling empire. He had expanded Tyco over a decade from a $3 billion enterprise into a $35 billion titan, much of it through acquisition after acquisition. But in his buying binge—$62 billion for nine hundred companies, averaging a rate of one new purchase per week—Kozlowski had pulled together widely disparate operations, ranging from Watts Waterworks and Submarine Systems to Central Sprinkler and US Surgical under a single umbrella.

And regardless of how related the acquisitions were to one another, some of the business lines were simply marginal producers. Tyco's revival, Breen concluded, depended on its conversion from a buying machine with uneven performers to a coherent and successful set of producers. Breen worked to rein in the sprawl by streamlining operations, disposing of dozens of marginal ones, and then he cut to the core, or, rather, created new cores out of what had been no core.

Fortunately, Tyco's new lead director, John A. Krol, a former chief executive of DuPont, proved an ally in arms. He was already in agreement with Breen on the immediate need to shed the company's weakest assets. They also concurred that the company's streamlining would have to be disciplined and methodical, in complete contrast to its ad hoc formation.

Breen assigned a new Tyco executive, Martina Hund-Mejean, the task of identifying in detail which units should go. Did an operating division generate enough value to justify Tyco's capital invested in it? If not, did it support other units, offer turnaround potential, or promise rapid growth? Hund-Mejean identified 130 units that did not meet these standards. Some were modest but others hefty, assets running into the hundreds of millions of dollars. One—TyCom, a provider of undersea cable—was hemorrhaging so much cash, some $300 million annually, that Breen decided to dispose of it immediately.[5]

With Hund-Mejean's methodical appraisals in hand, Breen narrowed the list to sixty units for disposal. Directors pressed him to explain the financial and strategic pros and cons of each. They also questioned timing: If all sixty went on the block at the same moment, would that not depress the prices they all might fetch? They also queried Breen about each unit's management: Might the top team, or a better one, resurrect the operation? And they asked about the strategic plan for each: Why exactly was it not working? In several instances, the directors concluded that the case for divestiture was not compelling or the timing not right, but otherwise the board gave the go-ahead. Breen liquidated rather than sold some of the units, but he disposed of them all, one way or another.

A turning point came when Breen's new CFO informed him that a convertible bond offering had been oversubscribed by a factor of thirty-two. "That was the day that we knew we got ourselves out of trouble," Breen recalled, the happiest day of his business career to date. Investors had given his restorative leadership a resounding vote of confidence.

With Tyco's marginal business units gone and new cash in hand, Breen turned to a far larger agenda. One of his four enduring leadership principles, setting company strategy, had come up against the troubling fact that Tyco's business bundle just no longer seemed right for the times. Even after streamlining, divisions as sundry as auto parts and security systems were still under the same roof.

In the eyes of institutional investors and equity analysts, as we saw earlier with ITT, diversified firms were hard to understand and confounding to run. A specialist in the oil industry, for instance, would balk at appraising the steel part of USX Corporation, packaged together from U.S. Steel and Marathon Oil, and a specialist in the steel industry would balk at appraising the oil part of USX, each not understanding enough about the company's other half. Mounting academic research comparing the performance of diversified companies like ITT, Tyco, and USX with the results of more narrowly defined companies offered compelling confirmation for the skepticism.[6]

Breen's early experience in saving Tyco would inform two successive rounds of transformation. He divided Tyco into three large, stand-alone enterprises in 2007, and then, five years later, he cut one of those spin-offs into two more pieces. Each of the five progenies became entirely separate, with their own directors, executives, and investors. Institutional holders and equity analysts applauded. In the view of an equity analyst at JPMorgan, for instance, the company broken apart was likely to be worth more than two and a half times Tyco's preseparation value of $20 billion, given that prospective buyers would find "strategic rationale in the different pieces" that they had not seen in the conglomerate itself. An analyst with Standard and Poor's also foresaw added value at the top since "management may be able to focus more strictly on each individual area."[7]

Several of Tyco's offspring proved especially alluring to other companies. Johnson Controls acquired one of the spin-offs for $16 billion, and Medtronic another for $50 billion. Tyco's market value in July 2002, when Breen had come in, had stood at $16 billion; fifteen years later, the company's descendants had achieved a combined value of $107 billion. Business leadership is devoted to creating value, and Breen certainly had done that, even though it meant pursuing disaggregation—the opposite of the acquisition strategy he had embraced as head of General Instruments. It was not an inconsistency, but simply an application of an enduring axiom: address the crisis at hand, whether it required triage or transformation.

EDWARD BREEN'S TRANSFORMATION OF DUPONT

Until 2013, Ed Breen continued to run one of the Tyco spin-offs, retaining the Tyco moniker and presiding over a work force of one hundred thousand. Just fifty-six years of age but already a veteran of four executive suites, he made a compelling candidate for search firms, and among several offers and near offers was the top job at General Electric. After considering his many options, Breen agreed to join the DuPont board in 2015.

Here was an opportunity to deeply engage again, without the all-consuming commitment of line management. The company was industrial, diversified, and massive, just as Tyco had been when Breen had first arrived. He found DuPont ripe too for restructuring, and some of its owners clamored for just that. Activist investor Nelson Peltz led the charge. His $11 billion Trian Fund had acquired 2.7 percent of DuPont's shares, not enough to gain control, but more than enough to rattle the cage. Peltz openly questioned whether DuPont's management was "capable of achieving best-in-class revenue growth." He wanted the company to "eliminate corporate bureaucracy," and most far-reaching of all, to "separate the portfolio," that is, to break it up. Other activist investors and the premier governance advisory services—Glass, Lewis & Co. and Institutional Shareholder Services—agreed. "We believe Trian has presented a compelling argument that Mr. Peltz is capable of working" with DuPont, said Glass Lewis, on its "ongoing transformation process." Institutional Shareholder Services was more blunt: "Instead of addressing the core issues," it said, DuPont's board and management "are more inclined to obfuscation than accountability." In other words, change or be changed.[8]

DuPont, however, recruited a second executive, James Gallogly, former CEO of LyondellBasell Industries (a chemical company), to join the DuPont board. He and Breen would, said the company, bring "deep expertise" to its transformation. Left unsaid: their business reputations ought to give Peltz and his allies pause.

Bringing on Breen and Gallogly, though, failed to repel the activist investor, and the Trian Fund turned against the company with a resolution for DuPont shareholder approval to add its own directors to the board, who would press for a breakup. The proxy campaign fell short, with 46 percent of the investor vote going for Peltz and his three hand-picked candidates, including former GE executive John Myers. And though that assault failed to deliver a knockout punch, it came close at a time when DuPont's share price was languishing, down by 27 percent in the run-up to the proxy fight.

Five months later, DuPont's chief executive, Ellen Kullman, stepped down after seven years at the helm. Then, in an unusual but not unknown move, seen already at Boeing and later at General Electric, DuPont directors turned to one of their own to take charge. Boeing directors had selected fellow director James Mc-Nerney, General Electric directors selected their fellow director Larry Culp, and DuPont directors now selected their fellow director Edward Breen to serve as chief executive. DuPont was not facing a wholesale crisis quite yet, but a calamity was not far ahead unless the board secured the right leadership for the company.[9]

The DuPont directors picked Breen to furnish that leadership now. He was well-known for his cost-cutting, value-creating, and turn-around experience, for both his triage and transformational leadership. Not surprisingly, Breen found that DuPont had become both too diverse in products and too limited in scale at a time when the chemical industry was consolidating, leaving just a few barons in each of the three main product arenas. If DuPont did not combine with another major player for heft, then redivide according to those three market segments, it ran the risk of falling fatally behind the industry's four dominant players: Germany's Bayer and BASF, Switzerland's Syngenta, and a dark horse, China National Chemical Corporation.

In the field of agriculture, for instance, where DuPont sold fertilizers, insecticides, and seeds, the advantages of global scale most likely would allow just two large producers to survive worldwide. But for DuPont to be one of the two, it needed to move fast. Syngenta and chemical maker Monsanto had been in merger talks (Monsanto was more a seed company, Syngenta more a crop-protection company), and though their negotiations fell through, their mutual interest signaled that consolidation was in the air. Indeed it was, with China National Chemical soon acquiring Syngenta for $43 billion. "It looked like the whole industry was going to the major players," Breen observed, and DuPont seemed on its way to the second tier.

For avoiding relegation to the lesser rank, Dow Chemical had become in Breen's mind the logical and still available partner for DuPont. Dow and DuPont were already the two largest American chemical firms, they operated in the same three industries, and if combined and then separated into those three markets, each of the spin-off combinations would have the requisite focus and heft to stay on top. "We knew we wanted to be with Dow to get this balanced portfolio," said Breen. "We need to take the first mover advantage and merge with somebody and create a powerhouse," he explained, "or we're going to be left behind and really destroy a lot of value."

Merging with Dow also presented a unique opportunity to double research and development, capital spending, and product sales in their shared product areas of agriscience, materials science, and specialty products. Breen also concluded that DuPont's budget could be cut by at least $1 billion, paralleling the $3 billion he had taken out of Tyco a decade earlier.

A DuPont streamlining also would accelerate its decision cycles, which to Breen seemed ponderous and without a "line of sight for fast decision-making," a judgment Nelson Peltz shared that was later confirmed by consulting firm McKinsey. For this perspective, Breen had his early experience at General Instrument to thank.

It had gone private before Motorola purchased it, and without shareholders looking over his shoulders, Breen had found that he could speed up decisions and production. To do the same at Dow-DuPont, to be a publicly traded company, he had to make fast cycle times a priority.[10]

Only days after his arrival at DuPont's top office, Breen met in Princeton, New Jersey, with the chief executive of Dow Chemical Company, Andrew Liveris, who had independently reached much the same "merge-and-divide" conclusion. They talked for four hours, resolved to move ahead, and within weeks had hammered out an agreement that followed the "industrial logic" of that moment. The two companies would temporarily combine, then separate into three less diversified entities:

Corteva Agriscience, with agriculture products, including seeds and crop protection;

(New) Dow Inc., with materials sciences, including performance chemicals, plastics, and materials; and

(New) DuPont, with specialty products, including biotechnology, nutrition and health, fibers and foams, solar panels, and alternative fuels.

Breen would run the third.

OUR SIMILARITIES ARE SIMILAR

Baseball legend Yogi Berra is famous for offering up life's wisdom through memorable malaprops. Among the better known: "When you come to a fork in the road, take it." When his son, Dale Berra, also a professional baseball player, was asked if he was similar to his father, he responded: "The similarities between me and my father are different." The same was true of Breen's leadership across seven major corporations (and twice at one), from General Instrument to the new DuPont. He led Tyco and DuPont in similar ways—but also in some very different ways.

Figure 8.1. Seven Companies Led by Edward Breen, 1997–2020.

Company	Title	Years
General Instrument Corp.	Chief Executive Officer	1997–2000
Motorola	Chief Operating Officer	2000–2001
Tyco International	Chief Executive	2002–12
New Tyco	Board chair	2012–15
DuPont	Chief Executive	2015–17
DowDuPont Inc.	Chief Executive	2017–19
New DuPont	Chief Executive (twice)	2019, 2020–

Evident in all seven of Breen's corporate incarnations, summarized in Figure 8.1, was his fourfold leadership template, directed as his companies' culture, strategy, risk, and top team. But at the same time, "Tyco was very different than DowDuPont," he said, "because of the liquidity and bankruptcy concerns at Tyco." So he dealt with "different issues."[11]

While Breen's personal leadership foundation remained constant, he was thus also adept at incorporating additional skills when the apparent similarities turned out, on closer examination, to be differences. Ultimately, he said, "I am being paid to create long-term sustainable value," no matter what the venue. "I do a lot of things, but this is the most important," regardless of the company.[12]

In each of these positions, Breen had seen around corners to anticipate where industries were going and their implications for his enterprise. "I'm a big believer," he explained, "in looking at the big strategic issues." No technical know-how here, just a lot of weekend reading and directors as sounding boards.

Breen allocated a majority of his board meetings to the companies' strategic issues, focusing on just two questions: "How do we grow the business and what are the biggest risks?" Those questions were the same for both Tyco and DuPont; but the roadmaps were very different. Tyco required triage and later being broken up into five stand-alone pieces. At DuPont, the path was to merge with Dow, then immediately break the new combination into three separate enterprises. Taking the leadership template he had developed in his General Instrument and Motorola days, Breen adapted it for the triage required at Tyco and then customized it for the transformation at DuPont.

At both Tyco and DuPont, Breen explained, "I am constantly looking over my left and right shoulders to see what's coming at me," and as one device for doing so, he regularly asked himself if he were a hedge fund principal, how he would plot a takeover of his own enterprise. "If you leave the door open," he warned, "you will get an activist." To help keep the door closed, Breen had long followed a habit of giving much of his weekend to his biggest downside worries and how they could be addressed the following week. By Sunday evening he had identified his two or three priorities for the coming days, and on Monday morning he instructed his direct reports on their resulting agenda for the week.

IN CHARGE OF CHANGE

Across his seven-company career as a top executive, Breen let run his lifelong penchant for taking charge of change when redirection was due. Many business leaders would duck the wrenching remakes called for at Tyco and DuPont, but Breen readily embraced them. "I like restructuring," he explained. "I don't mind turnarounds . . . and I kind of found them fun." At each company, he also drew on data analytics and operational discipline for the redirections. In leading them, he concluded as well that his impact was most enduring and his leadership most consequential in the small number of pivotal decisions he reached at each.

Through the years, following his core leadership principles in ways both similar and different, Breen came to appreciate the singular importance of getting the biggest actions done, and done right. "By the time I make a major decision" now, he said, "I am confident in it. [I've] done it before."

At Tyco, the most critical concern was restoring director and executive integrity. At DuPont, by contrast, the most immediate concern was executive underperformance and overstaffing. Having forced out the top tier at Tyco, Breen might have carried that practice into his leadership at DuPont. Building a loyal team of his own might have seemed the experience-informed pathway for the knotty restructuring that he planned to lead there as well. After all, DuPont's incumbents were partly responsible for the firm's overdue reconfiguration. But instead, Breen did the opposite.

After interviewing each of the top executives at DuPont, Breen concluded that he already had, in his words, "a lot of great people around me." At Tyco "it was a bad culture and the wrong people," he explained, while by "total contrast" he found "a great team at DuPont."

He had already learned to serve as a tough-minded judge of personnel, a vital capacity for leading any organization, but now he also learned to judge his direct reports with a lens that fit the specific moment, not necessarily all moments. Some executives prefer to bring in a loyal inner circle, while others have sometimes thrown out the baby with the bathwater. Breen committed to a still different line of consideration: What capacities do I need to lead this company now? he asked himself. The answers at Tyco and at DuPont were very different from each other.

Other pathways differed as well. When Breen first moved into the executive suite at DuPont, he asked McKinsey to benchmark his costs in human resources, legal service, and his major operating divisions against those in peer companies, including Honeywell International and 3M Company. To his chagrin, the numbers indicated that DuPont was more than twice as expensive to run as similar industrials. Confirming what the McKinsey statistics implied, his senior managers did not challenge the expense ratios or the conclusions Breen drew from them. They already knew.

Breen also found that DuPont's managers were enmeshed in a debilitating matrix, with many executives reporting to several bosses, and he eliminated the multiple authority lines, making each executive responsible and accountable for results. Now, he told each, your subordinates report only to you, and it is up to you "to get the job done." The larger remake, however, was to reconfigure the company to better fit the markets that had emerged around it.

At Tyco, however, Breen's agenda had instead been to "save the company, fix the company, and then grow the company." For that, he had to clean-out corruption, sell or close operations that were performing poorly, and then create stand-alone firms from operations within the company.

ADAPTING LEADERSHIP AT THE TOP

Few managers have served as top executives of even two major companies, let alone seven, but Edward Breen's life course gives us an opportunity to learn how to simultaneously stay fixed on a leadership foundation and still build out as needed. It might have been expected that Breen would execute his serial leadership in much the same way across all seven enterprises. And, in fact, facets of his leadership remained constant at all of them, as he prioritized company values, strategy, and risks.

But he was not reluctant to redirect an enterprise when its strategy was out of kilter with the changing market, as at DuPont, or, alternatively, to rescue an enterprise when it was reeling from a self-inflicted disaster, as at Tyco. He varied his ways of leading most notably according to whether the company was growing or imploding.

In other areas, his approaches were more similar, plain and simple. Dating back to his General Instrument days, for instance, Breen had incorporated into his leadership model a guiding premise that he had to know what each executive was best at, and that he had to intervene quickly if the executive was in the wrong position or faltering in an assignment. Decades later he still adhered to that belief.

Behind it all, Breen found in running companies that talent management can be as important as business direction. Strategic thinking, of course, remained a defining feature of the leadership he brought to his varied enterprises, but the first corollary from it was having people in place who could bring the firm's strategy to life.

STILL TRUE: PERSONAL RESOLVE

For years, Breen's annual compensation had been in the millions of dollars. As chief executive of DuPont in 2018, for instance, his income from the company totaled $14.6 million, with $1.9 million coming from salary and $12.7 million from long-term incentives. Though he had been serving as a nonexecutive director on the DuPont governing board when it was considering an executive change, he did not throw in his hat, or even tip his hand to show he would be interested. Instead, several of DuPont's independent directors initiated the unusual step of asking a fellow director, a part-time obligation, to take full-time leadership of the firm.[13]

I asked Breen to explain why he accepted the job, which included the burden of commuting from his family home some ninety minutes away from his DuPont office in Wilmington, Delaware, every day. Certainly, he did not need the money. And he'd received enough media attention and personal accolades to last a lifetime—including being named as one of the "100 Most Influential People in Business Ethics" in 2009 by Ethisphere Institute, a nonprofit organization concerned with corporate conduct. What attracted him, Breen told me, was the intrinsic challenge of running a company, guiding its strategy, optimizing it architecture, and defining its risk.[14]

For Breen, company leadership had long been a personal calling, and it remained so over the years. It entailed serving as an effective "operator," ensuring that products were efficiently made and sold, that customers received what they sought, and that whatever needed to be bettered indeed was. In his own words, "I've always felt passionate about running a company, in part because I'm very intrigued by business strategy." If he was not doing something along this line, he confessed, "I'd be bored."

Boredom would become Ed Breen's least worry in 2020, when another crisis hit with the arrival of the coronavirus. He had just come back to serve again as chief executive of the DuPont spinoff from the merger of Dow and DuPont, and his company ran more than twenty manufacturing facilities in China, including one in Wuhan, the early epicenter of the outbreak. As a result, Breen learned early on how to sustain manufacturing with social distancing and how to shut down plants in locked-out regions, giving him a head start on managing his more than ninety facilities in Germany, the US, and dozens of other countries when the pandemic reached them. And once more, he said, the value of thinking about both company strategy and risk management could not have been more vital as he reached dozens of wrenching decisions on how to sustain a company safely in a world largely shuttered by COVID-19. Here again, he would have to lead both similarly and differently, in this case strategically for the first and with triage—but not transformation—for the second.

CHAPTER 9

REINVENTING THE CULTURE

Johnson & Johnson CEO Alex Gorsky
Modernizes the Credo to Choreograph Performance

The credo is "not an option, it's an heirloom,
and we have to protect [and] apply it."

L eading a frontline team is very much a contact sport, with work
deadlines, children's recitals, and private worries all part of the
Sturm und Drang of office talk. Yet as mangers move up the ranks,
opportunities for informal, drop-by conversations are increasingly
out of reach with anyone but one's innermost circle. The greater
the organizational responsibility, the lesser the personal means for
exercising it.

In 2020, COVID-19 all but eliminated face-to-face contact of
any kind. Consider an office in a gleaming fifty-two-story building
at 7 World Trade Center in Manhattan that drew just two hundred
daily visitors in midsummer, down from more than four thousand
before the crisis. The building's eerily empty offices, reported a lone
worker in one, felt "like the Twilight Zone." Personal belongings
remained from the occupants' hasty exit months before, but almost
nobody had returned for them—or for work. The remote-only ar-
rangement could last for months or more. Google parent Alphabet
decided its employees would not be back in the office until at least
the summer of 2021, and Facebook declared the same. How could a
manager even begin to sustain purpose, direction, and energy with
human interactions limited to Zoom?[1]

For leading hundreds or even thousands of employees that you manage but may never encounter, whether by virtue of company scale or a global pandemic, additional mediums are thus required, and for this we turn to Johnson & Johnson, which had already mastered the challenges of remote leadership through a deceptively simple means before the outbreak. Comprising a sprawling combination of consumer goods, pharmaceuticals, and medical devices, J&J offers everything from Band-Aids and pain relievers to infection medications and hip-replacement hardware, making it one of America's largest corporations, among the top fifty in the Fortune 500. It works through some 260 operating companies, and its annual revenue totals more than a third of a trillion dollars. But the firm has also faced its share of billion-dollar recalls and penalties for faulty or allegedly harmful insulin cartridges, birth-control pills, implantable stents, opioid tablets, and even talcum powder.[2]

Many decades after its founding in 1886, as the company expanded and took on more and more employees, its executives had supplemented their face-to-face leadership with a written credo articulating the company's values. The terse avowal of enterprise purpose was intended to guide all employees without the company's leaders having to directly instruct them individually. The resulting declaration has since become one of J&J's trademarks, a tightly phrased expression of company ideals that everybody is asked to share, a kind of universal template for guiding their behavior within the corporate sphere.

Though a number of companies circulate credo-like statements, over its history J&J has stressed its creed more than most, applying and reinforcing it repeatedly. In effect it has created a vehicle for leveraging the chief executive's leadership across the firm, communicating what the CEO wants without his having to convey it in person. But while a credo can guide a firm's culture for years—at J&J it is set in stone—its language can also fall behind the times and impair its impact.

When Alex Gorsky, J&J's seventh chief executive, took charge in 2012, he came to believe that the written guidance he'd inherited had indeed become dusty, its words and phrases antiquated, its impact enervated. He would somehow have to update and modernize it if it was to leverage his leadership, but he would also have to tread carefully.

JOHNSON & JOHNSON'S ALEX GORSKY

Alex Gorsky brought a bottom-up view of Johnson & Johnson to his leadership of it, appreciating how it worked from his own experience at almost every level in it. After graduating from the US Military Academy at West Point, New York, then serving as an Army Ranger, reaching the rank of captain, he began his business career in 1988 as an entry-level sales representative for one of J&J's many companies, Janssen Pharmaceutica. He swiftly rose to become Janssen's chief in a little over a decade. He went on to run the parent's pharmaceutical business in Europe, the Middle East, and Africa; then directed the company's entire medical devices and diagnostic segment; and then became vice chair of J&J's executive committee. Along the way he decamped for four years to run the North American operations of Novartis Pharmaceutical Corporation, one of J&J's archrivals.

With his gold-plated résumé, Gorsky became one of two finalists to succeed the company's chief executive, William Weldon, who had run the firm for a decade. The company arranged for an outside consultant to conduct a 360-degree feedback assessment of the finalists, asking subordinates, peers, and bosses what they thought of each. Company insiders reportedly had been betting on Gorsky's competitor, but a former J&J executive familiar with the process reported that the 360-evaluations of the two finalists were actually so similar that "you could barely slide a piece of paper" between them. In the end, the board opted for Gorsky, purportedly because of his greater operational and supply-chain experience, and because of his role in securing the company's $21 billion acquisition of orthopedic device-maker Synthes, J&J's largest purchase to date.[3]

In April 2012, when Gorsky assumed Johnson & Johnson's highest office at the relatively young age of fifty-two, he confronted daunting challenges. Beyond the need to ensure that investors stayed in the stock, employees made the products, regulators approved the results, and customers bought the goods, he faced claims of asbestos being in one of the company's premier products, talc-based baby powder, and the loss of patent protections for top-selling medicines, including the antipsychotic drug Risperdal. J&J also had just abandoned a $4 billion market in stents, the small metal devices for propping open clogged heart arteries. A warning by a stock analyst several years later could have applied to almost any year around this time: "there are clear signs that J&J's moat," its ability to ward off its rivals, "is eroding."[4]

Gorsky, of course, accepted ultimate responsibility for surmounting the setbacks, repairing the moat, and sustaining performance. It was he and his top team who had to ensure that tens of thousands of middle managers and frontline workers develop and deliver a vast array of goods, from baby shampoo to an Ebola vaccine. And it was he and his lieutenants who had to prepare the company for digital disruption, global competition, and viral contagion.

Still, Gorsky presided over a juggernaut that sold more than $6 billion's worth of products every month. J&J had become a blue chip among the bluest, a ranking performer among the thirty companies that constituted the Dow Jones Industrial Average. Its market value in 2020 had risen above $400 billion, more than that of ExxonMobil or Walmart.

Fortunately, Gorsky's experience at Novartis added a competitor's perspective to a well-established, insider vantage point. But with the company's workforce of more than 135,000, the days of leading through individual oversight and personal instruction were long past. Instead, he turned to his company's culture to help reach those whom he would never see nor personally instruct. That is, all but a tiny fraction of his employees. J&J maintained a multilayered hierarchy, like all large enterprises, but the firm's cultural heritage also allowed Gorsky to go outside that chain of command. This was where the company's credo came in.

Gorsky's forerunners had created the credo—a statement of just three hundred words that encapsulated the company's ideals and intent—to stimulate and align the actions of all. Yet after months of questioning, Gorsky concluded that its present version stressed cost-cutting more than company strategy, job security more than work purpose, and competent management more than capable leadership.

The chief executive would have to revise the hymnal if he was to continue to lead with it, but there was, however, a massive road-block—almost literally. One of his predecessors had carved the entire credo into a six-ton limestone-and-quartz slab spanning the headquarters' lobby. Sometimes though, even wisdom etched in stone has to be recarved.

CULTURE AND CREDO

The J&J credo arose to serve an enterprise that dated back to the nineteenth century. Two brothers, Charles Johnson and William Johnson, had enlisted in the Union Army during the Civil War, a time when surgeons neither sterilized gloves nor sanitized in-struments. The two survived the war, and a third brother, Robert Wood Johnson, heard from them about the appalling losses from infection among soldiers injured on the battlefields of Chancellors-ville and Gettysburg.

The images still haunted Robert Wood Johnson a decade later when he came upon a lecture, a kind of Ted Talk of its era, at the Centennial Exposition of 1876, in Philadelphia. Joseph Lister, a controversial British surgeon, was advocating the seemingly mod-est step of sanitizing medical instruments. With hospital infec-tion rates running as high as 90 percent, Johnson instantly foresaw the commercial potential of sanitation. He and his brothers incor-porated in 1886 to make and sell sterilized dressing and sanitized sutures. In doing so, they saw the prospect not only of profiting personally but of benefiting humanity.

Six decades later, Robert Wood Johnson II, president and chair of Johnson & Johnson, decided to list the enterprise on the New York Stock Exchange. In going public, however, he worried that the dictates of the new arm's-length owners—stockholders and Wall Streeters—could push his company toward shareholder supremacy at the expense of customer primacy—a core value of the enterprise. To avert that prospect, Johnson asked his governing board to ratify a company charter, "Our Industrial Credo," affirming his operating principles. The board approved Johnson's company-defining message in 1944, making it *the* tangible and teachable expression of the firm's values and purpose for at least the next seventy-five years (Figure 9.1).

Curiously, the new creed positioned shareholders at the bottom and customers at the top, akin to Abraham Maslow's famous

FIGURE 9.1. Johnson & Johnson's First Credo, 1944.

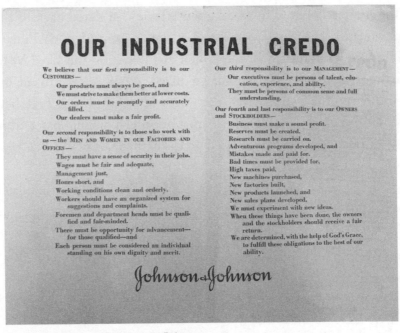

Source: Courtesy of Johnson & Johnson.

hierarchy of human needs, in which he placed personal survival at the bottom and transcendent purpose at the top. Putting shareholders last on the list of those to be served would, for a while, appear quaint, but ultimately it was far ahead of its time. As investor capitalism ascended in America during in the decades ahead, Milton Friedman of the University of Chicago and Michael Jensen of Harvard Business School would push the opposite view, exemplified by General Electric CEO Jack Welch's riveted focus on total shareholder return. After decades of shareholder dominance, though, the American Business Roundtable, an association of corporate CEOs including Alex Gorsky, would issue a radical break with its past, declaring in 2019 that the purpose of a corporation is to also serve customers, employees, suppliers, and communities, not just stockholders. Though owners were not necessarily demoted to last in line, they were also no longer always first.[5]

The J&J board's ratification of Johnson's proclamation would have proved an empty gesture, however, if it weren't vivified in the minds of the employees. Management consequently stepped forward to bring the credo's values to life among all staffers during their daily decisions, with methods ranging from recurrent recitations to prominent postings in the headquarters lobby, the CEO's corner office, and just about everywhere else. Periodic company-wide "Credo Days" reminded employees of the importance of applying the firm's values to their most vexing actions.

The creed as a result served as a kind of collective compass, pointing tens of thousands of employees, located in hundreds of separate operations, in the same direction without further intervention by the chief. But to help employees better translate those company directives into their daily decision-making, later CEOs updated and expanded the basic tenets over the years.

In 1948, Johnson & Johnson brought out an employee-friendlier version that was less a staccato pledge and more a personal narrative. Like later revisions, it was intended to bolster the credo's persuasiveness and behavioral consequence (Figure 9.2).

154

FIGURE 9.2. Johnson & Johnson's Credo, 1948.

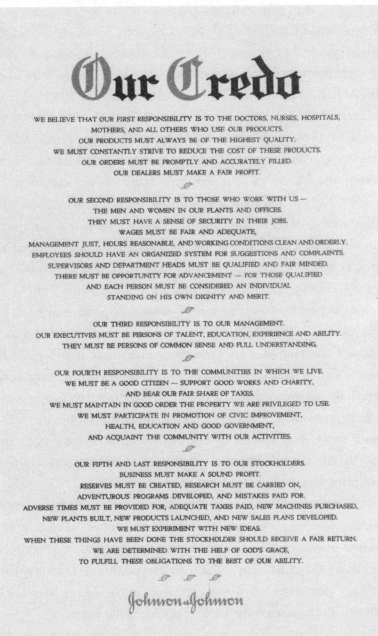

Source: Courtesy of Johnson & Johnson.

The 1948 update referenced doctors, nurses, hospitals, and mothers in place of the more-abstract and less-emotive category of "customers"; replaced "foremen" with "supervisors"; added responsibility to "the communities in which we live"; and freshly advocated that "we must experiment with new ideas." Unaltered in the final paragraph, though, was the callout to stockholders, "Business must make a sound profit," and a pledge that with the help of "God's Grace," the company would "fulfill these obligations to the best of our ability."

Years later, in 1979, J&J's chief executive James Burke replaced "customers" with "patients"; referenced the "world community," where the company increasingly operated; and with concerns for clean air and water coming to the fore, added protection of the "environment." Gone were the gothic title, the uppercase text, "responsibility" to "management," and dependence on "God's Grace" (Figure 9.3). And this revision asked decision-makers to incorporate the vantage points of just four constituencies: patients, employees, communities, and owners, dropping management.

In 1982, these values would be put to the test. Seven J&J customers in the Chicago area—including two brothers and their sister-in-law, as well as a twelve-year-old girl, Mary Kellerman—died after ingesting capsules from one of J&J's best-known and best-selling products, Extra Strength Tylenol. While the source of the poisoning was not immediately known—it would later be determined that someone had placed potassium cyanide inside the capsules, but the culprit was never found—its near-term implications for the company were crystal clear. Tylenol held a 37 percent market share at the time, outselling the next four painkillers combined. It also accounted for a fifth of the company's income. Had the Tylenol operation been spun-off as a separate company, it would have stood among the Fortune 250. But now 31 million of its capsules still on retail shelves were called into doubt.

Even though no regulator stepped in nor did the Federal Bureau of Investigation, Burke appealed for an immediate recall of

FIGURE 9.3. Johnson & Johnson Credo, 1979.

Source: Courtesy of Johnson & Johnson.

all Tylenol containers by his workforce. The company credo had directed the frontlines to place consumer interests ahead of others, and in most cases, J&J employees proceeded to remove the capsules with little explicit direction from above. In the end, the recall cost the company more than $100 million and dropped the product's market share to just 7 percent, not good for the near-term wealth of the shareholders—but certainly good for the near-term health of its customers.

Johnson & Johnson's across-the-board recall of Tylenol became one of the most widely assigned teaching cases in business schools, a benchmark for future managers to remember, and at the core of the case was the credo. When the editors of *Fortune* magazine later identified the "greatest business decisions of all time," they included J&J's decision to create the credo, on a par with Boeing's decision to build the 707 and Apple's decision to bring back its prodigal son, Steve Jobs. The Tylenol recall, said *Fortune*, was the "gold standard of crisis management," and its massive and swift execution followed the credo's mantra, "the shareholder comes last."[6]

In 1987, CEO Burke updated the credo yet again, adding "fathers" to "mothers" and calling for "employees to fulfill their family responsibilities," again limited but important adjustments for revitalizing the message. After all, loving fathers were as concerned about their children's wellness as mothers, and employees were increasingly drawn to balancing their work and family obligations.

In one reaffirming and oft-repeated account, a visitor to the home office, seeing the revised credo now etched in stone at headquarters (Figure 9.4), asked chief executive Ralph Larsen, who served from 1989 to 2002, "Suppose you want to change it?" Larsen politely informed the inquisitive guest that he had missed the point. The credo was so central to the company's identity that it was indeed "carved in stone." Much of the company's growth, Larson explained, could be attributed to the credo's directing powers, aligning employee decisions in ways he could not personally. The credo had even become a selling point in recruitment. The company

FIGURE 9.4. The Johnson & Johnson Credo in Stone at Headquarters.

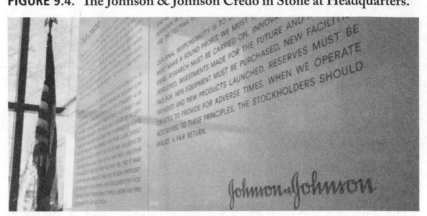

Source: Courtesy of Johnson and Johnson.

reported that its new hires singled-out the credo as one of their top three reasons for accepting a position with J&J.

As the years passed, the company's credo and its behavioral norms came to transcend the executives who devised them, embraced by one generation after another, a leadership template for all. It came as no surprise, then, that when Alex Gorsky took the helm in 2012, he devoted twenty minutes of his prepared remarks at his first stockholders meeting to affirming the leadership value of the creed. "Our Credo will remain at the core of what drives our actions," he declared. "It reflects our values, our beliefs, and our aspirations. It defines our core responsibilities to our stakeholders. It enables us to make a real, lasting, and profound difference in the world."[7]

When visiting J&J locations around the world, Gorsky came to regularly open his remarks by referencing the credo, declaring its principles to be his own leadership principles as well. "It is the glue, the thread, the inspiration" for everybody. "I use the credo every day," he explained, in reaching decisions concerning centralizing and decentralizing company functions, relying on internal manufacturing or external sourcing, or protecting patient safety. If he did not always get every decision right, he nonetheless had made it a habit to frame each decision with direct reference to credo principles, starting with, "We believe our first responsibility is to the patients, doctors and nurses, to mothers and fathers and all others who use our products and services."

THE CREDO'S ACCEPTANCE

While embraced at the top, the credo's value for propagating the chief executive's leadership was only as good as its reception within the ranks, and over the years the firm had pressed for universal acceptance. J&J asked all managers to prepare "credo action plans" for their employees, with "credo ambassadors" ready to assist, and it held supervisors responsible for their outcomes. Managers received a company rating on credo concurrence from their subordinates, and when subpar, the firm required managers to detail a plan to bolster the credo's acceptance in their ranks.

As a result, the 1987 credo came to be broadly accepted among rank-and-file employees by the time of Alex Gorsky's ascension in 2012. This was evident in the company's annual surveys of its employees. In 2013 and 2014, for instance, Johnson & Johnson asked the rank and file if they agreed that eight specific values of the credo were being enacted, including whether company managers passed up commercial opportunities if they compromised the credo's values, and whether managers held employees accountable if they violated those values. Strong majorities agreed in both years, with three-quarters or more concurring that each of the eight credo principles was being enacted (Figure 9.5).

Several years further into Alex Gorsky's term, the company focused in even greater detail on the credo's acceptance. It found that three-quarters or more of the surveyed employees reported their agreement with each of thirty-five separate elements in the 1987 credo's four paragraphs on patients and customers, leadership and work, communities, and owners (Figure 9.6). Since becoming CEO in 2012, Gorky had by 2018 grown his company's revenue by

FIGURE 9.5. Employee Rating of the Eight Credo Values, 2013 and 2014. Percentage of Employees Agreeing or Strongly Agreeing.

Credo Values	2014 84%	2013 84%
Management at my company would turn down business or other opportunities if it meant compromising our Credo values.	83	80
Management at my company sets a good example of ethical business behavior.	84	82
Senior management at my company takes appropriate action upon unethical or inappropriate behaviors and practices.	82	79
Unethical behavior is not tolerated in my department.	87	88
Ethical expectations have been clearly communicated to me by my company.	91	90
I feel I could report unethical business practices without fear of reprisal.	79	79
Employees are held accountable if they are caught violating our Credo values.	81	82
People in my work area are protected from health and safety hazards.	89	90

Source: Johnson & Johnson. Figure presents the percentage of employees strongly agreeing or agreeing with an item (lower rating categories: neutral, disagree, and strongly disagree).

more than 20 percent and its share price by more than 40 percent—and he was sustaining the credo's acceptance rates at better than 80 percent.

The credo could help align employee actions only if it was widely known and well accepted, and it was evident from employee surveys that such a foundation had indeed been set. Yet company executives

FIGURE 9.6. Employee Rating of the Credo's Four Sections, 2016 and 2018. Percentage of Employees Agreeing or Strongly Agreeing.

Credo Paragraphs and Questions	2018	2016
Patients and Customers	**89%**	**89%**
Is committed to the needs of doctors and nurses.	92	91
Is committed to the needs of patients.	93	93
Is committed to the needs of consumers.	92	92
Delivers high quality in everything we do.	89	89
Strives to reduce costs.	86	86
Strives to maintain good value for our products.	90	90
Ensures customer orders are serviced promptly and accurately.	87	88
Strives to ensure suppliers and distributors have opportunity for fair profit.	83	84
Leadership and Work	**80**	**80**
Is committed to the needs of employees.	78	78
Considers all employees as individuals.	80	80
Respects the dignity of all employees.	85	84
Provides employees with a sense of security in their jobs.	72	71
Provides employees with compensation that is fair.	74	74
Maintains working conditions that are clean and orderly.	91	91
Maintains working conditions that are safe.	94	94
Is committed to helping employees fulfill their family responsibilities.	82	81
Promotes an environment in which employees feel free to make suggestions and complaints.	78	78
Is committed to equal advancement opportunities for those qualified.	71	71

continues

FIGURE 9.6. *continued*

Credo Paragraphs and Questions	2018	2016
Leadership and Work (continued)	80	80
Provides capable management.	78	78
Provides management that acts in just and ethical ways.	81	81
Communities	89	89
Is committed to the communities in which employees live and work.	87	88
Supports good works and charities.	92	92
Ensures our business pays our fair share of taxes.	88	88
Encourages civic improvements in the community.	87	87
Encourages better health and education in the community.	89	89
Maintains the property in which employees use, by protecting the environment and natural resources.	90	90
Owners	87	87
Is committed to our stockholders.	94	94
Ensures our business makes a sound profit.	94	94
Experiments with new ideas.	84	85
Promotes continual research and the development of innovative programs.	87	87
Is committed to paying for mistakes.	80	81
Is committed to providing new facilities.	80	81
Is committed to launching new products.	91	91
Is committed to creating financial reserves to provide for adverse times.	85	85

Source: Johnson & Johnson. Figure presents the percentage of employees strongly agreeing or agreeing with a credo value (lower rating categories: neutral, disagree, and strongly disagree).

also cautioned that the credo could not by itself help resolve every leadership question they might have to confront. The greater the responsibility in the company, explained one senior manager, the larger were the ambiguities, and thus "rarely is there a 'credo answer'" for the most wrenching questions. Instead, the creed was more intended to remind its holders of the diverse and sometimes conflicting priorities that must be considered in making a decision. It called managers, for instance, to protect the health of patients, as identified in the first paragraph, and at the very same time ensure a "fair return" for shareholders, as signaled in the fourth paragraph.

As a case in point, an executive responsible for the company's vision-care business, which ranged from eye drops to cataract surgery equipment, had just launched a new contact lens when she learned that it caused extreme burning in some patients. If the executive withdrew the product it would result in a poor financial year for her division, and the burning was extremely rare—just three cases per million. For those reasons, her staff cautioned against a precipitous recall. The executive worried, however, about the product's long-term impact on patients and their trust in the company, and she decided on her own to pull it off the market. The credo's values were sufficiently directive, in her mind, to cancel the launch, and despite the resulting losses for the division and the company, home-office executives applauded the credo-driven action.

J&J appraised promotion candidates not only for their business results but also for their "credo leadership." Senior managers often referred to the credo when they reviewed subordinates for promotion, asking not only if they performed well in their business but also if they applied credo values to their operations. When making recommendations on senior advancements, the chief human resources executive, Peter Fasolo, reported that the credo helped him compare the values and commitments of the finalists in difficult personnel calls. If "you are not a 'credo leader,'" he warned, your upward mobility will be impaired. Similarly, when Alex Gorsky interviewed finalists for the senior-most positions in the company, he asked each to detail an example of their application of the credo. And to remind himself of the importance of following the credo, Gorsky placed a blown-up version of it in white letters with a red background on a wall facing his corner-office desk.

A NEW TIME HAD COME

Recurrently cited, repeatedly applied, the credo had not been updated, however, for more than a quarter century, and employees were terming it "quaint." In the mid-2010s, its modernization had emerged as a quiet but compelling concern for the CEO.

Updating the creed, however, would require a concerted act of leadership itself. Like all deeply held human ideals, once accepted, company charters resist easy amendment. "The Credo is like the Constitution or Magna Carta," warned a company historian, "only changed once a generation as society changes." In Gorsky's view, that generational moment had come.

Johnson & Johnson's market had become more global, customers more diverse, employees more purposeful, and litigation more damaging. Looking at younger generations in the ranks— Gen X, Gen Y, and millennials—Gorsky found that they "want to be part of something bigger than themselves." And to him, the credo's words seemed less resonant, some of its edicts no longer clear, others no longer appropriate. The credo had aligned thousands during the Tylenol crisis, but in Gorsky's view its power for doing so in a future crisis—perhaps a pandemic—was perceptibly waning. Still, it had served as the company's inertial guidance for some seventy-five years, most of it was still relevant, and the cost to his stature of wrongly amending it would be high.[8]

After privately pondering the possibility and the risks for several years, Gorsky finally raised the revision question with his top team, the company's executive committee, and the dozen heads of his operating divisions and company functions, including consumer products, medical devices, pharmaceuticals, human resources, supply chains, and finance. These were the officers through whom his leadership was directly exercised, and their active acceptance of a revision would be a *sine qua non* for its execution.

The executive committee's initial reaction confirmed Gorsky's cautionary reluctance. Some members were for updating the credo in principle, but they needed to see what was proposed. Others opposed any modification on principle. Why change the wording, some said, when the company was doing well and thus, by implication, was well served by the credo.

Undaunted, Gorsky brought forward a marked-up version of the credo for the executive committee's further counsel. To test his sense that an update was in order, he sought to engage the rank and file, asking each executive committee member to arrange at least a half dozen "credo challenges" in their own operation. They were to ask inductively, inquiring, If you could change the credo, what would you alter? General counsel Michael Ullmann took it to the extreme, arranging more than twenty such vettings. With so many suggestions now pouring in, there would be no turning back.

In all, some three thousand employees weighed in, and with their input Gorsky revised and resubmitted the credo to his executive committee. He asked three members—Michael Ullmann, communication chief Michael Sneed, and human resources executive Peter Fasolo—to devote further attention to fine-tuning the revisions. The general counsel would have to ensure that the revised statement carried no legal baggage; the communication executive would have to be sure it would resonate with the ranks; and the HR executive would have to be clear on how it could guide personnel planning.

After several months of rumination and a final weekend redrafting at home, Gorsky presented a revised version of the credo to his executive committee and the governing board for a last vetting. The final approval, however was to be his alone, and the final version appears in Figure 9.7.

The revisions are summarized in Figure 9.8, and we see that the changes and additions made patients first among company

FIGURE 9.7. Johnson & Johnson's Credo, 2018.

Our Credo

We believe our first responsibility is to the patients, doctors and nurses, to mothers and fathers and all others who use our products and services. In meeting their needs everything we do must be of high quality. We must constantly strive to provide value, reduce our costs and maintain reasonable prices. Customers' orders must be serviced promptly and accurately. Our business partners must have an opportunity to make a fair profit.

We are responsible to our employees who work with us throughout the world. We must provide an inclusive work environment where each person must be considered as an individual. We must respect their diversity and dignity and recognize their merit. They must have a sense of security, fulfillment and purpose in their jobs. Compensation must be fair and adequate and working conditions clean, orderly and safe. We must support the health and well-being of our employees and help them fulfill their family and other personal responsibilities. Employees must feel free to make suggestions and complaints. There must be equal opportunity for employment, development and advancement for those qualified. We must provide highly capable leaders and their actions must be just and ethical.

We are responsible to the communities in which we live and work and to the world community as well. We must help people be healthier by supporting better access and care in more places around the world. We must be good citizens — support good works and charities, better health and education, and bear our fair share of taxes. We must maintain in good order the property we are privileged to use, protecting the environment and natural resources.

Our final responsibility is to our stockholders. Business must make a sound profit. We must experiment with new ideas. Research must be carried on, innovative programs developed, investments made for the future and mistakes paid for. New equipment must be purchased, new facilities provided and new products launched. Reserves must be created to provide for adverse times. When we operate according to these principles, the stockholders should realize a fair return.

Johnson&Johnson

Source: Courtesy of Johnson and Johnson.

responsibilities, now ahead of doctors and nurses; focused the company on strategy, not just cost cutting; called for purpose in work, not just job security; added diversity to workplace dignity; pressed for "capable leaders" in place of "competent management"; added public health as a priority; and stressed research and innovation for the long haul. I believe that readers will generally agree that these changes and additions resonate better with contemporary employee values.

Gorsky's subsequent leadership challenge was to communicate the revised credo to the company's employees so that it would stick;

FIGURE 9.8. Johnson & Johnson's 1987 and 2018 Credos.

1987 Credo	2018 Credo	Change or Addition
Patients & Customers		
We believe our first responsibility is to the doctors, nurses and patients . . .	We believe our first responsibility is to the patients, doctors and nurses . . .	Putting patients first
We must constantly strive to reduce our costs . . .	We must constantly strive to provide value . . .	Focusing on company strategy, not just cost cutting
Our suppliers and distributors must have an opportunity to make a fair profit.	Our business partners must have an opportunity to make a fair profit.	Including more than suppliers and distributors among its partners
Leadership & Work		
Everyone must be considered as an individual.	We must provide an inclusive work environment where each person must be considered as an individual.	Adding inclusion
They must have a sense of security in their jobs.	They must have a sense of security, fulfillment and purpose in their jobs.	Inserting fulfillment and purpose

continues

FIGURE 9.8. *continued*

1987 Credo	2018 Credo	Change or Addition
We must respect their dignity . . .	We must respect their diversity and dignity . . .	Including diversity
We must provide competent management . . .	We must provide highly capable leaders . . .	Stressing capable leaders instead of competent managers
Communities		
[Nothing]	We must help people be healthier by supporting better access and care in more places around the world.	Adding public health
Stockholders		
Research must be carried on, innovative programs developed and mistakes paid for.	Research must be carried on, innovative programs developed, investments made for the future and mistakes paid for.	Stressing long-term investments

otherwise, it would remain just empty rhetoric. He introduced his new version of the company's values to them in September 2018 during a private telecast to the entire J&J workforce. He asked that every manager meet monthly with his or her direct reports on the implications of the new credo for their own actions. Symptomatic of the high stakes and leadership significance, the chief executive's voice broke at several points during the presentation. Then, on December 13, 2018, he added a "town hall" extravaganza, a company-wide recognition and promotion of the new text.

The event drew 1,200 participants in person, almost all, including the CEO and his executive committee members, clad in the same red shirts emblazoned with CREDO 75. The only jacket in sight was the one I wore. The company broadcast the event in two-way video to another 40,000 employees, from Cape Town and Dubai to São Paulo and Shanghai. The simple but unequivocal purpose, explained the chief human resources officer, Peter Fasolo, was to align "people's values with those of the company"—as newly expressed.

"Today we celebrate this event together," Gorsky declared, as "a great opportunity to reaffirm our commitments to the communities that we serve." The revised credo, he said, is for "putting patients first, for diversity and inclusion," for "our unwavering support of our health," and "I could not be more proud" of it. Moreover, "it's not an option, it's an heirloom, and we have to protect" and "apply it." He explained the reasons for its revision and offered a call to embrace it: "We are responding to the world that is changing" and the new credo will be at "the core of all that we do for generations to come." And now, we "have to bring it to life every day."

Presidential historian Doris Kearns Goodwin reported that although Abraham Lincoln had drafted the Emancipation Proclamation in mid-1862, he opted to delay its issuance until a major event provided evidence that the Union would ultimately prevail in the Civil War, and that the moment came in the aftermath of the Battle of Antietam on September 17, 1862. The engagement was more of a draw than an outright Federal victory, but after a string of Union defeats, Lincoln decided that it was sufficient, issuing the historic declaration on January 1, 1863, and transforming the purpose and course of the war.

Alex Gorsky had originally planned to introduce the credo's changes earlier in the year, but had to rethink its timing. Johnson & Johnson had been ordered by a court in July 2018 to pay more than $4 billion to twenty-two women charging that one of its products had caused their ovarian cancer (an appeals court reaffirmed the verdict in June 2020, though it cut the damage amount by more than half). In the judgment of the general counsel, waiting six months after the court verdict "was not too early and it was not too late" to make the credo changes and lift some of the cloud. An unveiling on December 13, 2018, also came with a piece of history: it was seventy-five years to the day since Robert Wood Johnson II had presented the original credo to his board for ratification.[9]

At the town hall presentation, General Counsel Ullmann added a personal connection by introducing John B. Gibson, seated in the front row. John J. Gibson, grandfather of John B., had served as corporate secretary when the governing board adopted the first iteration of the credo. Gibson's presence was intended to represent historic continuity. "The core values of our credo have never changed," explained one executive. "But over time the wording has shifted to reflect new realities in the world and in the workplace."

But that feel-good moment hardly meant that J&J would face calm seas ahead. In the months that followed, the state of Oklahoma initiated a civil trial against the company for its production of opioids, and the company reached cash settlements in other litigation against it, including $387 million for a blood thinner and $1 billion for its hip implants.

CULTURE LEADS

We often think of a company's culture as a distinctive set of operating values, behavioral norms, and even a way of life that sets a firm apart from other enterprises. Remove the nameplate from the headquarters of General Electric, Google, or Progressive, and most job applicants would still have no problem knowing which of the companies they had entered. Each has its own ethos and, aware of that, both hiring managers and job candidates look for a good match between a firm's philosophy and an applicant's values.[10]

That said, company culture is often underappreciated for the leadership leverage it can provide above and beyond the initial alignment at the point of hiring. It allows midlevel managers and senior executives to extend their sway to hundreds if not thousands in ways not otherwise achievable. When well-conceived and widely accepted, a firm's culture can thus serve as a force multiplier for a manager's leadership.

With only hundreds of employees, face-to-face leadership had been possible at Johnson & Johnson, but with 135,000, its values and norms, contemporarily articulated and repeatedly expressed, became a company-wide instrument for employee direction. Ron Williams, a former chief executive of the healthcare company Aetna Inc., repeats the oft-heard expression "culture eats strategy," but with the proviso that culture is not "just what the leadership says it is." Rather, it is "what people actually experience every day."[11]

Academic researchers have long cited the value of social purpose driven from the top, as we have seen at Johnson & Johnson, for boosting personal commitment and employee identification with the firm. Evidence from a survey of a half million employees at 429 US companies confirmed that these enhancements also result in better recruitment of new workers and stronger efforts from those who have been hired. "Making meaning" and actively pressing it produced strengthened commitments from middle managers that bolstered the firms' accounting and stock performance, though the perceptions among hourly workers were less consequential.[12]

The first management step for building that leverage is to construct a channel for articulating the culture, as Robert Wood Johnson II did in creating Johnson & Johnson's original credo in 1944. A second, follow-on action is for company leaders to actively instill and sustain the culture, as Johnson and his CEO successors sought to do through their "Credo Days" and town halls. But over time, as a firm and its markets evolve, rigid maintenance of the culture will come to defeat its leadership purpose. Then, a third management action becomes essential, reworking and modernizing the culture from time to time, preserving its core while also adapting it to the current era and its emerging mores.

As skillful as J&J has been in doing so, it is by no means alone. In 2009, Netflix, Inc., defined its own values in a 125-slide presentation. Its "culture deck" stressed employee autonomy—face few spending controls, it exhorted, and take whatever vacation time you like—*and* alignment—"act in Netflix's best interest"—and it emerged as a kind of bible among Netflix's high-tech peers. The chief operating officer of Facebook, Sheryl Sandberg, declared it "the most important document ever to come out of the Valley," and by 2017 it had been viewed online more than sixteen million times.

But it, too, would become dated, and CEO Reed Hastings also instigated an update. He converted bullet points into a narrative, akin to J&J's 1948 credo revision, and he now stressed diversity, inclusion, mutual respect, parental leave, and globalization (Netflix had by then expanded from just the US to more than 190 countries). The fundamentals of passion and innovation were still at its core, and the purpose remained unchanged—employees were still to be "loosely coupled" yet "highly aligned"—but other features spoke to contemporary sensibilities.

As Alex Gorsky characterized the enduring power of J&J's credo, if periodically and properly updated, its company-wide leadership value was sure to "outlive us" all.[13]

CHAPTER 10

MASTERING THE FIELD
TO WIN IT ALL

NFL Team Owner Jeffrey Lurie Orchestrates
His Team to a Super Bowl Victory

"An individual can make a difference,"
a "team can make a miracle."

I n 2018, Alphabet reported record profits of $31 billion. Apple racked up $59 billion. Impressive, certainly, among the best numbers ever reported. But only one organization could claim *the* trophy that year. By which I mean the sterling-silver, Tiffany-designed, twenty-two-inch-high Vince Lombardi Trophy, topped with a silver football matching the real thing. It goes to *the* football franchise that has triumphed in the National Football League's championship, the Super Bowl.[1]

Like every owner of the NFL's thirty-two teams, the Philadelphia Eagles' Jeffrey Lurie had long imagined the jubilation of the trophy being handed to him as the winning team's owner with tens of millions of fans tuned in. His team had reached the Super Bowl in 2004, but there it succumbed to the league's defending champion, the New England Patriots. In a rematch in the fifty-second Super Bowl on February 4, 2018, however, Lurie finally savored the ultimate moment in American football.

The New England Patriots had been leading 33–32 with 9 minutes and 22 seconds to go. Favored by 4.5 points going in, the Patriots had already won the Super Bowl in 2017, 2015, 2005, 2004, and 2002. And in this latest contest, Patriots quarterback Tom Brady had been on a roll, ultimately passing for 505 yards, the most ever in the game of games.

But the Philadelphia Eagles, with a backup quarterback on the field, would add 10 unanswered points in the game's final nine minutes. It was an upset that would inspire a city long starved for a football championship, along with fans nationwide, who savored the improbable—an upstart that beat the odds.

THE PHILADELPHIA EAGLES' JEFFREY LURIE

Few owners and executives follow a linear path to the top, instead taking unexpected turns along the way or sometimes just being in the right place at the right time. But Jeffrey Lurie seemed an especially improbable owner of a sports franchise. With a doctorate in social policy from Brandeis University—his thesis was on the depiction of women in Hollywood films—he began his career by teaching at Boston University. Filmmaking, however, beckoned more.

Lurie joined his family's firm, General Cinema Corporation, in 1983, and in 1985 founded his own movie studio, Chestnut Hill Productions. *Inside Job*, a film he produced about the 2008–2009 financial crisis, won the Academy Award in 2011 for best documentary feature film; *Inocente*, about a homeless girl in California, for which he served as executive producer, also won the Oscar for best documentary short film. Lurie actually performed in other films, including *Jerry Maguire*, in which he made a cameo appearance as himself.

But leading football players instead of film crews had become Lurie's passion. After failing to acquire the New England Patriots in 1993, in 1994 he successfully bought the Philadelphia Eagles for $195 million. The Eagles had won only half their games the year before, and a Super Bowl win for the midtier team seemed a very long way off. Lurie realized that the road to the Lombardi trophy would somehow depend on enlarging his leadership repertoire.

Fundamentals such as strategic thinking, persuasive communication, and decisive action would remain the same. Over time, however, Lurie learned to incorporate three additional leadership capacities: connecting the talent, completing the inner circle, and taking calculated risks. It took nearly a quarter century to master all three, and his experience stands as a potent reminder that there is no quick fix for learning to lead, or even just supplementing the traditional with what is new.

CONNECTING THE TALENT

Recruiting the right team leader is, of course, one of any firm's most consequential choices. Company owners and governing boards consistently confirm that their greatest decision is picking the top executive. To this end, as the Eagles' chair and chief executive, Lurie had sought a head coach who could bring out the collective performance of the entire team. The best players are not necessarily the best team members unless pulled together, and here the coach's leadership skills loom large.

Vince Lombardi, the legendary head coach for the Green Bay Packers from 1959 to 1967 for whom the Super Bowl trophy is named, captured one of the most important leadership precepts for bringing out a team's performance: "Perfection is not attainable," he said, but "if we chase perfection, we can catch excellence." The head coach of the New England Patriots since 2000, Bill Belichick, stressed the same collective pursuit: "On a team, it's not the strength of the individual players, but it is the strength of the unit and how they all function together."[2]

In the new owner's mind, the Eagles had to be far more than just a sum of the perfections of its parts, and he extended that mindset to nonplayers as well. If the organization could better sync its players and staffers around shared purpose, the team ought to be better able to move the ball when it really mattered, say with 9:22 to go in the ultimate game. Yet finding a head coach who could deliver proved more intractable than Lurie had imagined, and it required three tries.

Jeffrey Lurie's search for a head coach who could create connectedness started with his hiring of Andy Reid in 1999. Having served as a quarterback coach for a Green Bay Packers team that finished its 1998 season with eleven wins over five losses, Reid came with a promising résumé. He delivered in Philadelphia as well, with a win rate of 58 percent, and the team contending in four consecutive National Football Conference championship games, the semifinals in postseason play. But Reid fell short in earning the Super Bowl Championship that was the owner's ultimate goal.

Though Lurie and his senior staffers regarded Reid as a hall-of-fame-caliber coach, after fourteen seasons, and with no rancor, they made a change. Reid went on to lead the Kansas City Chiefs to a come-from-behind Super Bowl victory over the San Francisco 49ers in 2020. His most important legacy for the Eagles, though, was strengthening a culture of inclusiveness within not only the team but across the club, which Lurie and his lieutenants worked to sustain as they brought in a replacement.

The Eagles cast a wide net, interviewing more than a dozen candidates and finally hiring Chip Kelly, a coach with an innovative but risky approach to the game. Kelly too brought a promising résumé, having just taken the University of Oregon to great heights, including three conference championships and the college national championship game in 2014. While inclusiveness was not Kelly's strong suit, Lurie and his lieutenants believed that between Reid's legacy and their own backing of the principle, they would not lose the connected mindset. "We felt like we had the culture accounted for between Jeffrey, Don [Smolenski, the Eagle's president], and me," reported football operations head Howard Roseman. "What we needed was Chip's approach of aggressive risk-taking."

But Kelly's style of keeping players and staffers at arm's-length proved too much. All decisions, whether about which free agents to recruit, which players to field, or which staffers to retain, had to be on Kelly's terms.

Kelly remade the roster—trading away prominent fan favorites—and recast the executive suite, forcing Roseman out of football operations altogether. "Culture beats scheme every time," Kelly had declared, though his top-down mindset was not the one the organization had in mind when they hired him. Kelly brought in a chief of staff, for instance, who in the eyes of Lurie, Roseman, and Smolenski proved too self-absorbed, but Kelly thwarted calls for his replacement, insisting on retaining authority over all personnel matters. "As long as I win on the field," Kelly explained, "that's what counts."

As sometimes seen among promising chief executives early in their terms, Kelly was winning his battles for the moment, but ultimately, he would lose the war. While his "my way or the highway" attitude might work well elsewhere—and momentarily did with the Eagles—it got in the way of the engagement that Lurie had been seeking from both players and staff in his organization.[3]

It became evident to the owner and his deputies that Kelly's resistance to inclusiveness also was getting in the way of their Super Bowl aspirations, and Lurie dismissed him in a fashion intended to signal a strategic redirection to both the players and the fans. Most head coach firings come *after* the season's final game, but in 2015, Philadelphia moved Kelly out a week *before* the final game. Lurie explained the dismissal directly to the players, and then, displaying a tenet of the culture he wanted to bolster, he asked them what *they* wanted in a replacement. Many said they wanted a coach who could personally connect with them both on and off the field, a person who could talk with them, inform them, listen to them, and not mislead them.

Underscoring his connectedness principle during a press conference just after Kelly's dismissal, Lurie set forth what he now sought in a replacement. "The best approach is a real collaborative approach," Lurie explained. He wanted a head coach who "interacts very well and communicates clearly with everyone he comes in touch with." That required a human touch on top of technical mastery. The Eagles would be searching for a coach, the owner explained, who had "a sharp football mind, a style of leadership that values information, including football analytics" and "all the resources that are provided." He also wanted a coach whose "emotional intelligence" would draw in all, and somebody who expressed his thinking before he imposed it

As he narrowed a shortlist of candidates to replace Kelly, Lurie focused on one criterion in particular. The "right fit" would be a candidate with a talent-connecting mandate, someone focused on "bringing the building back together" in the words of Jake Rosenberg, the vice president of football administration, rather than a coach who insisted on unquestioned authority. The owner, the president, and the head of football operations all added that the new coach should be "quarterback centric," as at many NFL teams, meaning that the choice of quarterback, the plays fashioned around him, and the coaching of him were sure to be fateful. A successor would also have to be a risk-taker, but within a larger package that nevertheless prioritized inclusiveness. We will still "not tolerate a dictatorship," affirmed Lurie.

Lurie focused on Doug Pederson, a former quarterback and later a quarterback coach for the Eagles during Andy Reid's tenure, offensive coordinator at the time for the Kansas City Chiefs. Given that Kansas City was still in the playoffs, NFL rules precluded the Eagles from approaching him right away, but its executives already knew much about him, and everyone, including Reid, thought highly of him. Reid and Lurie had maintained a working relationship since their separation, a reminder that staying close to your former associates, even if now rivals, can prove of enduring advantage.

Recruited as head coach for the Eagles' 2016 season, Doug Pederson openly explained his lineup decisions to players and invited their counsel. "What do you want your team to look like?" he asked. New assignments went for review before anybody was moved. "It's not about me," Pederson pleaded. "You're the ones who play. I can't play anymore." He encouraged his guys to propose strategies, criticize techniques, even interrupt instruction. "I don't want robots in here," as offensive line coach, Jeff Stoutland explained, because "you might know even more than I know."[4]

The new mindset gained traction—"taking off" in Pederson's words—as skepticism receded, and by his second season players came to appreciate his engagement with them, even as he had to make decisions about their futures. Pederson found, as intended, that his linebackers, receivers, safeties, and other specialists began to coach one another. The players displayed the connectedness that Pederson had challenged them to embrace, driven in part by his own ability to connect with them. "Doug sparked buy in through his level of empathy for players after a twelve-year career," said Shaun Huls, responsible for player development as director of "high performance" for the Eagles. "He was constantly reminding players, 'I understand how you feel.'"

Moreover, the coach was on the same page with the owner. In Lurie's view, unquestioned authority had to give way to two-way discourse. We "don't want fifty-three leaders or fifty-three followers" on the team, but rather a "strong mix of leaders and followers." In the case of two defensive backs, for instance, the players consulted each other both on and off the field, nudging each other to adjust or act. "I know his buttons," said one, and "some guys do better when you prod them." For that to work, "you have to know each team member, you have to figure out" what motivates them.

Supported by Howie Roseman, Doug Pederson informed players more frequently and consulted more widely. "We try for everyone to know everything," Roseman explained. When anticipating adding a new player to the roster, for instance, he and Pederson articulated their rationale to the whole team. "Before we make a move," Roseman said, "key players need to know." And then, once players came to understand more about the moving parts, they began to accept greater responsibility for the pieces, even suggesting, for instance, which players should be moved into the lineup, out of the lineup, or elsewhere on the lineup. "We don't want anyone to learn of a move by reading about in the paper," said Roseman. The players, Roseman explained, "take ownership if you let them," and they did.

At the same time, as a carryover from the Kelly years and consistent with what Lurie saw in Pederson, the new coach moved to resolve uncertain questions quickly and aggressively. "If we wanted to be a Super Bowl contender," explained Roseman, "we couldn't do it the way everyone else did it." Player development director Shaun Huls added, we "needed our own way, and we all needed to take risks." To that end, Pederson retained several of Kelly's deputies, including the director of high performance, the offensive line coach, the running backs coach, and the special teams coach. Roseman brought the same. "Howie isn't afraid to take risks, and his personality matches the personality of the organization," said Lurie. "We'll never slow each other down, and building trust means there is no putting on the brakes." That trust was extended through the ranks. The best thing Roseman did for him, Huls reported, "was to say 'I trust you. I trust you at every opportunity.'"

RISK AND TRUST

The power of the risk-and-trust formula to help the team surmount setbacks was perhaps nowhere more evident than in the aftermath of the Eagles' loss of its principal quarterback, Carson Wentz (more on him shortly), when he was sidelined with an anterior cruciate ligament—ACL—injury three games before the end of the regular season in 2017. "If there ever was a time" for the players to help fill in the gap, Pederson recalled, it was now.

Following this devastating injury on a Sunday, the players took Monday off, and as the coach wrestled alone with his star's sidelining, he received a one-line morale booster from his own son. "An individual can make a difference," his son texted. "A team can make a miracle." This private gesture jump-started Pederson's own psychic repair, and at a team meeting on Tuesday, he sought the same from his players.

The assembled players remained eerily still as Pederson entered their meeting room, the pessimism palpable. The Eagles had already secured a place in the NFL's postseason playoffs, but the team was still vying for the number one seed and home-field advantage, and their prospects seemed gloomy. WITH CARSON WENTZ OUT FOR THE SEASON, the *New York Times* headlined, EAGLES' DREAMS TURN TO DREAD.

"Guys, we're sitting here, our hearts are heavy, we lost Carson, and this sucks," Pederson began. "But if one man can make a difference, a team can make a miracle." Body language warmed, and Pederson pressed the case. "You're still a good team," and "we're still number two or three in defense." Let's "focus now on what we have, not on what we lost."[5]

And what they had not lost was the players' connectedness that came with the risk-and-trust mindset that their leadership had created. "The players are our partners," explained the owner, not just "pieces on a chessboard." We "started the season as a family, and we'll finish the season as a family." Lurie attended every team practice, excusing himself from an interview with me and a colleague to join one of them. Carson Wentz was now on the sidelines but working with his replacement.

Lurie and his top tier worked hard to extend the logic and value of connectedness not just to the players and executives but to the entire Eagles' staff. The owner left his office door open, inviting casual drop-ins from anybody since, in his view, "the equipment manager was as important as a star running back." To say it more tangibly, as the Super Bowl in Minneapolis approached, the Eagles provided each staff member with two game tickets, two airline tickets, and a free hotel room. When the Eagles won, Eagles president Don Smolenski brought staff members to join the players on the field. And during the Eagles' five-mile parade four days later in Philadelphia, staff and families joined with players and their families in a victory ride through a sea of three million fans.

Better connecting the players and the staff, reasoned Lurie, would also be facilitated by them building a deeper bond with the people and institutions of the Philadelphia region, sustaining a camaraderie during the off-season when there was no action on the field. Its particular form was influenced by Lurie's experience during his own youth in Boston, where he came to appreciate how his city's major league baseball franchise, the Red Sox, had long energized itself through sustained partnership with the Jimmy Fund, a private foundation for cancer care. Lurie decided to build the same camaraderie in Philadelphia. "You can get caught up with the thirty-two teams in the NFL," he explained, "but you have to remember that you are there for your own fans."

An international organization dedicated to social change, Beyond Sport, recognized the Eagles as the "global sports team of the year" for its community endeavors, including eyesight and literacy campaigns, pink merchandise for breast cancer research, and a "Go Green" renewable energy initiative. Small acts of community engagement contributed as well. Don Smolenski joined the tailgate party of a longtime season ticket holder to present a game ball in honor of a recently deceased family member.[6]

At the heart of the Eagles' principle of talent connectedness was a code of inclusiveness that extended to gender in the front office. Though nearly half of NFL fans are women, less than a third of the employees of the thirty-two NFL franchises were women in 2018, and that dropped to 18 percent among those serving as vice president or higher. At the Eagles, however, more than half of Lurie's top managers were women, and when searching for Chip Kelly's replacement as head coach, a number of women advised Lurie on the pick, including Tina D'Orazio, a vice president and the owner's chief of staff. "It was a little bit different of a process this time around," she recalled.[7]

Connecting the talent among the players and staffers thus proved one of Lurie's most providential leadership additions. By engaging, consulting, and empowering everyone on payroll, the owner and his senior staff in turn received guidance and commitment from across the franchise, a direct product of the ironic principle of reciprocity: That in giving more away, we receive more in return. Managers who take the time to engage with others get more than those hours back as others contribute more of their time. Those who ask for guidance, relinquishing some of their decision-making authority, become more authoritative as their decisions become better informed.[8]

"Leadership, at its core, isn't about you," wrote two company observers, Frances Frei of the Harvard Business School and leadership coach Anne Morriss. "Instead, it's about how effective you are at empowering *other* people and unleashing *their* full potential." The owner of the Eagles had long been drawn to the concept of two-way personal connections for these reasons, and he finally found a coach who could deliver on it.[9]

COMPLETING THE INNER CIRCLE

The leadership of any organization, I appreciate from both personal experience and academic research, begins not only with the top executive—the owner in this case—but also the top team—here the owner, president, head coach, and head of football operations. Given the quarterback's centrality to the Eagles' strategy, he and his immediate backup were included as well.

Similarly, a firm's top team, its "inner circle," is first defined by its job titles—the denizens of the C-suite—but its impact depends on the solidarity within it. A cohesive inner circle, with a shared vision, mutual respect, and complementary expertise, should achieve more than a throng of siloed executives. We know from studies of organizational performance that firms with more cross-boundary collaboration report better results—and in this instance, it became an axiom of the Eagles' owner as well.[10]

In the wake of Kelly's ouster in 2015, Lurie sought to renew the strength of his inner circle. Lurie and Reid had earlier emphasized it, and though Kelly had disrupted the leadership puzzle, Lurie managed to put the pieces back together. The owner,

FIGURE 10.1. The Eagles' Inner Circle.

Individual	Position	Joined
Nick Foles	Backup Quarterback	2017*
Jeffrey Lurie	Owner	1994
Doug Pederson	Head Coach	2016*
Howie Roseman	Head of Football Operations	2000
Don Smolenski	President	1998
Carson Wentz	Quarterback	2016

* Nick Foles had earlier served as a starting quarterback for the Eagles from 2013 to 2015; Douglas Pederson had served as a starting quarterback for the Eagles in 1998.

president, head coach, and head of football operations had come to work more independently during Kelly's reign, focusing on executing their own functions and consulting less with one another. But realizing that their responsibilities were more interdependent than they might have supposed, they now sought to transcend their job titles. They retained clear lines of authority, each attending to their own knitting, but now they also worked on sharing their wisdom. With Pederson in place—recruited in part for that very purpose—they tightened their circle.

Eagles president Don Smolenski and football operations head Roseman, for instance, opted to watch all of the Eagles' games together, whether at home or away—a lapsed practice they had begun more than fifteen years prior and now resumed as top executives. One had to have the stadium ready for a game, the other had to have the players ready for the game, and their day-to-day responsibilities could not have been more different. But their objectives were the same, and from sideline banter about the action on the field, their shared understanding of what would make a difference both on and off the field became mutually reinforcing. They added frequent sit-downs together, talking both football and business, and so did Lurie and Roseman, who worked hand-in-hand on player drafts and trading deadlines.

Three-quarters of the inner circle's members had been on payroll for some time. Lurie himself had taken ownership in 1995, and Pederson had earlier been with the Eagles as well, albeit as Reid's quarterback and then offensive coach. Roseman had come in 2000, a year after Reid had joined as head coach, and Smolenski went back that far as well. Kelly's arrival in 2013 had weakened those sinews. Reid left for Kansas City, Pederson followed, and Roseman was demoted from frontline oversight to back office observer, or in the colorful phrasing of a former president of another NFL team, from "the penthouse to the outhouse."

But Lurie reasoned that his football team would perform better on the field if his top leaders also behaved like a team. He retrieved Roseman and restored his responsibility for player decisions as executive vice president of football operations. Lurie later reported that this was one of the most complex—but also one of the best—decisions he had ever made."[11]

The Eagles enlarged the concept of a connected inner circle of top managers to a "team of teams" scheme, a model developed by US General Stanley McChrystal. Functional groups work to achieve their own goals, but they must also do so in a collaborative fashion to advance company objectives. In the US Army, for instance, lapel colors signal an officer's specialty, green for special forces, yellow for armor, blue for infantry. Yet when an officer is promoted to the rank of general, they wear black, regardless of their function, signaling that they are now responsible for the whole organization, even as they perform specific functions within it. In the case of the Eagles, players assigned to a given position became one of the building blocks, part of "the players room," and their elected representatives in turn pulled together on a players council that worked with other blocks, including the coaching staff, top management, and staff specialists focused on sports science, stadium operations, and community relations.[12]

"NFL players are prideful guys; they want the ball," explained player Brent Celek, then the longest-tenured player on the Eagles. Despite that, he said, "Doug gets everyone involved, there are plays for everyone. You know that you are a big part of the team. The game strategy he creates means there is a role for everyone." It led directly to a running-back-by-committee approach, implemented by the running back coach, that kept both veterans and rookies engaged. The team-of-teams metaphor was felt off the field as well. Players who filled the same slot in the lineup regularly dined together or devoted time to the community together. "When we ask a player to visit a school or the children's hospital, there's an immediate sense of 'I get it,'" reported Julie Hirshey, director of community relations. "There's no blocking energy, and because a player wants to do it, the whole position group goes."[13]

Completing the inner circle within was thus also one of Jeffrey Lurie's most consequential leadership initiatives. By rejoining the C-suite occupants more actively in common cause, the owner and his staff strengthened a kind of lateral bond that transcended their separate functions, bolstering the operations of each as well as the shared performance of all. "When people know that the leaders at the top trust each other, that trickles down into the whole organization," reported Tina D'Orazio, the owner's chief of staff. "The football side and the business side can have tensions, but we see them talk it out and hash it out."

TAKING CALCULATED RISKS

The early leadership decisions, vital as they were to connecting the players, the staff, and the inner circle, had set the stage, but now it was up to the players to perform. And for that, the owner doubled down on calculated risk-taking. "Never be risk averse!" Lurie declared. He sought a mindset that, in the words of coach Doug Pederson, "feared nothing" and "attacked everything." Kelly had followed this "Don't be cautious!" dictum, even if he had fallen short on Lurie's other two leadership components, connecting talent and completing the inner circle.

Roseman took the marching orders to heart in constructing the roster. "*Aggressive* is valued," he affirmed, and that meant that he had to reach for it with expensive trades. At the same time, the "calculated" qualifier in front of "risk" loomed large as well. Depth research, data analytics, psychological profiles, scouting reports, medical appraisals, and face time were all deployed. And that was because "you have to be especially smart," explained Lurie, if you are especially aggressive. "With using data as a complementary tool, you're taking less risk," he said, warning that it is always "riskier to fall back on instinct."

With that in mind, Lurie, Pederson, Roseman, and Smolenski had turned to the quarterback decision, a critical choice for their strategy, and their attention converged on a star performer from a less well-known school, North Dakota State University. Would the player have equally stood out, they wondered, if he had played for one of the top teams in the Big Ten or Pac-12 football conferences? They concluded he likely would have, though it was hardly a sure thing. Compensating for some of that performance risk, however, was the prospect's personal presence. "We were looking for that rare combination of leadership, healthy confidence, and a genuine personality," Lurie explained. They wanted a player who aspired to be great in the role, but they also wanted a player who could personally relate to all those outside that role, even groundskeepers and equipment managers.

Through Roseman's negotiating, the Eagles secured the second pick in the annual NFL draft, heightening their prospect of securing North Dakota's Carson Wentz. "One player can change your team," argued Roseman, and the Eagles drafted Wentz on April 28, 2016. But then again, maybe Wentz wouldn't. He was the highest pick ever for a football player coming out of the second-tier Football Championship Subdivision, formerly Division I-AA.

"This was the big decision," recalled Pederson, referencing the potential downside. The Wentz selection was closely followed by the Eagles' next-biggest quarterback verdict, which was to trade away their veteran Sam Bradford and to start Wentz in his first season. In betting on the yet-untested Wentz, the organization was chancing much, and that was where risk mitigation also came in. For every starting player, including the quarterback, the Eagles had decided that a fully prepared backup had to be at the ready. "We coach all the players like they are starters," Roseman explained. And the risk of not doing so was readily apparent. His wife warned him bluntly, "This is career suicide if you get it wrong."

In case the actual starter faltered, Roseman explained, "We wanted to be a quarterback factory." So Plan B was fortunately ready in 2017 when Carson Wentz was sidelined with his torn ACL three games before the end of the regular season. The back-up quarterback Nick Foles came in to finish the game. A five-year veteran of the NFL, including a noteworthy season three years earlier with the Eagles, Foles had rejoined the club in the spring of 2017, then received his battlefield promotion in December when Wentz was injured. With less than a year on the roster, he went on to become the Super Bowl's Most Valuable Player. Roseman cited the decision to bring Foles back—and release seasoned backup Chase Daniels at significant financial cost—as a decision a year overdue but fortunately in time.

With players, coaches, and staffers connected, and with the top circle reconnected, everyone could take larger risks, and the organization could better manage the risks being taken. In the words of staff member Shaun Huls, it became "an environment of growth where I can contribute back to the organization. I wasn't just empowered, I was commanded to take risks and make a difference."

Before the 2018 Super Bowl the head coach had solicited fresh ideas from his players and coaches, and one suggested a bizarre option in which the quarterback became a pass receiver. Though they'd tested in practice, the Eagles had never called it in a game, but near the end of first half of the Super Bowl game, with the

Eagles at fourth-and-goal, Foles veered to the sideline with a suggestion. "You want Philly, Philly?" he asked the coach. Pederson's face lit up. "Yeah, let's do it." A rookie running back took the hike instead of the quarterback, the rookie pitched the ball to a third-string tight end who had never thrown a pass in the NFL, and the tight end successfully threw to the backup quarterback who had never caught a pass. But Foles did, and he scored. A three-point field goal would have been a safer option, but the far riskier six-point "Philly Special" proved better. "How do you figure?" a shocked NBC broadcaster wondered, and his cohost implied it could not be. "This is an unbelievable call!"[14]

Lurie had pressed everyone to be part of the aggressive risk-taking. "I've been in places where you are instructed not to talk to the coach," reported Shaun Huls. "It's so different here, there's a cross-pollination of ideas. And it's not just the coaching staff. Ideas come from unexpected places." Indeed, the Philly Special was not invented in Philadelphia, coming instead via a circuitous route through high school, college, and other professional teams before being cribbed by assistant quarterback coach Press Taylor from the Chicago Bears, who'd played it against the Minnesota Vikings at the end of the prior season.[15]

Calculated risk-taking can be viewed abstractly as making reasoned choices among strategic alternatives, yet in the hands of Lurie and his inner circle, it turned into a source of advantage and a tenet of the upstart's culture. Julie Hirshey, director of community relations, captured the point: "No matter who you are, you are empowered to find a way and to do it," whether on the field, with the fans, or in the community. "The message from Jeffrey and from Don is quite clear." We "have you so you can do some of that risk-taking. You can jump and we will catch you.'"

A PLAYBOOK FOR THE UPSTART

Winning is never a sure thing, of course, and leadership is often a matter of simply improving the odds. With Kelly as coach, the team had won 52 percent of the time during the regular season games; with Reid, 58 percent; and with Pederson, 60 percent. For the postseason, the percentages rose from 0 for Kelly to 50 for Reid and 80 for Pederson. The winning ratios were up, and so, too, was the value of the franchise. The owner had acquired it in 1994 for less than $200 million. After the 2018 Super Bowl, its estimated worth approached $3 billion.

What emerges from the experience of this upstart enterprise that achieved a winning season and an improbable victory is a three-faceted leadership roadmap built over many seasons. The Reid epoch brought football smarts and personal connectedness into the team, the Kelly era added risk-taking onto the field, and the Pederson years strengthened both and added an inner circle at the top. If the earlier coaches had served without a leader's complete playbook, owner Jeffrey Lurie and his lieutenants had finally instituted a more rounded-out version. Talent connectedness, inner-circle completeness, and calculated risk-taking all figured in, and though none alone sufficed, together they worked.

Four days after the Eagles' Super Bowl victory, team president Donald Smolenski sent out this message: "It is not only our locker room that is filled with special people; our entire organization is filled with special people."

The talent connectedness was further evidenced on June 14, 2018, a little more than four months after the victory. The winning players, an active roster of fifty-three and a practice squad of ten, gathered in Philadelphia for another larger-than-life moment. They paused one-by-one for an embrace and a photo onstage with Jeffrey Lurie as their personal highlights were projected onto a giant screen. With thunderous applause from three hundred family members and Eagles staffers, they received their Super Bowl rings from the owner. On each were the player's name, an engraved signature, a reference to the Philly Special, and the word *family*.

Then the owner asked the groundskeepers and equipment managers, the data crunchers, the team doctors, the talent scouts, and the community liaisons—all 336 people on payroll—to each accept a Super Bowl ring of their own. The staff rings came as an inclusive and high-priced gesture: identical to the players' rings, each was studded with 219 diamonds. The ring, the owner declared, "is for all of us." It was just "one more chance," explained Smolenski, "to show our thanks."[16]

The final moment in the "inclusiveness" trifecta was a quieter one, occurring a few months later as training camp was unfolding and preparations for the next football season were under way. Lurie announced that he had extended the contract of Executive Vice President for Football Operations Howard Roseman through 2022. The owner cited his aggressive risk-taking and ability to relate to all kinds of people—players, coaches, personnel, and fans alike—as reasons for his decision.[17]

What also emerges from a close look at this enterprise is the long-term nature of leadership development. It had taken more than twenty years for owner Jeffrey Lurie to build out the three leadership features that became the foundation for the Super Bowl win. To his credit—and to us a reminder—is the guiding principle of leading with what you already have but also adding to it. What also emerges is that single-bullet solutions can be red herrings, appealing but misleading. Lurie had to connect the players, unite his inner circle, and take calculated risks, even if they required years together before he would hoist the trophy.

CHAPTER 11

OVERCOMING DOUBTS
TO TAKE COMMAND

*George Washington Takes Charge
of the Continental Army*

"From the day I enter upon the command of the American
armies, I date my fall, and the ruin of my reputation."

B ritain's King George III ruled over his more than two million
American subjects with the largest and most disciplined military
force of the era. Yet an increasingly seditious Continental Congress
voted in 1775 to raise its own army, and in 1776 to declare a new
Confederation of English colonies, independent of the Crown.
Having now committed the capital offense of treason against the
Crown, Congress turned to the critical question of choosing some-
one to create an army and lead it in combat.[1]

John Adams of Massachusetts set forward his criteria for the
commander: "A gentleman whose skill and experience as an officer,
whose independent fortune, great talents and excellent universal
character would command the approbation of all America." John
Hancock, also of Massachusetts, was among the potential candidates, but Adams instead proposed a forty-three-year-old delegate
from Virginia. No others were suggested, and with unanimous
consent by the sixty-nine delegates, on June 15, 1775, Congress appointed Colonel George Washington to serve as commander in
chief of the Continental Army.[2]

FIGURE 11.1. Charles Willson Peale's *Washington as Colonel in the Virginia Regiment.*

Source: Courtesy of Museums at Washington and Lee University.

Washington seemed a natural, given his military bearing, personal probity, and brevity in speech. He was the only delegate dressed in military uniform, he was a Southerner at a time of regional rivalries, he had offered to raise a thousand men and pay for a march on the British Army in Boston, and he ws personally respected. As Abigail Adams would later observe: "He is polite with dignity, affable without formality, distant without haughtiness, grave without austerity; modest, wise and good."[3]

By the conventions of today, however, Washington's military résumé would hardly seem propitious for the momentous responsibilities suddenly thrust upon him. Army commands are now granted only to those with years of uniformed service. Terry R.

Ferrell, in 2020 the three-star commanding general of the US Army Central (dating back to the Continental Army), had been commissioned since 1984. Washington's military service had been far, far briefer, and he was well aware of its limitations.

During a brief acceptance speech on June 16, 1775, Washington confessed, "I do not think myself equal to the Command." He was reported to have confided to a fellow delegate, Patrick Henry, "From the day I enter upon the command of the American armies, I date my fall, and the ruin of my reputation." Later, he would complain to his brother, "I have often thought how much happier I should have been, if, instead of accepting of a command under such circumstances, I had taken my musket upon my shoulder and entered the ranks" or "retired to the back country, and lived in a wigwam." Though Washington's self-critical admissions were no doubt informed by the self-effacing hyperbole of the era, they hinted at his inexperience and insecurity.[4]

Whatever his personal hesitancy, Washington's charge was to transform a ragtag assembly of mostly amateur soldiers camped near Boston into a disciplined band that could defeat the British Army. Washington came to the calling with little schooling or formal training, and he had had only several years of service as a uniformed officer, and even then with only a colonel's duties. But with that experience as a starting foundation and despite his diffidence, Washington would in time master a radically expanded skill set, enough to ultimately force a British Army with nine thousand soldiers to surrender at Yorktown, Virginia, in 1781, and the Crown to fully capitulate upon signing the Treaty of Paris two years later, formally recognizing American independence.[5]

LEARNING TO COMMAND

Washington can serve as an inspiration for those among us who do not yet feel fully prepared to lead a team or an enterprise in the coming era, a model for how we might prepare ourselves for doing so. How did he learn to build and transform a loose assemblage of armed volunteers in 1775 and lead them to victory? And how did he come to do so despite his materiel disadvantage throughout the fighting years, directing a smaller, less well-equipped, and less disciplined cadre against the world's largest armed force? Washington confirms that we can all, if determined, step up to assume far greater responsibility however incomplete our background may be. He shows that our future capabilities are never limited to what we have mastered in the past.

On July 3, 1775, at age forty-three Washington assumed official command of the Continental Army on Cambridge Common, facing Harvard University and across the Charles River from Boston. Though formally in control from that moment, he would have to earn his actual authority in the months ahead. While his persona had served him well when he had earlier been responsible for hundreds of soldiers, he would need far more than that if he was to motivate and discipline tens of thousands, some several ranks away, stretching down the eastern seaboard and out to the western frontier.[6]

Washington was not without combat experience. Two decades earlier, the governor of Virginia, Robert Dinwiddie, had dispatched a small armed force to warn France to withdraw from part of Ohio country claimed by Virginia. Following the accidental death of the force's most senior officer, the governor elevated George Washington, age twenty-one, to command the Virginia Regiment.

Fearing imminent attack, Washington had ordered the construction of a circular, palisaded fort, named, for good reason, Fort Necessity. He brought in fresh troops, including British regulars, increasing the number of defenders to four hundred. Even so, on July 3, 1754, they were attacked by a larger force of six hundred French soldiers aided by one hundred Indian allies. French commander Louis Coulon de Villiers demanded the garrison's surrender, but he allowed that Washington and his soldiers would be free to return to Virginia. With safe passage assured, Washington agreed to the capitulation.

While Washington's first full command was hardly a victory, it also fell short of a rout. He had centered himself in the midst of the maelstrom, using his personal presence to ward off the French attack for the better part of a day, then secure the face-saving exit. With a loss of fewer than three dozen of his combatants, Washington had evaded disaster, though in signing the French-language surrender, he inadvertently confirmed that he had "assassinated" the French commander's brother just five weeks earlier, an assertion later denied by Washington but one that would shadow him for years to come. Yet the clash also brought him an early whiff of public recognition. He wrote his brother, "I heard Bullets whistle and believe me there was something charming in the Sound," and when that note of bravado reached the press, Virginia newspapers declared Washington one of the colony's first war heroes.[7]

A second field promotion followed a year later. When a thousand French and Indian fighters surrounded a British force twice its size on its way to capture France's Fort Duquesne (located in modern-day Pittsburgh) in 1755, the attackers fatally shot General Edward Braddock, the commander in chief of the British Army in America. As aide-de-camp for Braddock, Washington informally took command and helped organize a retreat of the bedraggled survivors, ending one of the greatest British defeats in North America at the time.

Now in Cambridge, twenty-one years later, Washington rose to command a far larger force, some fifteen thousand American irregulars who were, in his own words, "a mixed multitude of people under very little discipline, order or government." He soon realized that his prestige and personal qualities would take him only so far. He was no longer running a small shop, and regimentation and regularity would be needed for the exercise of a vastly expanded reach.

Leading the Continental Army, Washington realized, would require clear lines of authority, standardized training and weapons, and regular protocols for command and control. He thus divided his new force into three wings, each overseen by a general who was also part of a war council, and he asked the generals to operate both separately on his behalf and as a team of teams under his authority, mobilizing and directing the entire army, not just the parts in close proximity. As he scaled up, Washington also delegated out, drawing on trusted lieutenants to construct a scaffolding through which he could direct thousands into battle.[8]

In late 1777, Washington took his army into winter quarters at Valley Forge, twenty miles outside of Philadelphia. At Fort Necessity, he had been able to give direct instructions to fighters just feet from him, but by Valley Forge, he imposed direction through an extended hierarchy. There, he and his staff, with the special assistance of Baron von Steuben, a Prussian general turned drillmaster, worked to create the discipline that is the backbone of any large-scale army. Von Steuben instilled a regimen to ensure more-unified battlefield movement among the units of the Continental Army. Washington also insisted on a dignified and authoritative presence for himself, riding with officers around him as he learned to master the power of a leadership that could no longer be exercised through his personal presence alone.[9]

FIGURE 11.2. William T. Trego's *The March to Valley Forge*.

Source: Image courtesy of the Museum of the American Revolution.

BECOMING DELIBERATIVE

As Washington was building the power of the Continental Army, he was also learning how it should be applied. He was already of an attack mindset, preferring clashes, even if impetuous, over inaction. In a letter to his brother during one of his army's stand-still moments, he complained, for instance, that the "inactive state we lie in is exceedingly disagreeable." He expanded in a letter to John Hancock. The "state of inactivity," he said, "in which this army has lain for some time, by no means corresponds with my wishes, by some decisive stroke, to relieve my country from the heavy expense its subsistence must create." Yet he and his army had to also be ready to face any perils given the ambitions of the American Revolution. As he explained more grandly to the governor of Rhode Island, "No danger is to be considered when put in competition with the magnitude of the cause."[10]

The British and American armies would face off first at Boston in the latter half of 1775 and early months of 1776, with the British occupying the city proper and the Americans the surrounding area. The moment was almost perfect for bringing out Washington's aggressive mindset, but it also revealed a sometimes-mechanical approach—take charge and move forward—that did not carefully weigh likely gains and losses. Boston was surrounded by water—a river, a marsh, and a harbor—except for a thin isthmus, just 120 feet wide at high tide, known as Boston Neck. Despite the peninsula's nearly unassailable defensive advantage, Washington pressed for a way to pierce it, and to do so immediately.

Washington went ahead with an ill-fated attack elsewhere. Believing that the entire eastern half of North America would sooner or later be brought into the conflict, and with scant knowledge of the terrain and its winter conditions, on December 31, 1775, he sent 1,200 troops 350 miles north to attack Quebec City. The British outnumbered the exhausted American force as it arrived, and the relative losses proved staggering: five hundred American casualties against twenty on the British side. "It is difficult to imagine such a campaign ever being contemplated later in the war," observed modern-day historian James Ellis, "but at this early stage Washington shared the prevalent belief that patriotic fervor, combined with sheer courage, could defeat the elements and the odds."[11]

Washington continued to argue for direct attack on the British garrison in Boston. A "stroke, well aim'd at this critical juncture," he wrote, "might put a final end to the War." One of his proposals was for an amphibious landing, another for a charge across Boston Neck, and a third for skating the frozen harbor at night. And it was best not to delay, urged Washington, because many of his soldiers, all volunteers, might soon decamp for home, while the British combatants could not. As he feared, the American numbers shrank from fifteen thousand to nine thousand as the months dragged on, leaving Washington to face a still-undiminished British force.[12]

Fortunately, Washington had staffed his war council with senior officers who were not only militant but also strategic. Among them were General Charles Lee, Washington's second in command and a former British officer widely thought to have the best military mind of Washington's inner circle, and General Artemus Ward, who had served as army commander before Washington arrived on the scene.

To these more strategic-minded officers of his war council, some of Washington's ideas looked dubious at best. The enemy was dug in, they argued, Boston Neck would prove a deathtrap, and skating into battle seemed ludicrous. In the end, his lieutenants prevailed, and though it could not be foreseen at the time, all Washington had to do anyway was wait several months to let another of his plans play out. Mastering the art of leadership ironically demands hearing those below you, especially when they may have a better understanding of the issues than you.[13]

In the spring of 1776, Washington armed Dorchester Heights, a hill overlooking the Boston peninsula, with some fifty cannons from Fort Ticonderoga in New York, guns that had been disassembled and hauled on sleds by a detachment led by Henry Knox. Shocked by the freshly positioned fire power, the British commander, General William Howe, abruptly ordered the complete abandonment of Boston by ship, for good, on March 17, 1776. Ending their eleven-month siege, the Americans had forced the British out with no attack at all.

Washington complained that the sudden British evacuation denied him the direct confrontation he had been advocating for months. But the wisdom of listening to his more experienced staff was graphically driven home when Washington walked through Boston after the British evacuation. Their defenses were "amazingly strong," he reported, "almost impregnable, every avenue fortified." A frontal attack might well have led to another catastrophe, whereas strategic patience had resulted in victory—without a single American casualty.[14]

With Boston free of redcoats, Washington moved his own forces south, where he met the British again in what became known as the Battle of Brooklyn (also known as the Battle of Long Island) on August 27, 1776. There he experienced the sting of battlefield defeat, suffering some two thousand casualties against Britain's four hundred. The setback finally delivered the combat lesson that his subordinates had failed to make stick until then. The enemy ranks were well led, more disciplined, and better armed.

As a result, Washington embraced a new leadership principle for the duration of the war: he should never engage unless there was a "moral certainty" of winning. Taking charge and leading change remained vital principles throughout the war for him, but a fuller template for exercising his leadership had now come to the fore, one that included strategic thinking, seeing ahead before moving ahead, and anticipating what could happen before it did happen, especially regarding low-probability but high-consequence reversals. In 1777, for instance, he would caution one of his officers then planning an attack on the British in Newport, Rhode Island: "Unless your Strength and Circumstances be such, that you can reasonably promise yourself a more certainty of succeeding, I would have you by all means to relinquish the undertaking, and confine yourself, in the main, to a defensive operation."[15]

As a tangible result of his now more strategic mindset, Washington was coming to see that he did not have to triumph on the battlefield to win the war. He anticipated that, eventually, the British Parliament would lose its will to fight, yielding the colonies a victory through its own exhaustion. Accordingly, he shifted to a strategy of attrition, though with an asterisk. Fearing that his soldiers might lose their own fighting spirit, he would still seek to win offensive victories from time to time, even if only tactical, if they would bolster American morale. He also sought more modest wins to help sustain the commitment of the Continental Congress and its backers. "Everything depends on public opinion," Washington observed, one more principle in his expanding sense of how to lead an army, and one day—though he could not yet foresee it—a nation.

Washington also sought tactical advances because of the pain they imposed on his adversaries. "Let's make it impossible for them to live here," he explained, anticipating one of Mao Tse-tung's strategies during China's revolution nearly two centuries later: "We fight, we lose, we attack again." Washington's deliberative thinking became not only more evident in his leadership but more subtle in its application. "The way to win the war," as Washington's blueprint was characterized by historian Joseph Ellis, "was not to lose it." A similar theory was expressed by North Vietnamese Minister of Defense General Vo Nguyen Giap, one of the masterminds of the defeat of France and the United States in Indochina. According to US Senator John McCain, a former naval aviator and war prisoner in North Vietnam from 1967 to 1973, Giap had said to the French, "You will kill 10 of us, we will kill one of you," but "in the end, you will tire of it first." McCain similarly characterized Giap's later fight against the US: "He beat us in war but never in battle."[16]

Washington's emergent thinking could be seen in his successful attacks on small British units at Trenton on December 26, 1776, and at Princeton on January 3, 1777. In each instance, the colonial forces had overwhelming local superiority. At Trenton, 2,400 Americans assaulted 1,500 British defenders, and at Princeton, 4,500 Americans assailed 1,200 British. In both cases British losses far outnumbered American (more than four hundred British casualties in Princeton versus fewer than one hundred Americans). As Washington had hoped, American desertions slowed and reenlistments grew in the months that followed.

One last principle expanded his leadership template: while thinking of ambitious strategies, focus as well on small maneuvers that can help catalyze the grand. The cross-river assault on Trenton would be memorialized in one of the more compelling depictions of the war and Washington's leadership of it, Emanuel Leutze's *Washington Crossing the Delaware*. Though painted many decades later, in 1851, it captured Washington's use of modest but heroic moments for public advantage.

FIGURE 11.3. Emanuel Leutze's *Washington Crossing the Delaware*.

Source: Metropolitan Museum of Art.

LEARNING TO LEAD

Today, many general army officers reach that grade only after four years of study at the US Military Academy at West Point, or another college or university, and then twenty to thirty years of professional service. More than 80 percent of all active-duty officers in 2015 held at least a bachelor's degree, and 42 percent held an advanced degree. Joseph F. Dunford Jr. joined the Marine Corps in 1977, for instance, and served in uniform for thirty-seven years before becoming chairman of the Joint Chiefs of Staff in 2015.[17]

For our first supreme commander, however, formal schooling ended with the passing of his father, when Washington was only eleven, and his time in uniform totaled just five years when he took control of the Continental Army. He had experience in logistics from his earlier commands, but little direct exposure to other military branches, including cavalry, artillery, engineering, and naval operations. Little wonder then that historians attribute his eagerness to attack the nearly impregnable British defenses in Boston and Quebec in 1775—and to challenge the far larger British forces in Brooklyn in 1776—to inexperience and undertraining. Yet Washington nonetheless proved he could learn to lead an entire army on the job.

Earlier in his career, Washington had focused less on leadership and more on his own advancement and personal stature. But much like Jim Collins's "Level 5" leaders, who put company prosperity well ahead of their personal gain, Washington came to replace individual ambition with patriotic purpose. On his way to becoming commander in Cambridge in 1775, Washington thus announced his more transcendent objectives: "Every exertion of my worthy colleagues and myself," he declared, will be "extended to the re-establishment of peace and harmony between the mother country and the colonies." Personal credit was not his purpose, nor was conquered ground. They were just the means to a far larger goal:

"Neither glory nor extent of territory," did he seek, "but a defense of all that is dear and valuable in life."[18]

When appointing Washington as commander in chief of the Continental Army on June 16, 1775, the Continental Congress resolved to provide him $500 per month. Washington accepted the position but rejected the pay: "I beg leave to assure the Congress, that, as no pecuniary consideration could have tempted me to have accepted this arduous employment, at the expense of my domestic ease and happiness, I do not wish to make any profit from it. I will keep an exact account of my expenses," and "that is all I desire." During the six years of warfare that followed, throughout attacks, sieges, retreats, and encampments, he returned home to Mount Vernon for just ten days.[19]

In 1781, after years of lethal conflict, Washington finally achieved the decisive military victory at Yorktown that forced a complete British withdrawal. From the day he took command in 1775, until the Yorktown triumph, he had lost more battles than he had won, but along the way he had learned to be more deliberative in his strategy, and to build the public support and political will that would also prove vital for the American Revolution. Washington's acquired skills—strengthened of necessity from his siege of Boston to the victory at Yorktown—included

- maintaining relentless realism, fighting the fights he could win, not the ones he simply wanted to, as evident in his decision to heed his lieutenants and not attack Boston;
- "making haste slowly," waiting for opportunities rather that moving impetuously, as he demonstrated when deciding to take six months off the battlefield to build military discipline at Valley Forge;
- managing morale, as he did by bucking up esprit de corps and public backing with tactical successes like the attacks on Trenton and Princeton;
- projecting character to leverage rank; and

- subordinating himself to the cause, placing common purpose ahead of self-interest, as when he decided to forego his
  personal compensation and home stays for the duration of
  the war.

Through a combination of listening to direct reports and learning from setbacks, Washington mastered a world he had not come
of age in and prevailed over it. He learned how to vanquish a vastly
more dominant opponent, and he came to appreciate why leadership in all its many facets had become so critical—and also why
achieving ends with the right calculus was so vital to those who
supported him. "No rational person will condemn you for not
fighting with the odds against you and while so much is depending
on it," he wrote to one of his senior officers, the Marquis de Lafayette, in 1781, "but all will censure a rash step if it is not attended
with success." And he found that success by learning to lead at his
edge, even if it took him years to do so.[20]

CHAPTER 12

BREAK THE BUBBLE

Expanding Your Edge

"Many believe leaders are born with some innate charisma,"
but "the vast majority of leadership is learned."

I am always struck by the answer both company managers and
MBA students respond with when asked what gave the edge to
premier twentieth-century leaders such as Nelson Mandela, George
C. Marshall, Mother Teresa, and Margaret Thatcher. Setting forth
a vision, advancing common purpose, and honoring their followers
are all singled out.[1]

These same qualities seem to apply whether the country is South
Africa, the US, India, or the UK. They are considered indispens-
able whether the era is the midcentury, when George Marshall
served as the US Army chief of staff and transformed a small, un-
prepared military into a fighting machine during World War II;
or several decades later, when Margaret Thatcher presided as the
UK prime minister and ushered in Euroscepticism, limited government, and free-market philosophy. The leadership capacities also
stretched across these figures' personal callings, whether Mother
Teresa's dedication to the poor in India or Nelson Mandela's service to South Africa.

The same is true in business, where we can see that making a
product or marketing a service relies on many of the equivalent
skills whether the firm is headquartered in China, India, or the US,
or it is the nineteenth, twentieth, or twenty-first century. Industries

and cultures vary radically across eras and borders, but the foundational principles for leading enterprises are very much the same.[2]

Yet we can also appreciate from the lives of the chief executives
in this book that those foundational principles need to be supplemented to maintain an edge in the present era. Traditional precepts
such as strategic thinking, persuasive communication, and decisive
decision-making are still foundational, the building blocks needed
to reach the edge, but additional tenets are needed as well for the
challenges ahead. How these leaders model the additional principles required provide a learning opportunity for us.[3]

> From Vanguard's Bill McNabb, we can see the value of iden-
> tifying and then accelerating a self-reinforcing flywheel for
> growth.
> From Progressive Corporation's Tricia Griffith, we can see the
> benefit of more lateral and more inclusive leadership.
> From WSFS's Mark Turner, we saw the value of taking a step
> away from daily demands to appreciate the way technologies
> may be changing how we lead and our own timing for step-
> ping down.
> From Estée Lauder's William Lauder and Fabrizio Freda, we
> learned to partner for change to open new channels for mar-
> keting products before traditional avenues close off.
> From ITT's Denise Ramos, we saw the value of rounding out
> your leadership skills holistically to serve as a general man-
> ager, then picking a successor with a new and different skill
> set that's better suited to the challenges that lie ahead.
> From Nokia Growth Partners' Bo Ilsoe, we were reminded
> that a company may be struggling for traction not because
> its strategy is misdirected, but because it has the wrong in-
> dividual at the top, and that for finding the right leader a
> meticulous and disciplined appraisal is essential for ensuring
> effective execution of the firm's strategy.
> From seeing his markets imploding, splitting, or consolidating,
> Ed Breen faced one crisis after another, but he confronted

each with a fresh eye, triaging his firm in one case, dividing and recombining the firm in another, and confronting a virus in a third.

From Johnson & Johnson's Alex Gorsky, we learned that culture can serve as an invaluable vector for aligning the behavior of those beyond your direct instruction—though only if modernized from time to time as the world changes.

From the Philadelphia Eagles' Jeffrey Lurie, we were reminded that single-bullet solutions are appealing but misleading as he learned to connect the players, unite his inner circle, and embrace calculated risk-taking.

From the Continental Army's George Washington, we came to better appreciate that leadership can be learned across a lifetime—and that it can take a lifetime to master.

All of these leaders learned to lead more effectively from their own on-the-ground experience, from both their tangible setbacks and their hard-fought successes. And few of their leadership insights came as a bolt from the blue. William Lauder spent five years in the corner office before he recruited Fabrizio Freda as a comrade in arms; Denise Ramos required many seasons in the finance function to come to think like a CEO; Jeffrey Lurie recruited two coaches before he found the right combination of skills in a third; and George Washington learned from setback after setback that his far more powerful adversary could not be defeated through direct assaults. In finding their own ways forward, sometimes over years, our exemplars taken together provide us with an instructive roadmap for designing our own ways forward.

WHAT ELSE SHOULD BE ON A ROADMAP

From the close study of these contemporary executives and one historic leader, we can also see that most if not all the leadership capacities on the basic, foundational roadmap described in the first chapter remained true. Nothing from my interviews, observations,

FIGURE 12.1. An Expanded Roadmap for Leading at the Edge.

1. Accelerate your flywheel for growth
2. Mobilize and engage holistically
3. Take a learning sabbatical
4. Partner to lead change
5. Think like a chief executive
6. Bring in better leadership
7. Reconfigure for evolving markets
8. Reinvent the company culture
9. Connect and unite all the players
10. Learn to lead across a lifetime

and fly-on-the-wall trailing of the executives and those who worked with them suggests that articulating a vision or thinking and acting strategically are now passé, nor did anyone push back at the idea of building a diverse top team and placing common interest first. In fact, all the leaders made at least passing reference to the salience of most of these eternal verities. But we've also come upon a set of new ideas to supplement that foundational roadmap, summarized in Figure 12.1.

The brief phrases captured in the figure are, of course, just shorthand for the more detailed enacting principles seen in the leadership profiles in this book. And keep in mind that while each of these additional capacities is necessary, none is sufficient on its own. Falling short on any one of these mission-critical principles is like a commercial pilot checking everything except an aircraft's fuel before takeoff, or an orthopedic surgeon checking everything but which joint is to be replaced before operating (yes, both have happened).

But our expanded roadmap will even then never be fully complete. Newer dimensions will have to added as time goes on, and several are already very evident.

MANAGE RISK

Taking certain calculated risks and avoiding others has and should become an intrinsic part of any firm's agenda, and thus its leader's template. The most vital questions increasingly facing executives are which risks to avoid, which to take, and how to hedge against the downsides of the latter.

In the 1990s, the World Economic Forum devoted only a few sessions at its annual meeting in Davos to risk. Of its nearly 250 total sessions at the 1997 meeting, just a dozen focused explicitly on the topic. By the mid-2000s, a third of its sessions touched on risk, and by the 2010s nearly half.[4]

The soaring interest in managing risk reflects a soaring rise in risk itself. Annual inflation-adjusted losses from natural disasters— such as hurricanes, earthquakes, and epidemics—totaled $50 million in 1985 but over $350 billion by 2012. Because of the coronavirus, that sum is sure to reach $1 trillion or more in 2020. The number of people afflicted by such disasters also is mounting: by mid-December 2020, more than 70 million COVID-19 cases had been reported worldwide.[5]

When Standard and Poor's appraised the robustness of enterprise risk management (ERM) among large American insurance companies in 2013, it found that firms whose leaders had strengthened their risk management capabilities had much lower volatility in their return on equity compared to others that did not give risk management a high priority. The study also reported that companies with strong ERM measures in place outperformed the S&P 500 index by nearly 20 percent, while those with weak risk management underperformed by 40 percent.[6]

Other research has found that executives who experienced modest disasters early in their lives are more risk seeking later on—but less risk prone if they had faced major calamities. One study of the childhood experiences of chief executives of S&P 1500 firms, for example, focused on whether they had been exposed—from ages

five to fifteen—to an earthquake, hurricane, wildfire, or other natural disaster in the area where they lived. Years later, those CEOs
who had experienced childhood events that caused a small number
of fatalities were more likely to accept operating risks, including
greater debt for financing, higher interest rates, lower rating for
company debt, and greater volatility in their stock prices, compared with CEOs who had witnessed no fatal disasters in their
childhoods.

By contrast, those chief executives who had faced major disasters in their early years, with large losses of life, tended to build
up greater cash reserves, make fewer acquisitions, and allow less
share volatility than those who had no exposure to fatal disasters. A
study of CEOs who had grown up during the Great Depression—
another extreme disruption—found much the same: children of the
Depression were more likely to avoid borrowing and to depend
less on external financing. The same might be anticipated of young
managers coming of age during the coronavirus crisis of 2020.[7]

Whatever role CEOs' personal experiences play in their readiness to incorporate risk management onto their leadership roadmap,
long-term upward risk trends have pressed all company leaders to
do so, whether because of climate change, financial meltdowns, or
terrorist attacks. To document the inroads that enterprise risk management has made into the executive suite, a colleague and I interviewed a hundred-plus company leaders in the mid-2010s, asking
each how they anticipated and then responded to their company's
threats and disruptions. We learned that executives are generally
now appraising their threats and disruptions in a more explicit and
deliberative fashion, making risk management a more integral part
of their business leadership.[8]

Understanding and managing risk are thus no longer the province of company specialists. Threats and disruptions have entered
executive deliberations as top managers have come to appreciate that cyclones and cyberattacks can dampen their firm's performance, and their own reputations, as much as a floundering

strategy. And executive misbehavior itself, as we earlier saw at Tyco International, can cause as much or even greater damage. Consider, for example, the German automaker Volkswagen Group, whose leaders encouraged engineers to install devices to prevent regulators from detecting excessive emissions, and America's Wells Fargo Bank, whose leaders encouraged sales representatives to create false accounts for unwitting customers.

VW admitted in 2016 that it had placed "defeat devices" in a half million vehicles sold with diesel engines in the United States and in millions more abroad. The illicit software detected when a vehicle was being tested for emissions, then activated engine equipment to reduce emissions of nitrous oxide, a well-known cause of respiratory disease. Once back on the road, the software then instructed the engine to return to its normal levels of effluence, far exceeding legal limits. The company had promoted its diesel vehicles as both cost effective and environmentally sound, but in fact they gave off some forty times more nitrous oxide on the road than in a lab.

When the deception came to light, the Volkswagen chief executive denied that he had authorized or even known of it, attributing it to "the terrible mistakes of a few people." But the head of VW for America confirmed that it was actually a leadership authorization: "We have totally screwed up," he admitted. "Our company was dishonest with the EPA." Researchers estimated that the excess emissions from the company's vehicles resulted in 60 premature deaths in the US and 1,200 in Europe. Under siege, Volkswagen's CEO resigned; the company posted an annual loss of $2 billion, the worst-ever financial result in its eight decades of operations; and it set aside $18 billion for customer claims in the US alone. On the first trading day after the defeat device became publicly known, VW's stock price plunged 17 percent, and on the next trading day, another 17 percent.[9]

A similar set of events unfolded at Wells Fargo Bank in 2016. Incentivized by a draconian pay-for-performance system that required frontline employees to meet aggressive sales goals, the bank created two million fake bank and credit card accounts in the names of customers without their knowledge. As these results became known within the bank, executives forced out thousands of sales representatives over several years, even though the representatives had been threatened with firing if they did not meet their aggressive targets. Bank executives retained the illicit incentive system until it became public.

The defective system at Wells Fargo was not a hidden middle-management misstep—it was instituted by top company executives and known to their directors. Warren Buffett, chief executive of Berkshire Hathaway, Wells Fargo's largest single shareholder, condemned the reckless management at the top that forced employees to disserve their customers and then fired them when they did so: "It was a bad incentive system," he said, and the "main problem is that they didn't act when they learned about it." The absence of adequate enterprise risk management in Wells Fargo's leadership cost the company billions of dollars in litigation expenses, settlement costs, and foregone revenue, and it led the US Federal Reserve to cap Wells Fargo's deposit taking until its executives instituted a full-throated risk management system.[10]

The salience of enterprise risk management for all company leaders became starkly evident during the outbreak of the coronavirus in 2020. Its rapid spread from China to the US, Europe, Asia, and beyond pressed business executives and directors to protect employees, reduce expenses, cancel meetings, cut pay, restrict travel, reconfigure supply chains, and shutter operations. Other executives went further, pressing for collective action. Rachel Romer Carlson, chief executive of a group devoted to employee education, and Kenneth Chenault, former chief executive of American Express, secured commitments from more than 1,500 chief executives to donate cash in support of COVID-19 recovery efforts.[11]

Since no two "black swans" are ever the same, however, preparing for a highly unlikely event after the fact is most likely a fool's errand. But building readiness and resilience for any crisis, whatever the form, has emerged as an additional calling for those responsible for company well-being. As two public health research-ers have urged, the "coronavirus outbreak is officially a crisis—let's not waste it"; now is the time, they insisted, for company executives and directors to invest in "preparedness, prevention, mitigation and response" beyond the pandemic.[12]

DISCIPLINED NONMARKET BEHAVIOR

Three hurricanes hammered the US in just two months in 2017, leaving a $200 billion swath of destruction from Puerto Rico to Texas. Several months later, a raging wildfire destroyed more than 8,500 buildings in northern California. It was a frightful year abroad, too. A magnitude 8.2 earthquake rocked Mexico, monsoon flooding killed 1,200 in Bangladesh, and extreme temperatures scorched India.[13]

But 2017 is by no means the worst year on record for natural disasters. That dreary distinction belongs to 2011, when the costs of natural disasters worldwide exceeded $350 billion. Yet the long-term trend line is moving unhappily upward: The inflation-adjusted costs of global calamities half decade by half decade have been rising, and they are now up more than fourfold from the early 1980s. Making matters worse, public and nonprofit sources of disaster assistance have not kept pace.[14]

Fortunately, private sector donations have made up for some of the humanitarian shortfall. My colleague Luis Ballesteros found in a detailed look at the three thousand largest companies worldwide that while less than a third had contributed anything to disaster relief in 2000, by 2015 more than 90 percent were doing so, and on average they had increased their donations tenfold. The fraction of the five hundred largest American corporations giving disaster relief soared as well, from less than 20 percent in 1990 to more than 95 percent by 2014.[15]

After so many natural disasters, company donations have become far more widespread and substantial, the aggregate sometimes exceeding all other forms of international aid. Following a magnitude 8.8 earthquake in Chile in 2010, firms contributed more toward national relief than foreign governments, private foundations, and multilateral agencies combined. The same happened after the magnitude 9.0 earthquake in Japan that killed more than twenty-four thousand people in 2011.

As a result, corporate giving has become a business norm, and falling short risks censure of leadership from both company stakeholders and the wider business community. Economist Milton Friedman famously argued that "the social responsibility of business is to increase its profits," and deemed other objectives irresponsible. Yet when well targeted, corporate giving benefits both the recipient country and the company—and is thus both socially responsible and business essential.[16]

Business norms have as a result become important arbiters of nonmarket engagement and top business leadership, meaning that firms and executives now look to one another for guidance on how much to give in the wake of a calamity. In nine out of ten natural disasters worldwide from 2000 to 2015, the donation of the first corporate giver was almost exactly matched by later givers, even though the latecomers differed greatly in their market value and financial performance. Within hours of Chile's 2010 earthquake, for example, multinational mining company Anglo American pledged $10 million for relief, the first major private donor to step forward, and in the days that followed, three major competitors pledged identical amounts.[17]

Luis Ballesteros, Tyler Wry, and I also found that giving in response to disasters benefits firms with good predisaster reputations. A first mover with a positive standing, for instance, gains considerably more in local revenue compared to a first mover of negative repute. Moreover, the revenue gains or losses far outstrip the cost of giving. For a first mover with a positive reputation, for instance, its revenue gain is eighteen times greater on average than the size of its gift itself. In other words, the value of corporate giving for the company depends much upon the ability of its executives to design the donation well, to lead their company effectively in its engaged giving.[18]

Nonmarket engagement also provides more benefits to the region receiving the aid when the contributing company already has its feet on the ground. If firms have operations in an afflicted region, as Walmart did in the hurricane-ravaged Gulf Coast in the wake of Hurricane Katrina in 2005, they are often better than outside agencies at identifying what is actually needed and how to tailor their responses accordingly.

Drawing on these and other research findings, still another principle is required for a complete leader's template: disciplined nonmarket behavior. Like all the principles on the leadership roadmap, this one comes with a number of subpoints. For firms operating in a country struck by a disaster, whether an earthquake or infectious disease, two of these subpoints are 1) that the emerging norm is for companies to give, and that failing to do so risks censure from both business and public leaders; and 2) that a company's giving for disaster victims achieves its greatest value in regions where the company already has an operating presence. Donating in these places can restore a region's development path and benefit the company over time, while an absence of donations can impair local development for a decade. With all due respect to Professor Friedman, company leadership can and should try to do good while also doing well.

DIVERSIFY STAKEHOLDERS

The nineteenth-century French chronicler of American ways Alexis de Tocqueville observed that Americans "are fond of explaining almost all the actions of their lives by the principle of self-interest rightly understood," and America's culture of individual achievement has long placed a premium on being clear minded about the pursuit of one's private purpose. Among publicly traded companies, this precept took form in the twentieth century and continued into the twenty-first century with total shareholder return—the increase in a company's market value and dividend payments over a given period, such as a quarter, a year, or more—as the chief criterion for judging enterprise performance and leadership results.[19]

But as previously noted, the Business Roundtable declared in 2019 that corporations should move away from a singular focus on shareholder value and embrace a broader commitment to customers, communities, employees, and suppliers as well. If this revised conception of corporate responsibility builds traction, still another mission-critical principle should be added to the leadership roadmap: committing to all of a firm's interested parties, not just shareholders. In the wake of widely publicized cases of extra-judicial killing of racial minorities in the US, major companies stepped forward in 2020 with programs and donations in response. "I have been personally outraged by the terrible killings of George Floyd and many other Black people within our U.S. communities," said Darius Adamczyk, chief executive of Honeywell International, a $35 billion maker of aerospace, home, and building materials, and "we will never tolerate racism at Honeywell." Company leaders will increasingly be called to bring greater inclusiveness into their ranks and to explicitly combat misogyny and racism.[20]

DIGITIZE THE FIRM

Understanding how to build and deploy artificial intelligence, data analytics, and digital technologies has also become an essential capability for leaders everywhere, as we have seen with CEO Mark Turner at WSFS Bank. As a sign of the times, the largest companies providing the foundations for the digitalization of business—Apple, Amazon, Google, and Microsoft—have now achieved market capitalizations of at least $1 trillion each. Company leaders will be required to apply these companies' and others' technologies to sustain their own market growth.

"The very concept of the firm," write two university researchers who studied the consequences, "is evolving as processes become embedded in software, and as data, analytics, and AI drive an increasing proportion of operating activities and managerial decisions." Company leaders will be called to refocus their firms on digital technologies that allow for rapid learning, massive scaling, and remote operating. Universities, including my own, are getting a good taste of that future as they have gone online during the pandemic not only in teaching but also in their operations. My colleagues and I advise students online, teach programs online, and monitor our health online.[21]

No arcane skill set is required here, just what has long been required for presiding over accounting, finance, marketing, operations, and research. What's needed is a deep appreciation for these and other functions, though not necessarily technical knowledge of each. This is the essence of general management: understanding the value of different functions and knowing how to take all into account at the same time. This capacity—the ability to simultaneously think not only financially but also strategically—helps explain why ITT promoted Denise Ramos to the helm of its spin-off, and why Nokia Growth Partners succeeded with Christian Tang-Jespersen at Heptagon, who came with more digital skills than his predecessor. These further-extended leadership principles are summarized in Figure 12.2.

FIGURE 12.2. The Further-Expanded Leadership Roadmap.

1. Manage risk
2. Discipline nonmarket behavior
3. Diversify stakeholders
4. Digitize the firm

APPLYING THE ROADMAP

In the years ahead, other mission-critical precepts are sure to emerge as well. From my personal engagement in a range of leadership development programs at both my own university and a number of companies and organizations, I have found that it is important to devise, customize, and direct your own learning methods for re-affirming your foundational roadmap and also for acquiring and applying updates in ways that are indelible.

In *Made to Stick*, academic and business experts Chip Heath and Dan Heath help us understand why some thoughts or experiences live on in our memory while others are soon forgotten. Compar-ing successful with failing efforts to communicate ideas—why, for instance, we remember President John F. Kennedy's call for civic engagement, "Ask not what your country can do for you—ask what you can do for your country," but not much else from his inaugural address—they point to the value of making the ideas concrete and credible.[22]

With leaders challenged to both identify and retain the addi-tional leadership tenets without forgetting the foundational ele-ments, it is for this reason that we've focused in this book on the lives of ten leaders, examining them through both their enduring and new challenges to glean transferable ideas that are concrete and credible.

To that end, Figures 12.1 and 12.2 are intended to provide a shorthand for current managers and upcoming executives who want to lead with what has always been true but also with what is now new. It is a matter of taking what you've already learned, applying it well, and then also looking to further expand your repertoire as needed. Mastering the latter should and can be straightforward, as former Aetna chief executive Ron Williams has concluded from his own experience. Most "people can learn to be an exceptional leader," he said, with simply the "right training, development, self-awareness, and feedback."[23]

George Washington became the commander in chief of the Continental Army with little confidence that he and his new forces would prevail, much less the military training or senior service ex-perience most would now think necessary. But he accepted his call-ing, ready to take charge and make the necessary changes in others and himself, learning along the way to become a master of the battlefield and, eventually, his new nation. Aetna's Williams summed up the learning point: "Many believe leaders are born with some innate charisma," but "the vast majority of leadership is learned."[24]

Finally, it is worth reminding ourselves just how vital it is to have the right leader with the right template in hand. We intuitively know how much of a difference even a single person can make in the fate of a company or a country. Despite hundreds of thousands of employees or hundreds of millions of citizens, the premier executive of a company or the top official of a country can have enormous impact, for better or for worse.

If we compare successor leaders in business or coaches in sports, research has recurrently confirmed, net of everything else that can drive company results or team victories, replacing an effectively performing executive or coach with an ineffective one can undercut a firm's or team's results by as much as 30 percent within several years. Getting the right person in high office with the right up-to-date leadership repertoire is thus as essential as anything for the long-term success of business firms, sports teams, and even nations.[25]

LEADING IN OUR TIMES

"We have a lot of work ahead of us
to unlock the value of GE."

Y ou have been called to your superior's office, advised in advance that you will be asked to accept a far more responsible role at your enterprise, moving you from leading tens or hundreds to thousands or more. One of your first questions is, What will give you the edge to lead in the years ahead? We know that success certainly requires the capacities that have proven tried and true for others in the past, many of which were evident in your predecessor. But we also know from the leadership measures of the people chronicled here that you will need fresh approaches as well.[1]

Consider Henry Lawrence "Larry" Culp Jr.'s concerns after his selection in 2018 to run General Electric. Since its apotheosis under Jack Welch, GE had come on hard times, dismissing one successor, John Flannery, after just fourteen months. The company's market value had sunk to $75 billion, a far cry from the more than $400 billion at its peak in 2000. Adding to the ignominy, Dow Jones had dropped GE from its blue-chip average of America's industrial leaders.

Larry Culp came to General Electric after having led a less known but well-regarded manufacturer, Danaher Corporation, for fifteen years. But as he sized up how he would resurrect GE, Culp appreciated that it would have to go well beyond what Jack Welch; Welch's successors, Jeffrey Immelt and John Flannery; and Culp himself had led with in the past.

"We have a lot of work ahead of us to unlock the value of GE," Culp explained, and he'd need an expanded leadership repertoire to do it. One new essential, he said, would be to reduce the runaway optimism that one of his predecessors, Immelt, had been tagged with in the past. "I'm most encouraged by how our team has embraced discussions around fostering greater candor, transparency, and humility," he reported. "Putting the good and the bad on the table in equal measure is not always easy, but it is critically important."[2]

Culp would follow two of Welch's trademark behaviors—thinking strategically and acting decisively—but he could also learn from Vanguard's Bill McNabb the worth of identifying and accelerating a company flywheel. From Estée Lauder's William Lauder and Fabrizio Freda, he could see the value in allying with other senior managers to retool the company's sales channels. From Progressive's Tricia Griffith he could be reminded to lead collaboratively as much as vertically. And from DuPont's Edward Breen, he could appreciate the benefit of freshly reconstituting the enterprise to better fit its very different markets.

From WSFS's Mark Turner and the Continental Army's George Washington, we are further reminded that the new can be mastered through a host of tangible, self-disciplined steps, ranging from traveling on a three-month sabbatical to heeding your dissident lieutenants. And from the Eagles' Jeffrey Lurie, we can see that no single one of these new or old principles can fully carry the day. A complete set of both long-standing and fresh principles are required for victory now.

The executives followed in this book have thus helped us visualize how to lead our own ways forward. By incorporating their leadership capacities, both old *and* new, we should be more able to pave our way. For the next generation of company leaders, incorporating the novel alongside the long-standing will be important for the class curriculum in MBA programs, promotion criteria in the ranks, and development programs everywhere.

And all of the capabilities we have seen in our ten leaders will be essential for leading through the great tests that lie ahead, some of which might spell opportunity and others, if not dealt with properly, catastrophe. For the upside challenges, consider the doors opened by digital computing and artificial intelligence. In the *Innovator's Dilemma*, academic researcher Clayton Christensen explained that pioneering incumbents are too often unable to transcend their own success, leaving the next breakthrough to other start-ups. For instance, engineers at Xerox Corporation had invented the computer cursor, but Apple engineers commercialized it. In Christensen's diagnostic, the leaders of successful first movers, as well as their customers, are naturally anchored in what they have already proved so good at. To counter this tendency, it is thus useful to leave a place on your leader's template for the contrary principle of looking for what may disrupt your current model—especially when you are doing well with it.[3]

As for the catastrophic challenges, consider the remorseless expansion of the coronavirus in 2020 across the US and abroad—with Britain, India, and Italy shutting down entirely at points—that made the daily routines of hundreds of millions virtually unrecognizable as they became victims of one of the most dreadful and far-reaching disasters of our era.[4]

We of course still hunger for leadership from the top, but when disasters like hurricanes, wildfires, and now the coronavirus upend our way of life, they call for every individual to step into the breach. Not just first responders or health workers, not only state governors or national leaders, but all of us.

We know from ample research that leadership makes the greatest difference when we are unsure what lies ahead. And we also know that its impact is greatest when it is coming not only from the apex but also from the middle ranks and frontlines. Not just from public officials and chief executives, but also from those who help run restaurants, service hospitals, and administer schools.[5]

To exercise our own leadership during the coronavirus crisis, let's start by recalling what's most essential during a crisis of this magnitude. At the top of the traditional roadmap are thinking strategically, communicating persuasively, and deciding decisively.

As a case in point on *thinking strategically*: When Vanguard Group faced the economy's near-total meltdown after the failure of Lehman Brothers in 2008, its chief executive, Bill McNabb, slashed salaries but laid nobody off. He theorized that when the market eventually came back—and it did of course—he would need all his people to service the returning clients. Vanguard is now one of the world's largest investment companies, with more than $6 trillion of assets under management, up from $1 trillion in 2005, not long before the global financial crisis.

Communicating persuasively: When two colleagues and I interviewed fourteen corporate CEOs in 2009 on what they were doing to weather the global financial crisis, they all said: connect with others. "If in doubt," advised the CEO of aerospace company Northrop Grumman, "communicate." Explained the top executive of Travelers Insurance: "Transparency in troubled times really matters!"[6]

Acting decisively: The owner of three crowded pizza stores in Johnson City, Tennessee, shut them down in mid-March, precisely because they were jammed. Patrons were not distancing themselves, so for their own sake, the owner sent them packing. And he did the same for his workers. If "I'm uncomfortable in my own spaces, how can I ask my employees to come in," he explained.

Less than a day later, a nearby restaurant shuttered itself for the same reason, with special thanks to the first mover. "As hard as it is," said the second owner, "it is beyond the right thing to do," reported the *New York Times*. The second owner credited the first's decision as a kind of personal catalyst or force multiplier, making his own "decision easier."[7]

Then there's the question of where to act during a crisis. The closer to home, the research confirms, the better, since that's where we have the most immediate, best-informed, and largest impact.

Intensive-care nurses can strengthen patient safety on their floors; grocery stockers can work to ensure safe produce is on their shelves; and auto companies can assemble life-saving respirators in their plants—all without being directed to do so.[8]

Another corollary is to act even when others around us are not doing so at first, as the Johnson City pizza store owner did. Our neighbors and colleagues could be too occupied at the moment with a sick child or isolated parents to act first. Stepping forward quickly can thus be additionally significant, whatever our status or responsibilities, since early exemplars at all levels can help inspire subsequent movers at every level.

Hundreds of volunteers, including survivors of the Andes air crash of 1972 (featured in the book and film *Alive*), streamed into Chile's northern desert in 2010 to help rescue thirty-three miners trapped a half mile below ground. And some of those miners in turn traveled to northern Thailand in 2018 to help retrieve a youth soccer team from a water-filled cave.[9]

And finally, let our actions to surmount the COVID-19 crisis also take guidance and inspiration from the fresh roadmap principles from the CEOs chronicled in this book. To cite just three: Following Vanguard's Bill McNabb, nations will want to shape their self-reinforcing actions against the virus into an accelerating flywheel, with lockdowns diminishing infections, which in turn will cut demand for hospital services, and then result in higher-quality care for the stricken. Taking a page from WSFS's Mark Turner, health providers and public authorities in the US will advisedly want to arrange learning sabbaticals when the crisis subsides to improve their readiness to combat future outbreaks. And like Tricia Griffith's employees at Progressive, we will all want official but relational directives during the catastrophe, with clear intent but no micromanagement, asking each of us to lend a hand in our own way.

In line with this last point, here is a final personal template, brought to the fore by the crisis of 2020 but also transferrable to whatever crisis is next.

- I can help prevent the spread of the coronavirus in my own neighborhood or workplace if I act now.
- Here, as I see it, is a short list of actions I can take that will likely help most.
- I am sure that nothing on my list can worsen the health or safety of those around me.
- I will take at least one of these actions today.

If we can make a difference, however small or large our realm, now is the time to step forward. The game has changed: we are in a more challenging era, and as we reinvent ourselves to confront it, may the learning moments of the CEOs we've followed better inform us at the edge.

ACKNOWLEDGMENTS

With their titles and affiliations at the time of an interview, presentation, or conversation, a special thanks to:

Paul Asel, managing partner, NGP Capital

Sherry S. Bahrambeygui, chief executive officer, PriceSmart, Inc.

Luis Ballesteros, assistant professor of international business, George Washington University

Joseph Bass, senior vice president, ASRC Federal

Edward D. Breen, chief executive officer, Tyco International; chief executive officer, DuPont Inc.

M. Grace Calhoun, director, Department of Athletics and Recreation, University of Pennsylvania.

Dennis Carey, vice chair, Korn Ferry International

Brent Celek, tight end, Philadelphia Eagles

Dara Chamides, vice president, Global Executive Education, Estée Lauder Companies

Ram Charan, independent consultant

Kevin Chuah, doctoral student, London Business School

Peter Cowen, independent writer, Wellesley, Massachusetts

Jennifer W. Davis, nonexecutive director, WSFS Financial Corporation

Danielle Devine, global leader, Enterprise, Strategy and Communication, Johnson & Johnson

Tina D'Orazio, vice president and owner's chief of staff, Philadelphia Eagles

Peggy H. Eddens, executive vice president, chief associate and customer experience officer, WSFS Bank

Peter Fasolo, executive vice president and chief human resources officer, Johnson & Johnson

Fabrizio Freda, chief executive officer, Estée Lauder Companies

Geoffrey Garrett, dean, Wharton School, University of Pennsylvania

Alex Gorsky, chair and CEO, Johnson & Johnson

Anne Greenhalgh, deputy director, McNulty Leadership Program, Wharton School, University of Pennsylvania

David Griffith, executive director and head coach, Episcopal Community Services, Philadelphia

Tricia Griffith, president and chief executive officer, Progressive Corporation

Rajiv L. Gupta, former chief executive officer, Rohm and Haas Company; former director, Tyco International

Margaret Gurowitz, chief historian, Johnson & Johnson

Andrew Heller, independent researcher and writer

Carol Heller, event manager, Wharton Risk Management and Decision Processes Center, University of Pennsylvania

Rebecca Henderson, university professor, Harvard Business School, Harvard University

Jane Hertzmark Hudis, group president, Estée Lauder Companies

Julie Hirshey, director of community relations, Philadelphia Eagles

Beth Hodge, executive communications, Vanguard Group

Shaun Huls, director of high performance, Philadelphia Eagles

Martina Hund-Mejean, treasurer, Tyco International

Bo Ilsoe, partner, NGP Capital

John D. Kelly, IV, MD, professor of clinical orthopaedic surgery, University of Pennsylvania Health System

Stephen Klasko, MD, president, Thomas Jefferson University; chief executive officer, Jefferson Health

Jeffrey Klein, executive director, McNulty Leadership Program, Wharton School, University of Pennsylvania

John A. Krol, former chief executive officer, DuPont Inc.; lead director, Tyco International

William P. Lauder, executive chair, Estée Lauder Companies

Vickie Leinhauser, Vanguard Group

Rodger Levenson, executive vice president and chief operating officer, WSFS Financial Corporation

L. Scott Levin, MD, chair, Department of Orthopaedic Surgery, University of Pennsylvania Health System

Jeffrey Lurie, chair, chief executive officer, and owner, Philadelphia Eagles

Frank T. MacInnis, chair, ITT Inc.

Timothy MacKinnon, lead, Surveys and Engagement Research, Human Resources—Workforce Analytics, Johnson & Johnson

Chris Maragos, special teamer and safety, Philadelphia Eagles

Kim Marshall, editor, the *Marshall Memo*

Philip Mead, director of curatorial affairs and chief historian, Museum of the American Revolution

Lori Niederst, chief human resources officer, Progressive Corporation

Indra Nooyi, chief executive officer, PepsiCo Inc.

James Norris, managing director, Vanguard International, Vanguard Group

Michael O'Hare, executive vice president, Global Human Resources, Estée Lauder Companies

William Patrick, independent editor and writer

Douglas Pederson, head coach, Philadelphia Eagles

Eric Pillmore, senior vice president, Tyco International

Phebe Farrow Port, senior vice president of global management strategies and chief of staff to the president and chief executive officer, Estée Lauder Companies

Eleanor Powell, executive director, Investor Relations, Estée Lauder Companies

Denise L. Ramos, chief executive officer, ITT Inc.

Glenn Reed, managing director, Strategy and Finance Group, Vanguard Group

Howie Roseman, executive vice president, Football Operations, Philadelphia Eagles

Jake Rosenberg, vice president, Football Administration, Philadelphia Eagles

Raphael Sagalyn, owner, ICM/Sagalyn

Tom Scalera, executive vice president and chief financial officer, ITT Inc.

Marvin Schoenhals, board chair and former chief executive officer, WSFS Financial Corporation

Nauman Shah, chief of staff, Office of the Chief Executive, Johnson & Johnson

Gregory P. Shea, senior fellow, Wharton Leadership Center, University of Pennsylvania

Don Smolenski, president, Philadelphia Eagles

Michael Sneed, executive vice president, Global Corporate Affairs and Chief Communication Officer, Johnson & Johnson

Duce Staley, assistant head coach/running backs coach, Philadelphia Eagles

R. Scott Stephenson, president and chief executive officer, Museum of the American Revolution

Claudia Stowers, vice president for advancement, Museum of the American Revolution

Christian Tang-Jespersen, former chief executive officer, Heptagon

Mark Turner, board chair and chief executive officer, WSFS Financial Corporation

Michael Ullmann, executive vice president and general counsel, Johnson & Johnson

Elizabeth Vale, senior fellow, Wharton Leadership Center, University of Pennsylvania

William C. Weldon, chair and chief executive officer, Johnson & Johnson

Tyler Wry, associate professor of management, Wharton School, University of Pennsylvania

A special thanks for permission to include photographs, paintings, and images to:

Bill McNabb, for the Vanguard Group flywheel

Patricia Griffith, for the photograph with Progressive employees on Halloween

Johnson & Johnson, for the Johnson and Johnson credos

Metropolitan Museum of Art, New York, New York: *Washington Crossing the Delaware* by Emanuel Leutze. Open Access, Creative Commons.

Museum of the American Revolution, Philadelphia, Pennsylvania: *The March by Valley Forge* by William T. Trego. Courtesy of the Museum of the American Revolution. The color of the image has been lightened for inclusion here.

Museums at Washington and Lee University, Lexington, Virginia: *George Washington as Colonel of the Virginia Regiment* (1772) by Charles Willson Peale, U1897.1.1. Courtesy of the Museums at Washington and Lee University.

NOTES

PROLOGUE:
THE GREATEST CEO OF THE CENTURY

1. Welch 2003.
2. Colvin 1999; Tichy 1997.
3. Khurana and Weber 2008; Pillmore 2003; Symonds 2001.
4. An American naval officer in 1813 sent a message reporting the capture of six British ships during the Battle of Lake Erie: "We have met the enemy and they are ours." The creator of the daily comic strip *Pogo*, Walt Kelly, parodied the quote in 1971 in a cartoon with an antipollution message on Earth Day: "We have met the enemy and he is us."
5. Useem 1998a, 2001; Useem, Davidson, and Wittenberg 2005; Useem and Useem 2014.
6. Pfanz 1998.
7. Freeman 1998, 567–574.
8. Wharton School, University of Pennsylvania, Leadership Ventures 2020.
9. Haass 2020.
10. Kanter 2020; Henderson 2020; Rubenstein 2020.
11. Martin and Burns 2020.
12. Higgins 2020; Lieber 2020; Sorenson 2020; Uber 2020.
13. Mann 2020.
14. When a source is not cited, I have observed or interviewed the referenced executive.

CHAPTER 1: FINDING YOUR EDGE

1. Flint and Schwartzel 2020.
2. Useem 2011.
3. Useem 1996.

4. Wachtell, Lipton, Rosen & Katz 2018; Wells Fargo 2018.

5. Feldman and Montgomery 2015.

6. Brown, Anderson, Salas, and Ward 2017.

7. Haddon 2019.

8. Haddon 2019.

9. Kang 2019.

10. Goldsmith 2007.

11. Chambers 2018; Chambers with Brady 2018; Zemmel, Cuddihy, and Carey 2018.

12. Anthony, Viguerie, and Waldeck 2016; Anthony, Viguerie, Schwartz, and Van Landeghem 2018. Estimates for 2018–2020.

13. Perry 2017.

14. Anthony, Viguerie, Schwartz, and Van Lendeghem 2018; Stangler and Arbesman 2012.

15. Groysberg, Abbott, and Baden 2018.

16. Gerstner 2003.

17. Fitch 2019; Langley 2015; Useem 2012; Vanian 2020.

18. EY 2019.

19. Barnes 2020a, 2020b.

20. Flint and Watson 2020.

21. Barnes 2020b; Friedman 2020; Schwartzel 2020; Smith 2020.

22. Public presentation, Wharton School, University of Pennsylvania, April 26, 2019.

23. Dempsey 2012.

24. *Chronicle of Higher Education* 2020; Koehn 2000; Zemsky, Shaman, and Baldridge 2002.

25. Useem 1984.

26. CEO Academy and Wharton Business School, University of Pennsylvania 2020a; CEO Academy and Wharton Business School, University of Pennsylvania 2020b.

27. Hernandez 2014; Kogut and Zander 1992.

28. Schmidt, Rosenberg, and Eagle 2019.

29. NBC News 2020.

CHAPTER 2: BUILDING A GROWTH
ENGINE WHEN THE CHIPS ARE DOWN

1. Useem 1996.

2. Furlong 2010; Segal 2018.

3. Useem 1998b.

4. McNabb 2008a, 2008b.

5. Rekenthaler 2019.

6. EY 2017.

7. Collins 2001.

8. Collins 2001.

9. Collins 2008.

10. Kennedy 2018.

11. The figures are for the end of 2008; Vanguard later closed its offices in two of the countries where it had operated. See also Xie and Lim 2019.

12. Lawler 1992; Pfeffer 1998; Charan, Barton, and Carey 2018.

13. *Chief Learning Officer* 2016.

14. Kahneman 2011.

15. Collins 2019; Dumaine 2020.

16. Bezos 2020.

CHAPTER 3:
INCLUSION AS A LEADERSHIP IMPERATIVE

1. Guzior 2018; Jenkins 2018.

2. Kilpatrick 2019.

3. Great Places to Work 2019

4. Griffith 2019a, 2019b.

5. Business Roundtable 2019a; *Fortune* 2019.

6. Wharton School of Business, University of Pennsylvania 2017.

7. Useem, Singh, Liang, and Cappelli 2017.

8. Griffith 2019a, 2019b.

9. Business Roundtable 2019b; Great Places to Work 2019; Griffith 2019b.

10. Progressive Corporation 2020.

11. Griffith 2019a, 2019b.

CHAPTER 4: STAYING AHEAD OF THE
GAME IN AN ALWAYS-ON/24-7 WORLD

1. This chapter draws on Ey 2018; Kline 2018; and Osborne 2019.

2. Marcec 2018.

3. Collins 2001.

4. Burns 2018.

5. Kline 2019; McCarthy 2020.

6. Gara 2020; Nassauer 2020

7. Clifford 2019; Guth 2005.

8. Bank Director 2021.

CHAPTER 5: RECRUITING A PARTNER
TO LEAD CHANGE BEFORE YOU HAVE TO

1. Dowling 2008.
2. Useem 2015.
3. Dowling 2008.
4. Gottfried 2012.
5. This chapter draws on Tully 2013.
6. Christensen 2018.
7. Gottfried 2012.
8. Christensen 2018.
9. Fine 2019.
10. The Estée Lauder Companies Inc., private communication. The figures for department stores sales include online sales through those stores; the figures for online sales include brand websites (such as Clinique.com), retailer websites (such as Macys.com), and third-party platforms (such as Tmall.com). Other sales channels, not displayed in the figure, include freestanding retail stores, travel retail (such as duty-free shops in airports), specialty-multi brand stores (such as Sephora, Ulta, or Boots), salons, spas, and perfumeries.
11. Estée Lauder Companies, private communication.
12. *Barron's* 2018; *Harvard Business Review* 2019a.
13. Fred H. Langhammer, the only other nonfamily member to serve as ELC's chief executive, was a twenty-five-year veteran of the company.
14. Spencer Stuart 2018; Heenan and Bennis 1999.
15. Estée Lauder Companies 2020; Fine 2020; Moss, Terlep, and Maloney 2020.

CHAPTER 6: COMPLETING AN
INCOMPLETE RÉSUMÉ TO THINK LIKE A CHIEF

1. Sampson 1973; Jensen 1972.
2. Sampson 1973; Tichy 1997.
3. Singh and Useem 2016.
4. Baird Equity Research 2018; Haskett 2018.
5. Haskett 2018.

CHAPTER 7: DOUBLING DOWN ON THE RIGHT TALENT

1. This chapter was prepared with the assistance of Nokia Growth Partners' Paul Asel.
2. Useem 2002.
3. Sjöberg 2018.

CHAPTER 8: TRIAGE OR TRANSFORMATION

1. Maremont and Markon 2002.

2. Maremont and Cohen 2002.

3. NBC News 2012.

4. Boselovic 2003; Dewar, Keller, Sneader, and Strovink 2020.

5. This section draws on Khurana and Weber 2008; Pillmore 2003; and Useem 2006.

6. Hoskisson and Hitt 1994; Useem 1996; Zieminski 2012; Zuckerman 2000.

7. Lublin and Tita 2011; Wong 2007.

8. Benoit 2015; Merced 2015; Trian Partners 2015.

9. DuPont 2015.

10. Bunge 2018.

11. Bunge 2018.

12. Bunge 2018.

13. DuPont 2019; Wallmine 2019.

14. Ethisphere Institute 2009.

CHAPTER 9: REINVENTING THE CULTURE

1. Kadet 2020; Bindley 2020.

2. Hoffman 2019.

3. Rockoff and Lublin 2012.

4. Speights 2019.

5. Business Roundtable 2019a, 2019b.

6. Harnish and the Editors of *Fortune* Magazine 2012.

7. Johnson & Johnson 2012.

8. Baron and Hannan 2002.

9. Goodwin 2018; Hsu 2018; Rabin 2020.

10. O'Reilly 2001; Sørensen 2002.

11. Williams 2019.

12. Gartenberg, Prat, and Serafeim 2019; Henderson and Van den Steen 2015.

13. Gartner 2017; Hass 2013; Netflix 2009, 2017.

CHAPTER 10: MASTERING THE FIELD TO WIN IT ALL

1. This chapter has been coauthored with Jeffrey Klein, and it draws on Klein and Useem 2019, and Pederson 2018.

2. Entis 2015.

3. Mosher 2015.

4. Prewitt 2018.

5. Shpigel 2017.

6. George 2011.

7. Beaton 2019.

8. Grant 2014.

9. Frei and Morriss 2020.

10. Casciaro, Edmondson, and Jang 2019.

11. Diamond 2017.

12. McChrystal 2015.

13. Prewitt 2018.

14. Best 2018.

15. Klemko 2018.

16. McManus 2018a, 2018b.

17. Berman 2018.

CHAPTER 11: OVERCOMING DOUBTS TO TAKE COMMAND

1. Henry Ruger and Jerry Useem provided research and guidance for this chapter. Henry Ruger at the time was a high school senior at Germantown Friends School in Philadelphia, Pennsylvania; Jerry Useem is an independent writer affiliated with *The Atlantic* and formerly a staff writer with *Inc.* and *Fortune* magazines. This chapter draws on many sources, including Chernow 2010; O'Connell 2019; Washington n.d.; and Wood 2002.

2. Tourtellot 2000; Charles Willson Peale, *George Washington as Colonel of the Virginia Regiment*, 1772.

3. Center for the Study of the American Constitution, University of Wisconsin–Madison n.d.

4. Ellis 2004.

5. Fried 2018.

6. Anderson 1999.

7. Ellis 2004.

8. Ott 2020.

9. William T. Trego, *The March to Valley Forge*, 1883.

10. Sears 2014; McCullough 2005.

11. Ellis 2004, 85-86.

12. Ellis 2004, 85.

13. Useem 2002.

14. McCullough 2005.

15. Weigley 1977.

16. Ellis 2004, 99; McCain 2013.

17. Parker, Cilluffo, and Stepler 2017; US Department of Defense, Office of the Deputy Assistant Secretary of Defense for Military Community and Family Policy 2015.

18. Collins 2001.

19. Library of Congress n.d. Words have been changed to their contemporary spelling and capitalization.

20. Washington 1781.

CHAPTER 12: BREAK THE BUBBLE

1. These qualities are similar to those that developmental psychologist Howard Gardner (1996) highlighted in his study of these four and other historical leaders of the last century. Based at the Harvard Graduate School of Education, Gardner is best known for his work on multiple forms of human intelligence.

2. Collins 2001; Goodwin 2018; Ibarra 2015; Isaacson 2012. Herminia Ibarra, for instance, argued in *Act Like a Leader, Think Like a Leader* that the primary foundation for any individual's leadership is to first behave like a leader and then accept that public identity as one's own. Jim Collins argued in *Good to Great* that leaders who take companies from average to eminent are riveted on their firm's success and not their own. Doris Kearns Goodwin wrote in *Leadership: In Turbulent Times* that successful American presidents acquired an exquisite sense of timing for when to hold back on a policy or edict—and when to move forward. And Walter Isaacson advocated in his biography of Steve Jobs that focus, simplicity, and perfection are among the qualities that not only defined Jobs's leadership at Apple but should apply to entrepreneurs everywhere.

3. Still, from other analyses we have found that on top of these boundary-spanning and time-invariant universals are a set of distinct country-coded principles. We came to appreciate this by talking directly with a number of company leaders in China and India. We interviewed 72 executives and directors of large nonstate-owned Chinese enterprises during the mid-2010s, and we interviewed 105 executives and directors among India's largest corporations between 2007 and 2009. The better-known companies included Alibaba and Lenovo in China, and Infosys and Tata in India. We sought to identify the distinctive leadership codes in these countries through the eyes of those who had been running their largest privately owned firms. With studies of American and British business executives serving as implicit contrast points, several characteristic Chinese and Indian leadership tenets stood out (Cappelli, Singh, Singh, and Useem 2010; Useem, Singh, Liang, and Cappelli 2017).

Chinese business leaders embraced a readiness to work with uncertainty and learn from experience rather than received wisdom; displayed an urgency to capitalize on emergent business opportunities; expressed high confidence and optimism and focused on executing; and proved passionate about company purpose and mission, with little concern for shareholder value. Indian business leaders, by contrast, sought to meet the needs of impoverished consumers with extreme efficiency; learned to rely on their wits and improvisation to circumvent recurrent hurdles; saw their employees as assets to be developed, not costs to be reduced; and emphasized not only enterprise success but also family prosperity, regional advance, and national renaissance.

We believe that the Chinese and Indian business leaders acquired their distinctive views of leadership because so many of them came of age at a time when private enterprise was barely tolerated. Since reforms of the 1990s in both China and India opened up their economies, a group of entrepreneurs created and expanded their companies with a set of practices that differed substantially from the previous period, when state constraints and a culture of hierarchy had stifled business innovation and flexibility. And though they shared basic leadership canons with executives and directors in the West—all emphasized strategic thought and action—these leaders had added distinctive leadership bundles that have come to constitute what might be termed a "China Way" and an "India Way."

4. Kunreuther and Useem 2018.

5. Munich Re Geo Research 2020; World Health Organization 2020.

6. Standard and Poor's 2013

7. Bernile, Bhatwat, and Rau 2017; Malmendier, Tate, and Yan 2011.

8. This section draws on Kunreuther and Useem 2018.

9. Chu 2017.

10. Kunreuther and Useem 2018.

11. Chenault and Carlson 2020a, 2020b; Judge 2020; Mann 2020.

12. Bloom and Cadarette 2020; Rodin 2014.

13. This section draws on Ballesteros, Useem, and Wry 2017; Ballesteros, Wry, and Useem 2020a; *Harvard Business Review* 2019a; Kunreuther and Useem 2018.

14. From Howard Kunreuther and Michael Useem 2018, based on data from Munich Re Geo Research 2015.

15. Ballesteros, Useem, and Wry 2017; Kunreuther and Useem 2018.

16. Ballesteros, Useem, and Wry 2017; Friedman 1970.

17. Ballesteros, Useem, and Wry 2017; Ballesteros, Wry, and Useem, 2020b; Kunreuther and Useem 2018.

18. Ballesteros, Wry, and Useem 2020b.

19. Tocqueville 1836; Useem 1996.

20. Adamczyki 2020.

21. Iansiti and Lakhani 2020.

22. Carey 2013; Heath and Heath 2007.

23. Williams 2019.

24. Williams 2019.

25. Berry and Fowler 2019; Lieberson and O'Connor 1972; Thomas 1988; Useem 1998a.

EPILOGUE: LEADING IN OUR TIMES

1. Neff and Citrin 2007.

2. Winoker 2019.

3. Christensen 1997.

4. This section draws on Useem 2020.

5. Waldman, Ramirez, House, and Puranan 2001.

6. Carey, Patsalos-Fox, and Useem 2009; similar redirections of executive behavior were reported by Carey, Charan, and Remick (2020) from interviews with a dozen chief executives in the wake of the coronavirus outbreak in 2020.

7. Plott and Medina 2020.

8. Ballesteros, Wry, and Useem 2020a.

9. Useem and Eavis 2018; Useem, Jordán, and Koljatic 2011.

REFERENCES

Adamczyki, Darius. 2020. "A Statement from Our Chairman and CEO on Our Opposition to Racism and Our Promotion of Equality and Opportunity." Honeywell International. June 17, 2020. www.honeywell.com/en-us/newsroom/pressreleases/2020/06/a-statement-from-our-chairman-and-ceo-on-our-opposition-to-racism-and-our-promotion-of-equality-and-opportunity.

Anderson, Fred W. 1999. "The Hinge of the Revolution: George Washington Confronts a People's Army, July 3, 1775." *Massachusetts Historical Review* 1: 20–48.

Anthony, Scott D., S. Patrick Viguerie, Evan I. Schwartz, and John Van Landeghem. 2018. "2018 Corporate Longevity Forecast: Creative Destruction Is Accelerating." Innosight. February 2018. www.innosight.com/wp-content/uploads/2017/11/Innosight-Corporate-Longevity-2018.pdf.

Anthony, Scott D., S. Patrick Viguerie, and Andrew Waldeck. 2016. "Corporate Longevity: Turbulence Ahead for Large Organizations." Innosight. Spring 2016. www.innosight.com/wp-content/uploads/2016/08/Corporate-Longevity-2016-Final.pdf.

Baird Equity Research. 2018. *ITT Inc.* August 3, 2018. https://seekingalpha.com/article/4194520-itt-itt-q2-2018-results-earnings-call-transcript.

Ballesteros, Luis, Michael Useem, and Tyler Wry. 2017. "Masters of Disasters? An Empirical Analysis of How Societies Benefit from Corporate Disaster Aid." *Academy of Management Journal* 60, no. 5: 1682–1708.

———. 2020. "Disruption Strikes, You're in Charge, Now What: When Companies Tackle Great Challenges." *European Business Review* (May–June 2020): 44–51.

Ballesteros, Luis, Tyler Wry, and Michael Useem. 2020a. "Halos or Horns? Reputation and the Contingent Financial Returns to Non-market Behavior." (working paper).

———. 2020b. "Rents from Nonmarket Action Under High Uncertainty: The Role of Corporate Reputation." (working paper).

Bank Director. 2021. "2021 Ranking Banking: Performance Powerhouses." www.bankdirector.com/rankingbanking/2021-rankingbanking-performance-powerhouses.

Barnes, Brooks. 2020a. "Center Stage at Disney After a Career out of the Spotlight." *New York Times*, February 26, 2020. www.nytimes.com/2020/02/26/business/media/bob-chapek-disney-ceo.html.

———. 2020b. "Disney Takes a Pandemic Hit, and There's Worse to Come." *New York Times*, May 5, 2020. www.nytimes.com/2020/05/05/business/media/coronavirus-disney-earnings.html.

Baron, James N., and Michael T. Hannan. 2002. "Organizational Blueprints for Success in High-Tech Start-Ups." *California Management Review* 44, no. 3: 8–36.

Barron's. 2018. "World's Best CEOs: 30 Leaders with Talent to Spare." May 26, 2018. www.barrons.com/articles/worlds-best-ceos-30-leaders-with-talent-to-spare-1527300812.

Barry, John M. 2004. *The Great Influenza: The Story of the Deadliest Pandemic in History*. Penguin Books.

Beaton, Andrew. 2019. "The NFL Team Run by Women." *Wall Street Journal*, September 25, 2019. www.wsj.com/articles/the-nfl-team-run-by-women-11569412442?mod=searchresults&page=1&pos=3.

Benoit, David. 2015. "Glass Lewis Backs Trian's Nelson Peltz for DuPont Board." *Wall Street Journal*, April 30, 2015. www.wsj.com/articles/glass-lewis-recommends-dupont-shareholders-elect-trians-nelson-peltz-1430365548.

Berman, Zack. 2018. "Eagles Coach Doug Pederson, Top Executive Howie Roseman Sign Contract Extensions Through 2022." *Philadelphia Inquirer*, August 5, 2018. www.philly.com/philly/sports/eagles/doug-pederson-howie-roseman-eagles-contract-extensions-20180805.html.

Bernile, Gennaro, Vineet Bhagwat, and P. Raghavendra Rau. 2017. "What Doesn't Kill You Will Only Make You More Risk-Loving: Early Life Disasters and CEO Behavior." *Journal of Finance* 72, no. 1: 167–206.

Berry, Christopher R., and Anthony Fowler. 2019. "How Much Do Coaches Matter?" *Counterpoints* (podcast). MIT Sloan Sports Analytics. March 21, 2019. sloanreview.mit.edu/audio/how-much-do-coaches-actually-matter.

Best, Neil. 2018. "Super Bowl LII: NBC Announcers Rise to Occasion of Historic Thriller." *Newsday*, February 5, 2018. www.newsday.com/sports/columnists/neil-best/super-bowl-lii-nbc-al-michaels-cris-collinsworth-1.16549263.

Bezos, Jeff. 2020. "2019 Letter to Shareholders." Amazon. https://blog
.aboutamazon.com/company-news/2019-letter-to-shareholders.

Bindley, Katherine. 2020. "Remote Work Is Reshaping San Francisco, as
Tech Workers Flee and Rents Fall." *Wall Street Journal*, August 14,
2020. www.wsj.com/articles/remote-work-is-reshaping-san-francisco
-as-tech-workers-flee-and-rents-fall-11597413602.

Block, Fang. 2020. "World's Top 100 Billionaires Lost US$408 Billion
in Two Months Due to Covid-19." *Barron's*, April 6, 2020. www
.barrons.com/articles/worlds-top-100-billionaires-lost-us-408
-billion-in-two-months-due-to-covid-19-01586210558.

Bloom, David E., and Daniel Cadarette. 2020. "Coronavirus: We Need
to Start Preparing for the Next Viral Outbreak Now." *The Conversation*, February 20, 2020.

Boselovic, Len. 2003. "Tough Decisions Awaited Tyco's New CEO,
Grove City's Breen." *Pittsburgh Post-Gazette*, November 16, 2003.
www.post-gazette.com/business/businessnews/2003/11/16/Tough
-decisions-awaited-Tyco-s-new-CEO-Grove-City-s-Breen/stories
/200311160103.

Brown, Jill A., Anne Anderson, Jesus M. Salas, and Andrew J. Ward.
2017. "Do Investors Care About Director Tenure? Insights from Executive Cognition and Social Capital Theories." *Organization Science*
28, no. 3: 471–494.

Buffett, Warren. 2014. "To the Shareholders of Berkshire Hathaway Inc."
Berkshire Hathaway. February 28, 2014. www.berkshirehathaway
.com/letters/2013ltr.pdf.

Bunge, Jacob. 2018. "Meet the Breakup Artist Taking Apart Dow
DuPont." *Wall Street Journal*, December 26, 2018. www.wsj.com
/articles/meet-the-breakup-artist-taking-apart-dowdupont
-11545832801.

Burns, Hillary. "WSFS Broke the Mold with Its Latest Deal. Other
Banks Should Take Note." *American Banker*, August 10, 2018. www
.americanbanker.com/opinion/wsfs-broke-the-mold-with-its
-latest-deal-others-banks-should-take-note.

Business Roundtable. 2019a. "*Business Roundtable* Redefines the Purpose of
a Corporation to Promote 'An Economy That Serves All Americans.'" August 19, 2019. www.businessroundtable.org/business
-roundtable-redefines-the-purpose-of-a-corporation-to-promote
-an-economy-that-serves-all-americans.

———. 2019b. "Tricia Griffith, President and CEO, The Progressive
Corporation." September 16, 2019. www.businessroundtable.org
/tricia-griffith-president-and-ceo-the-progressive-corporation.

Cappelli, Peter, Harbir Singh, Jitendra Singh, and Michael Useem. 2010. *The India Way: How India's Top Business Leaders Are Revolutionizing Management*. Harvard Business Press.

Carey, Benedict. 2013. *How We Learn*. Random House.

Carey, Dennis, Ram Charan, and Tierney Remick. 2020. "CEO Shift: How CEOs Are Using Crisis to Pivot to a Better Future." *Chief Executive*, April 24, 2020. https://chiefexecutive.net/ceo-shift-how -ceos-are-using-crisis-to-pivot-to-a-better-future.

Carey, Dennis, Michael Patsalos-Fox, and Michael Useem. 2009. "Leadership Lessons from Hard Times." *McKinsey Quarterly*, July 1, 2009. www.mckinsey.com/featured-insights/leadership/leadership -lessons-for-hard-times#.

Carton, Andrew M., Chad Murphy, and Jonathan R. Clark. 2014. "A (Blurry) Vision of the Future: How Leader Rhetoric About Ultimate Goals Influences Performance." *Academy of Management Journal*, 57, no. 6: 1544–1570.

Casciaro, Tiziana, Amy C. Edmondson, and Sujin Jang. 2019. "Cross-Silo Leadership." *Harvard Business Review* (May–June 2019). hbr .org/2019/05/cross-silo-leadership.

Center for the Study of the American Constitution, University of Wisconsin–Madison. n.d. "George Washington." https://csac .history.wisc.edu/multimedia/founders-on-the-founders/george -washington.

CEO Academy and Wharton Business School, University of Pennsylvania. 2020a. CEO Academy. www.ceo-academy.com.

———. 2020b. "CEO Academy." Executive Education. https://executive education.wharton.upenn.edu/for-individuals/all-programs /ceo-academy.

Chambers, John. 2018. "Leadership in Action." Interview by Michael Useem. *Wharton Business Radio*. SiriusXM. November 26, 2018. soundcloud.com/user-414944777/3-john-chambers-on-leadership -in-action?in=user-414944777/sets/leadership-in-action-top-5.

Chambers, John, with Diane Brady. 2018. *Connecting the Dots: Lessons for Leadership in a Startup World*. Hachette Books.

Charan, Ram, Dominic Barton, and Dennis Carey. 2018. *Talent Wins: The New Playbook for Putting People First*, Harvard Business Review Press.

Chenault, Kenneth I., and Rachel Romer Carlson. 2020a. "It's Time for the Business Community to Step Up." *New York Times*, March 18, 2020. www.nytimes.com/2020/03/18/opinion/business-coronavirus .html.

———. 2020b. "Stop the Spread—A Response to COVID-19." *Medium*, March 14, 2020. https://medium.com/@rachel.romer.carlson/leading-boldly-on-covid-19-b23ecb2f5093.

Chernow, Ron. 2010. *Washington: A Life*. Penguin Group.

Chief Learning Officer. 2016. "2016 Learning Elite Winners." August 11, 2016. https://learningelite.clomedia.com/2016/08/11/2016-learning-elite-winners.

Christensen, Clayton. 1997. *The Innovator's Dilemma: When New Technologies Cause Great Firms to Fail*. Harvard Business School Press.

Christensen, Karen 2018. "Staying Relevant in an Age of Transformation." *Rotman Magazine* (Winter: 2018). www.rotman.utoronto.ca/Connect/Rotman-MAG/Back-Issues/2018/Back-Issues---2018/Winter2018-CreativeDestruction/Winter2018-FreeFeatureArticle-FabrizioFreda.

Chronicle of Higher Education. 2020. *The Successful President for Tomorrow: The 5 Skills Future Leaders Will Need*. https://store.chronicle.com/collections/administration-leadership/products/the-successful-president-of-tomorrow-the-5-skills-future-leaders-need?variant=14947128410154.

Chu, Jennifer. 2017. "Study: Volkswagen's Excess Emissions Will Lead to 1,200 Premature Deaths in Europe." *MIT News*, March 3, 2017. https://news.mit.edu/2017/volkswagen-emissions-premature-deaths-europe-0303#:~:text=The%20team%20previously%20estimated%20that,premature%20deaths%20across%20the%20U.S.

Clifford, Catherine. 2019. "Bill Gates Took Solo 'Think Weeks' in a Cabin in the Woods—Why It's a Great Strategy." *CNBC*, July 28, 2019. www.cnbc.com/2019/07/26/bill-gates-took-solo-think-weeks-in-a-cabin-in-the-woods.html.

Collins, Jim. 2001. *Good to Great: Why Some Companies Make the Leap and Others Don't*. Harper Business.

———. 2008. *How the Mighty Fall*. JimCollins.

———. 2019. *Turning the Flywheel: Why Some Companies Build Momentum . . . and Others Don't*. Harper Business.

Colvin, Geoffrey. 1999. "The Ultimate Manager in a Time of Hidebound, Formulaic Thinking, General Electric's Jack Welch Gave Power to the Worker and the Shareholder. He Built One Hell of a Company in the Process." *Fortune*, November 22, 1999.

Dempsey, Martin. 2012. *Janes Defence Weekly*, September 26, 2012.

Dewar, Carolyn, Scott Keller, Kevin Sneader, and Kurt Strovink. 2020. "The CEO Moment: Leadership for a New Era." *McKinsey Quarterly*, July 2020. www.mckinsey.com/featured-insights/leadership/the-ceo-moment-leadership-for-a-new-era#.

Diamond, Jeff. 2017. "Eagles GM Howie Roseman Goes from Hot Seat to Catbird Seat in Less Than One Year." *Sporting News*, November 15, 2017. www.sportingnews.com/nfl/news/philadelphia-eagles -general-manager-gm-howie-roseman-carson-wentz-super-bowl /vst7d1utrg0u1m8o00dtn9h4f.

Dowling, Daisy Wademan. 2008. "The Best Advice I Ever Got: William P. Lauder, President and CEO, Estée Lauder Companies." *Harvard Business Review* (May 2008). https://hbr.org/2008/05/the -best-advice-i-ever-got-william-p-lauder-president-and-ceo-estee -lauder-companies.

Dumaine, Brian. 2020. *Bezonomics: How Amazon Is Changing Our Lives, and What the World's Best Companies Are Learning from It*. Scribner.

Dunsmuir, Lindsay, and Ann Saphir. 2020. "For U.S. Small Restaurants, Coronavirus Impact Is Swift and Brutal." *Reuters*, March 19, 2020. www.reuters.com/article/health-coronavirus-usa-eateries/for-u-s -small-restaurants-coronavirus-impact-is-swift-and-brutal-idUSL 1N2BA172.

DuPont. 2015. "DuPont Appoints Edward D. Breen and James L. Gallogly to Board of Directors." PR Newswire. February 5, 2015. www .prnewswire.com/news-releases/dupont-appoints-edward-d-breen -and-james-l-gallogly-to-board-of-directors-300031547.html.

———. 2019. Schedule 14A Proxy Statement. SEC. April 29, 2019. www.sec.gov/Archives/edgar/data/1666700/000119312519126249 /d728663ddef14a.htm#rom728663_18.

Ellis, Joseph J. 2004. *His Excellency George Washington*. Random House.

Entis, Laura. 2015. "10 Inspirational Quotes on Leadership from the NFL's Greatest Coaches." *Entrepreneur*, January 27, 2015. www .entrepreneur.com/article/242262#:~:text=A%20great%20football %20coach%20understands,the%20unrelenting%20desire%20to% 20win.

Estée Lauder Companies. 2020. *Fiscal 2020 Third Quarter Results*. May 1, 2020. https://media.elcompanies.com/files/e/estee-lauder-companies /universal/investors/earnings-and-financials/quarterly-earnings /2020/q3/q3-fiscal-2020-earnings-release.pdf.

Ethisphere Institute. 2009. "2009's 100 Most Influential People in Business Ethics." Covalence. www.covalence.ch/docs/2009s100Most InfluentialPeopleinBusinessEthics_EthisphereInstitute.htm.

EY. 2017. *Reshaping Around the Investor: Global ETF Research*.

——— 2019. "CEO Imperative Study."

Ey, Craig. 2018. "Announcing the *Philadelphia Business Journal*'s 2018 Most Admired CEOs: Mark Turner, WSFS Financial Corp. and WSFS Bank." November 6, 2018. https://www.bizjournals.com

/philadelphia/news/2018/11/06/announcing-thephiladelphia -business-journals-2018.html.

Feeley, Jef. 2019. "J&J Pays About $1 Billion to Resolve Pinnacle-Hip Suits." *Bloomberg*, May 7, 2019. www.bloomberg.com/news/articles /2019-05-07/j-j-said-to-pay-about-1-billion-to-resolve-pinnacle -hip-suits.

Feldman, Emilie R., and Cynthia A. Montgomery. 2015. "Are Incentives Without Expertise Sufficient? Evidence from Fortune 500 Firms." *Strategic Management Journal* 36, no. 1 (January): 113–122.

Fine, Jenny B. 2019. "The Freda Era." *BeautyInc*.

———. 2020. "Leading for the Long Term." *BeautyInc*, May 15, 2020.

Fitch, Asa. 2019. "IBM Closes Its Red Hat Purchase, a Deal with High Stakes for Rometty." *Wall Street Journal*, July 9, 2019. www.wsj.com /articles/ibms-biggest-purchase-ever-has-high-stakes-for -rometty-11562676754.

Flint, Joe, and Erich Schwartzel. 2020. "NBCUniversal CEO Jeff Shell Has No Time for Hollywood Egos." *Wall Street Journal*, June 20, 2020. www.wsj.com/articles/nbcuniversal-ceo-jeff-shell-has-no-time -for-hollywood-egos-11592625714.

Flint, Joe, and R. T. Watson. 2020. "Described as All Business, Disney's New CEO Is a Number-Crunching Tactician." *Wall Street Journal*, February 26, 2020.

Fortune. 2019. "Tricia Griffith." Most Powerful Women. https://fortune .com/most-powerful-women/2019/tricia-griffith.

Freeman, Douglas Southhall. 1998. *Lee's Lieutenants: A Study in Command*. Simon & Schuster.

Frei, Frances, and Anne Morriss. 2020. *Unleashed: The Unapologetic Leader's Guide to Empowering Everyone Around You*. Harvard Business Review Press.

Fried, Stephen. 2018. *Rush: Revolution, Madness, and the Visionary Doctor Who Became a Founding Father*. Crown.

Friedman, Milton. 1970. "The Social Responsibility of Business Is to Increase Its Profits." *New York Times Magazine*, September 13, 1970.

Friedman, Thomas. 2020. "Our New Historical Divide: B.C. and A.C.— the World Before Corona and the World After." *New York Times*, March 17, 2020. www.nytimes.com/2020/03/17/opinion/coronavirus -trends.html.

Furlong, Lisa. 2010. "The CEO of Vanguard on Thinking for the Long Term." *Dartmouth Alumni Magazine*, June 2010. https://dartmouth alumnimagazine.com/articles/william-mcnabb-%E2%80%9979.

Gara, Antoine. 2020. "The World's Best Banks: The Future of Banking Is Digital After Coronavirus." *Forbes*, June 8, 2020. www.forbes.com

/sites/antoinegara/2020/06/08/the-worlds-best-banks-the-future
-of-banking-is-digital-after-coronavirus/#2aa65eef2993.

Gardner, Howard, with Emma Laskin. 1996. *Leading Minds: An Anatomy of Leadership*. Basic Books.

Gartenberg, Claudine, Andrea Prat, and George Serafeim. 2019. "Corporate Purpose and Financial Performance." *Organization Science* 30, no. 1: 1–18.

Gartner. 2017. "Netflix Updates Its Famous Culture Document with Focus on Inclusion and Respect." June 22, 2017.

George, John. 2011. "Philadelphia Eagles Win International Award for Community Service Efforts." *Philadelphia Business Journal*, December 8, 2011. https://globalphiladelphia.org/news/philadelphia-eagles -win-international-award-community-service-efforts.

Gerstner, Louis V., Jr. 2003. *Who Says Elephants Can't Dance? How I Turned Around IBM*. HarperCollins.

Goldsmith, Marshall. 2007. *What Got You Here Won't Get You There*. Hyperion.

Goodwin, Doris Kearns. 2018. *Leadership: In Turbulent Times*. Simon & Schuster.

Gottfried, Miriam. "Estée Lauder's Makeover Man." *Barron's*, January 14, 2012. www.barrons.com/articles/SB50001424052748703535904577152833522554226.

Grant, Adam. 2014. *Give and Take: Why Helping Others Drives Our Success*. Penguin Books.

Great Places to Work. 2020. "Progressive Insurance." www.greatplace towork.com/certified-company/1000270.

Griffith, Tricia. 2019a. "When It's a Tough Call, Rely on Your Values." LinkedIn. July 8, 2019. www.linkedin.com/pulse/when-its-tough -call-rely-your-values-tricia-griffith.

———. 2019b. "Letter to Shareholders, Third Quarter." Progressive Corporation.

Grossman, Matt. "J&J Steps Up Trials for Covid-19 Vaccine." *Wall Street Journal*, March 31, 2020. www.wsj.com/articles/johnson-johnson -to-begin-human-trials-on-covid-19-vaccine-by-september-11585 569380.

Groysberg, Boris, Sarah Abbott, and Katherine Connolly Baden. 2018. "Resolving to Stay Relevant in 2018." *The Official Board's Blog*. www .theofficialboard.com/blog/hr/resolving-to-stay-relevant-in-2018.

Guth, Robert A. 2005. "In Secret Hideaway, Bill Gates Ponders Microsoft's Future." *Wall Street Journal*, March 28, 2005. www.wsj.com /articles/SB111196625830690477.

Guzior, Betsey. 2018. "A First for Progressive CEO Tricia Griffith." *Business Journals*, November 15, 2018. www.bizjournals.com/biz women/news/latest-news/2018/11/a-first-for-progressive-ceo-tricia -griffith.html?page=all.

Haass, Richard. 2020. *The World: A Brief Introduction*. Penguin.

Haddon, Heather. 2019. "Biggest Supermarket Company Struggles with Online Grocery Upheaval." *Wall Street Journal*, April 22, 2019. www .wsj.com/articles/americas-biggest-supermarket-company -struggles-with-online-grocery-upheaval-11555877123?mod=hp _featst_pos1.

Harnish, Verne, and the Editors of *Fortune* Magazine. 2012. *The Greatest Business Decisions of All Time: How Apple, Ford, IBM, Zappos, and Others Made Radical Choices That Changed the Course of Business*. TI Inc. Books.

Harvard Business Review. 2019a. "The CEO 100, 2019 Edition." (November–December 2019). https://hbr.org/2019/11/the-ceo-100 -2019-edition.

———. 2019b. "Giving After Disasters." (January–February 2019): 17–20.

Haskett, Gordon, Research Advisor. 2018. ITT. October 12, 2018.

Hass, Nancy. 2013. "And the Award for the Next HBO Goes to . . ." *GQ*, January 29, 2013. www.gq.com/story/netflix-founder-reed-hastings -house-of-cards-arrested-development.

Heath, Chip, and Dan Heath. 2007. *Made to Stick: Why Some Ideas Survive and Other Die*. Random House.

Heenan, David A., and Warren Bennis 1999. *Co-Leaders: The Power of Great Partnerships*. Wiley.

Henderson, Rebecca. 2020. *Reimagining Capitalism in a World on Fire*. PublicAffairs.

Henderson, Rebecca, and Eric Van den Steen. 2015. "Why Do Firms Have 'Purpose'? The Firm's Role as a Carrier of Identity and Reputation." *American Economic Review* 105, no. 5: 326–330.

Hernandez, Exequiel. 2014. "Finding a Home Away from Home: Effects of Immigrants on Firms' Foreign Location Choice and Performance." *Administrative Science Quarterly* 59, no. 1: 73–108.

Higgins, Tim. 2020. "Behind Elon Musk's Fight to Reopen Tesla in California: Keep Up with Detroit." *Wall Street Journal*, May 13, 2020. www.wsj.com/articles/elon-musk-pushes-to-reopen-tesla-in -california-and-keep-up-with-detroit-11589393592?mod= searchresults&page=1&pos=3.

Hoffman, Jan. 2019. "First Opioid Trial Takes Aim at Johnson & Johnson." *New York Times*, May 26, 2019. www.nytimes.com/2019/05/26 /health/opioid-trial-oklahoma-johnsonandjohnson.html.

Hoskisson, Robert E., and Michael A. Hitt. 1994. *Downscoping: How to Tame the Diversified Firm*. Oxford University Press.

Hsu, Tiffany. 2018. "Johnson & Johnson Told to Pay $4.7 Billion in Baby Powder Lawsuit." *New York Times*, July 12, 2018. www.nytimes.com/2018/07/12/business/johnson-johnson-talcum-powder.html.

Iansiti, Marco, and Karim R. Lakhani. 2020. *Competing in the Age of AI: Strategy and Leadership When Algorithms and Networks Run the World*. Harvard Business Review Press.

Ibarra, Herminia. 2015. *Act Like a Leader, Think Like a Leader*. Harvard Business Review Press.

Isaacson, Walter. 2012. "The Real Leadership Lessons of Steve Jobs." *Harvard Business Review* (April 2012). hbr.org/2012/04/the-real-leadership-lessons-of-steve-jobs.

Jargon, Julie. 2019. "Starbucks CEO Kevin Johnson Reins in Predecessor's Ambitions: 'I'm Not Howard.'" *Wall Street Journal*, January 7, 2019. www.wsj.com/articles/starbucks-ceo-kevin-johnson-reins-in-predecessors-ambitions-im-not-howard-11546857001?mod=searchresults&page=1&pos=1.

Jenkins, Aric. 2018. "Meet the CEO of the Insurance Company Growing Faster Than Apple." *Fortune*, November 15, 2018. https://fortune.com/2018/11/15/progressive-insurance-ceo-tricia-griffith.

Jensen, Michael C. 1972. "Tough I.T.T. Chief Harold Sydney Geneen." *New York Times*, March 10, 1972. www.nytimes.com/1972/03/10/archives/tough-itt-chief-harold-sydney-geneen.html.

Johnson & Johnson. 2012. "Johnson & Johnson Holds 2012 Annual Meeting of Shareholders." Johnson & Johnson. April 26, 2012. www.jnj.com/media-center/press-releases/johnson-johnson-holds-2012-annual-meeting-of-shareholders.

———. 2020. "Johnson & Johnson Announces a Lead Vaccine Candidate for COVID-19; Landmark New Partnership with U.S. Department of Health & Human Services; and Commitment to Supply One Billion Vaccines Worldwide for Emergency Pandemic Use." Johnson & Johnson. March 30, 2020. www.jnj.com/johnson-johnson-announces-a-lead-vaccine-candidate-for-covid-19-landmark-new-partnership-with-u-s-department-of-health-human-services-and-commitment-to-supply-one-billion-vaccines-worldwide-for-emergency-pandemic-use.

Judge, John. 2020. "Facility and Program Closures in Response to Covid-19." *Outdoors*, March 24, 2020.

Kadet, Anne. 2020. "'It Was Like the Twilight Zone': Few Return to Empty Manhattan Offices." *Wall Street Journal*, August 11, 2020.

www.wsj.com/articles/empty-manhattan-offices-coronavirus -reopen-workplace-lockdown-newyork-covid-economy-115971 57584?mod=hp_featst_pos5.

Kahneman, Daniel. 2011. *Thinking, Fast and Slow*. Farrar, Straus and Giroux.

Kang, Jaewon. 2019. "Kroger's Sales Rise After Digital Investments: Supermarket Chain Is Investing to Keep Up with Changes in Food Retail." *Wall Street Journal*, September 12, 2019. www.wsj.com /articles/krogers-sales-rise-after-digital-investments-11568295387.

Kanter, Rosabeth Moss. 2020. *Think Outside the Building: How Advanced Leaders Can Change the World One Smart Innovation at a Time.* PublicAffairs.

Kennedy, Liam. 2018. "Top 400 Asset Managers 2018: 10 Years of Asset Growth." *IPE Magazine*, June 2018. www.ipe.com/reports/special -reports/top-400-asset-managers/top-400-asset-managers-2018 -10-years-of-asset-growth/10025004.article.

Khurana, Rakesh, and James Weber. 2008. "Tyco International: Corporate Governance." Harvard Business School. November 2008. https://www.hbs.edu/faculty/Pages/item.aspx?num=35149.

Kilpatrick, Mary. 2019. "Tricia Griffith: Northeast Ohio's Influential Women." *Shatter*, May 14, 2019. www.cleveland.com/shatter/2019 /05/tricia-griffith-northeast-ohios-influential-women.html.

Klein, Jeffrey, and Michael Useem. 2019. "Leading an Upstart Victory: Fateful Decisions That Carried a Mid-Ranking American Football Team to a National Championship." *European Business Review* (September–October 2019). www.europeanbusinessreview.com/leading -an-upstart-victory-fateful-decisions-that-carried-a-mid-ranking -american-football-team-to-a-national-championship.

Klemko, Robert. 2018. "'Philly Special' Was Drawn Up by a Mad-Scientist Coach on a South Carolina Baseball Field in 2011." *Sports Illustrated*, February 21, 2018. www.si.com/nfl/2018/02/21/philly -special-eagles-trick-play-clemson-westlake-high-gray-military -academy-2011.

Kline, Alan. 2018. "Community Banker of the Year: WSFS Financial's Mark Turner." *American Banker*, November 27, 2018. www.american banker.com/news/community-banker-of-the-year-wsfs-financials -mark-turner.

———. 2019. "The Purpose-Driven Chief Executive." *American Banker* (May 2019).

Koehn, Nancy F. 2000. "Building a Powerful Prestige Brand: Estée Lauder and the Department Store Cosmetics Counter." Harvard

Business School Working Knowledge, October 30, 2000. https://
hbswk.hbs.edu/archive/building-a-powerful-prestige-brand-est
-eacute-e-lauder-and-the-department-store-cosmetics-counter.

Kogut, Bruce, and Udo Zander. 1992. "Knowledge of the Firm, Combi-
native Capabilities, and the Replication of Knowledge." *Organization Science* 3, no. 3: 383–397.

Kunreuther, Howard, and Michael Useem. 2018. *Mastering Catastrophic
Risk: How Companies Are Coping with Disruption.* Oxford University
Press.

Laird, Donald A., and Eleanor C. Laird. 1951. *Sizing Up People.*
McGraw-Hill.

Langley, Monica. 2015. "Behind Gini Rometty's Plan to Reboot IBM."
Wall Street Journal, April 20, 2015. www.wsj.com/articles/behind
-ginni-romettys-plan-to-reboot-ibm-1429577076.

Lawler, Edward E., III. 1992. *The Ultimate Advantage: Creating the
High-Involvement Organization.* Jossey Bass.

Library of Congress. n.d. "Washington Accepts His Appointment as
Commander of Continental Army, June 16, 1775." http://memory
.loc.gov/cgi-bin/query/r?ammem/hlaw:@field(DOCID+@
lit(jc00237)).

Lieber, Ron. 2020. "Big Lenders Slow to Promise Relief." *New York
Times*, March 18, 2020. www.nytimes.com/2020/03/17/your-money
/loan-waivers-coronavirus.html.

Lieberson, Stanley, and James F. O'Connor. 1972. "Leadership and Organizational Performance: A Study of Large Corporations." *American Sociological Review* 37, no. 2: 117–30.

Lublin, Joann S., and Bob Tita. 2011. "End of an Empire: Tyco Plans
Split." *Wall Street Journal*, September 20, 2011. www.wsj.com
/articles/SB10001424053111904106704576580251347533420.

Malmendier, Ulrike, Geoffrey Tate, and Jon Yan. 2011. "Overconfidence
and Early-Life Experiences: The Effect of Managerial Traits on
Corporate Financial Policies." *Journal of Finance* 66, no. 5:
1687–1733.

Mann, Ted. 2020. "Hit by Coronavirus, Amtrak Banks on Billion-Dollar
Bailout to Stay Afloat." *Wall Street Journal*, March 24, 2020. www
.wsj.com/articles/hit-by-coronavirus-amtrak-banks-on-billion
-dollar-bailout-to-stay-afloat-11584979346?mod=searchresults&
page=1&pos=1.

Marcec, Dan. 2018. "CEO Tenure Rates." Harvard Law School Forum
on Corporate Governance, February 12, 2018. https://corpgov.law
.harvard.edu/2018/02/12/ceo-tenure-rates.

Maremont, Mark, and Laurie P. Cohen. 2002. "Tyco Spent Millions for Benefit of Kozlowski, Its Former CEO." *Wall Street Journal*, August 7, 2002. www.wsj.com/articles/SB1028674808717845320.

Maremont, Mark, and Jerry Markon. 2002. "Tyco's Kozlowski Is Indicted on Charges of Tax Evasion." *Wall Street Journal*, June 5, 2002. www.wsj.com/articles/SB1023196847218251120.

Martin, Jonathan, and Alexander Burns. 2020. "In a Crisis, Governors Flexed Their Executive Muscles as the White House Balked." *New York Times*, March 18, 2020. www.nytimes.com/2020/03/17/us/politics/governors-coronavirus-trump.html.

McCain, John. 2013. "He Beat Us in War but Never in Battle." *Wall Street Journal*, October 6, 2013. www.wsj.com/articles/he-beat-us-in-war-but-never-in-battle-1381100852.

McCarthy, Ken. 2020. "Delaware Bank's Tech Overhaul Shifts into Higher Gear." *American Banker*, February 24, 2020. www.americanbanker.com/news/delaware-banks-tech-overhaul-shifts-into-higher-gear.

McChrystal, Stanley, with Tantum Collins, David Silverman, and Chris Fussell. 2015. *Team of Teams: New Rules of Engagement for a Complex World*. Portfolio.

McCullough, David. 2005. *1776*. Simon & Schuster.

McManus, Tim. 2018a. "Eagles Reunite to Receive 'Bling-ier' Super Bowl Rings." *ESPN*, June 14, 2018. www.espn.com/nfl/story/_/id/23797030/philadelphia-eagles-super-bowl-rings-219-diamonds-17-green-sapphires.

———. 2018b. "Eagles Surprise Executive Assistant Fired by Chip Kelly with Super Bowl Ring." *ESPN*, June 14, 2018. www.espn.com/nfl/story/_/id/23804871/philadelphia-eagles-surprise-former-team-secretary-super-bowl-ring.

McNabb, William. 2008a. Remarks, Vanguard Officers' Dinner. October 25, 2008.

———. 2008b. "What We've Learned Over 25 Years." Vanguard Vision Conference. December 4, 2008.

———. 2017. "Debrief from 2017 Jim Collins Offsite." Vanguard Group. April 2017.

Merced, Michael J. de la. 2015. "DuPont Shares Rise After Proxy Advisers Back Nelson Peltz." *New York Times*, April 27, 2015. https://www.nytimes.com/2015/04/28/business/dealbook/dupont-shares-rise-after-proxy-adviser-backs-nelson-peltz.html.

Mosher, Geoff. 2015. "How 'Culture Beats Scheme' Became Eagles' Motto." *NBC Sports*, July 29, 2015. www.nbcsports.com/philadelphia/philadelphia-eagles/how-culture-beats-scheme-became-eagles-motto.

Moss, Trefor, Sharon Terlep, and Jennifer Maloney. 2020. "U.S. Firms Get Another Boost from China." *Wall Street Journal*, November 6, 2020. https://www.wsj.com/articles/u-s-firms-get-another-boost -from-china-11604658601.

Mount, Ian. 2020. "Goldman Sachs Says Its Gloomy Prediction of 24% U.S. GDP Contraction in Q2 Wasn't Nearly Grim Enough." *Fortune*, March 31, 2020. www.msn.com/en-us/money/markets /goldman-sachs-says-its-gloomy-prediction-of-24percent-us-gdp -contraction-in-q2-wasnt-nearly-grim-enough/ar-BB16LvNK.

Munich Re Geo Research. 2015. Loss Events Worldwide 1980–2014.

———. 2020. "Natural Disasters of 2019 in Figures." September 1, 2020. www.munichre.com/topics-online/en/climate-change-and -natural-disasters/natural-disasters/natural-disasters-of-2019-in -figures-tropical-cyclones-cause-highest-losses.html.

Nadler, David A., and Michael L. Tushman. 1996. *Competing by Design: The Power of Organizational Design*. Oxford University Press.

Nassauer, Sarah. 2020. "Walmart's Coronavirus Challenge Is Just Staying Open." *Wall Street Journal*, April 18, 2020. www.wsj.com/articles /walmarts-coronavirus-challenge-is-just-staying-open-11587221657.

NBC News. 2012. "10 CEOs Who Went from the Boardroom to the Cell Block." May 21, 2012. www.nbcnews.com/business/markets /10-ceos-who-went-boardroom-cell-block-flna783944.

———. 2020. "Biden Says Trump Administration Outreach Has Been 'Sincere' as Transition Begins." November 24, 2020. www.nbcnews .com/politics/2020-election/biden-says-outreach-trump-admin -has-been-sincere-transition-begins-n1248873.

Neff, Thomas J., and James M. Citrin. 2007. *You're in Charge, Now What?* Currency.

Netflix, Inc. 2009. "Netflix Culture: Freedom and Responsibility." Slide-Share, August 1, 2009. www.slideshare.net/reed2001/culture-179 8664.

———. 2017. "Netflix Culture." https://jobs.netflix.com/culture.

New York Times. 2020. "Models Predicting Expected Spread of the Virus in the U.S. Paint a Grim Picture." March 31, 2020. www.nytimes .com/2020/03/31/world/coronavirus-news.html?action=click &module=Spotlight&pgtype=Homepage.

O'Connell, Robert. 2019. *Revolutionary: George Washington at War*. Penguin Random House.

O'Reilly, Charles. (1989) 2001. "Corporations, Culture, and Commitment: Motivation and Social Control in Organizations." *California Management Review* 31, no. 4: 9–25.

Osborne, Peter. 2019. "Parting Thoughts: Mark Turner Looks Back on Long Career." *Delaware Business Times*, January 31, 2019. https://delawarebusinesstimes.com/mark-turner-looks-back-at-long-career.

Ott, Tim. 2020. "How George Washington's Personal and Physical Characteristics Helped Him Win the Presidency." *Biography Newsletter*, February 7, 2020. www.biography.com/news/george-washington-character-presidency.

Parker, Kim, Anthony Cilluffo, and Renee Stepler. 2017. "6 Facts About the U.S. Military and Its Changing Demographics." Pew Research Center, April 13, 2017. www.pewresearch.org/fact-tank/2017/04/13/6-facts-about-the-u-s-military-and-its-changing-demographics.

Pederson, Doug. 2018. *Fearless: How an Underdog Becomes a Champion.* Hachette Books.

Perry, Mark J. 2017. "Fortune 500 Firms 1955 v. 2017: Only 60 Remain, Thanks to the Creative Destruction that Fuels Economic Prosperity." American Enterprise Institute, October 20, 2017. www.aei.org/carpe-diem/fortune-500-firms-1955-v-2017-only-12-remain-thanks-to-the-creative-destruction-that-fuels-economic-prosperity.

Pfanz, Donald C. 1998. *Richard S. Ewell: A Soldier's Life.* University of North Carolina Press.

Pfeffer, Jeffrey. 1998. *The Human Equation: Building Profits by Putting People First.* Harvard Business Review Press.

Pillmore, Eric M. 2003. "How We're Fixing Up Tyco." *Harvard Business Review* (December 2003). https://hbr.org/2003/12/how-were-fixing-up-tyco.

Plott, Elaina, and Jennifer Medina. 2020. "The People Leading When Leaders Do Not." *New York Times*, March 25, 2020. www.nytimes.com/2020/03/25/us/politics/coronavirus-tennessee-arizona-oklahoma.html.

Prewitt, Alex. 2018. "The Eagles' Brotherhood of Blockers." *Sports Illustrated*, July 18, 2018. www.si.com/nfl/2018/07/18/philadelphia-eagles-offensive-line.

Progressive Corporation. 2020. Apron Relief Program.

Rabin, Roni Caryn. 2020. "Women with Cancer Awarded Billions in Baby Powder Suit." *New York Times*, June 23, 2020. www.nytimes.com/2020/06/23/health/baby-powder-cancer.html.

Rabin, Roni Caryn, and Tiffany Hsu. 2018. "Asbestos Opens New Legal Front in Battle Over Johnson's Baby Powder." *New York Times*, December 14, 2018. www.nytimes.com/2018/12/14/business/baby-powder-asbestos-johnson-johnson.html.

Randazzo, Sara. 2019. "Bayer, Johnson & Johnson to Pay $775 Million to Settle Xarelto Litigation." *Wall Street Journal*, March 25, 2019. www .wsj.com/articles/bayer-johnson-johnson-to-pay-775-million -to-settle-xarelto-litigation-11553526678.

Rekenthaler, John. 2019. "Vanguard Won the Loser's Game." *Morningstar*, November 12, 2019. www.morningstar.com/articles/954274 /vanguard-won-the-losers-game.

Rockoff, Jonathan D., and Joann S. Lublin. 2012. "J&J Weldon Is Out." *Wall Street Journal*, February 22, 2012. www.wsj.com/articles/SB100 01424052970204909104577237642041667180.

Rodin, Judith. 2014. *The Resilience Dividend: Being Strong in a World Where Things Go Wrong*. PublicAffairs Press.

Rowland, Christopher, Carolyn Y. Johnson, and William Wan. 2020. "Even Finding a Covid-19 Vaccine Won't Be Enough to End the Pandemic." *Washington Post*, May 11, 2020. www.washingtonpost .com/business/2020/05/11/coronavirus-vaccine-global-supply.

Rubenstein, David M. 2020. *How to Lead: Wisdom from the World's Greatest CEOs, Founders, and Game Changers*. Simon & Schuster.

Sampson, Anthony. 1973. *The Sovereign State of ITT*. Stein and Day.

Schmidt, Eric, Jonathan Rosenberg, and Alan Eagle. 2019. *Trillion Dollar Coach: The Leadership Playbook of Silicon Valley's Bill Campbell*. Harper Business.

Schwartzel, Erich. 2020. "Disney Takes $1.4 Billion Hit to Earnings as Coronavirus Takes Hold." *Wall Street Journal*, May 6, 2020. www .wsj.com/articles/disneys-income-falls-as-coronavirus-takes -hold-11588710935.

Sears, Stephen W. 2014. *George B. McClellan: The Young Napoleon*. Houghton Mifflin Harcourt.

Segal, Julie. 2018. "Life After Vanguard." *Institutional Investor*, September 21, 2018. www.institutionalinvestor.com/article/b1b1nc7t5xtbk8 /Life-After-Vanguard.

Shpigel, Ben. 2017. "With Carson Wentz out for the Season, Eagles' Dreams Turn to Dread." *New York Times*, December 11, 2017. www .nytimes.com/2017/12/11/sports/carson-wentz-philadelphia-eagles .html.

Singh, Harbir, and Michael Useem. 2016. *The Strategic Leader's Roadmap: 6 Steps for Integrating Leadership and Strategy*. Wharton School Press.

Sjöberg, Annika. 2018. "The Untold Story Behind One of Europe's Largest Exits 2017—Heptagon." NGP Capital. February 21, 2018. www .ngpcap.com/news/the-untold-story-behind-one-of-europes -largest-exits-2017-heptagon.

Smith, Ben. 2020. "Bob Iger Thought He Was Leaving on Top. Now, He's Fighting for Disney's Life." *New York Times*, April 12, 2020. www.nytimes.com/2020/04/12/business/media/disney-ceo-corona virus.html.

Sorenson, Arne. 2020. "Honoring George Floyd with Real Change." LinkedIn. May 31, 2020. www.linkedin.com/pulse/honoring-george -floyd-real-change-arne-sorenson/?trackingId=FFBPtMI%2BRL mY7lm1j3mBNA%3D%3D.

Sørensen, Jesper B. 2002. "The Strength of Corporate Culture and the Reliability of Firm Performance." *Administrative Science Quarterly* 47, no. 1 (March): 70–91.

Speights, Keith. 2019. "Should Investors Worry About Johnson & Johnson's Eroding Moat?" *The Motley Fool*, November 27, 2019. www .fool.com/investing/2019/11/27/should-investors-worry-about -johnson-johnsons-erod.aspx.

Spencer Stuart. 2018. *2018 United States Spencer Stuart Board Index*. www .spencerstuart.com/-/media/2018/october/ssbi_2018.pdf.

Standard and Poor's. 2013. *Evaluating Insurers' Enterprise Risk Management Practice.* https://www.casact.org/education/infocus/2013 /handouts/Paper_2667_handout_1348_0.pdf.

Stangler, Dane, and Sam Arbesman. 2012. "What Does Fortune 500 Turnover Mean?" Kauffman Foundations. June 2012. www .kauffman.org/-/media/kauffman_org/research-reports-and-covers /2012/06/fortune_500_turnover.pdf.

Statista, Statistics and Studies. 2019. "Net Sales of Estée Lauder Worldwide from 2010 to 2020, by Region." twww.statista.com/statistics /267950/net-sales-of-Estée-lauder-worldwide-by-region.

Symonds, William C. 2001. "The Most Aggressive CEO: Many Executives Have Never Heard of Tyco's Dennis Kozlowski Until He's Acquired Their Companies." *Business Week*, May 28, 2001. www .bloomberg.com/news/articles/2001-05-27/the-most-aggressive -ceo.

Thomas, Alan Berkeley. 1988. "Does Leadership Make a Difference to Organizational Performance?" *Administrative Science Quarterly* 33, no. 3: 388–400.

Tichy, Noel. 1997. *The Leadership Engine: How Winning Companies Build Leaders at Every Level*. HarperBusiness.

Tocqueville, Alexis de. (1836) 2000. *Democracy in America*. Translated by Henry Reeve. Reprint. Bantam Classics.

Tourtellot, Arthur Bernon. 2000. *Lexington and Concord: The Beginning of the War of the American Revolution*. W. W. Norton.

Trian Partners. 2015. "DuPont: A Referendum on Performance and Accountability."

Tully, Shawn. 2013. "An Outsider in the Family Castle." *Fortune*, October 31, 2013. http://fortune.com/2013/10/31/an-outsider-in-the-family-castle.

Uber. 2020. "A Company That Moves People Is Asking You Not to Move." April 2020.

US Army Center of Military History. 2014. "Washington Takes Command of Continental Army in 1775." June 5, 2014. US Army. www.army.mil/article/40819/washington_takes_command_of_continental_army_in_1775.

US Department of Defense, Office of the Deputy Assistant Secretary of Defense for Military Community and Family Policy. 2015. *2015 Demographics, Profile of the Military Community.* https://download.militaryonesource.mil/12038/MOS/Reports/2015-Demographics-Report.pdf.

Useem, Michael. 1984. *The Inner Circle.* Oxford University Press.

———— 1996. *Investor Capitalism: How Money Managers Are Changing the Face of Corporate America.* New Basic Books/HarperCollins.

————. 1998a. *The Leadership Moment: Nine True Stories of Triumph and Disaster and Their Lessons for Us All.* Times Books/Random House.

————. 1998b. "Corporate Leadership in a Globalizing Equity Market." *Academy of Management Executive*, special issue on "Global Competition and Leadership in the 21st Century," 12, no. 4: 43–59.

————. 2001. "The Leadership Lessons of Mount Everest." *Harvard Business Review* (October 2001). hbr.org/2001/10/the-leadership-lessons-of-mount-everest.

————. 2002. *Leading Up: How to Lead Your Boss So You Both Win.* Crown Business/Random House.

————. 2006. "How Well-Run Boards Make Decisions." *Harvard Business Review* (November 2006). https://hbr.org/2006/11/how-well-run-boards-make-decisions.

————. 2011. *The Leader's Checklist.* Wharton School Press.

————. 2012. "IBM's Sam Palmisano: 'Always Put the Enterprise Ahead of the Individual.' *Knowledge@Wharton*, January 18, 2012. https://knowledge.wharton.upenn.edu/article/ibms-sam-palmisano-always-put-the-enterprise-ahead-of-the-individual.

————. 2015. "Learning to Lead from the Inside." In *Decision Making in the Leadership Chair.* Edited by William Lauder. Disruption Books and Estée Lauder Companies.

————. 2020. "It's Your Leadership Moment." *Knowledge@Wharton*, March 30, 2020. https://knowledge.wharton.upenn.edu/article/its-your-leadership-moment.

Useem, Michael, Mark Davidson, and Evan Wittenberg. 2005. "Leadership Development Beyond the Classroom: The Value of Leadership Ventures to Instruct Leadership Decision Making." *International Journal of Leadership Education* 1: 159–178.

Useem, Michael, and Andrew Eavis. 2018. "The Thai Cave Rescue: What Are the Leadership Lessons?" *Knowledge@Wharton*, July 16, 2018. https://knowledge.wharton.upenn.edu/article/leadership-lessons -thai-soccer-team-rescue.

Useem, Michael, Rodrigo Jordán, and Matko Koljatic. 2011. "How to Lead During a Crisis: Lessons from the Rescue of the Chilean Miners." *MIT Sloan Management Review* 53: 1–7.

Useem, Michael, Harbir Singh, Neng Liang, and Peter Cappelli. 2017. *Fortune Makers: The Leaders Creating China's Great Global Companies.* PublicAffairs.

Useem, Michael, and Andrea Useem. 2014. "Exceptional Frontline Performance: Learning from the Medal of Honor Tradition." *Organizational Dynamics* 43, no. 1: 37–43.

Vanian, Jonathan. 2020. "IBM CEO Ginny Rometty to Step Down." *Fortune*, January 30, 2020. https://fortune.com/2020/01/30/ibm-ceo -ginni-rometty-to-retire.

Wachtell, Lipton, Rosen & Katz. 2018. "Federal Reserve Takes Severe and Unprecedented Action Against Wells Fargo: Implications for Directors of All Public Companies." Harvard Law School Forum on Corporate Governance. February 4, 2018. corpgov.law.harvard.edu /2018/02/05/federal-reserve-takes-severe-and-unprecedented -action-against-wells-fargo-implication-for-directors-of-all -public-companies.

Waldman, D. A., G. G. Ramirez, R. J. House, and P. Puranan. 2001. "Does Leadership Matter? CEO Leadership Attributes and Profitability Under Conditions of Perceived Environmental Uncertainty." *Academy of Management Journal* 44, no. 1: 34–43.

Walker, Joseph, Peter Loftus, and Jared S. Hopkins. 2020. "Scientists Rush to Find Coronavirus Cure—but It Still Isn't Fast Enough." *Wall Street Journal*, April 6, 2020. www.wsj.com/articles/inside -the-race-to-find-a-coronavirus-cure-11586189463?mod=search results&page=1&pos=7.

Wallmine. 2020. "Edward Breen Net Worth." Last modified August 5, 2019. https://wallmine.com/people/6309/edward-d-breen.

Wall Street Journal. 2020. "The Month that Changed Everything." April 4–5, 2020.

Washington, George. n.d. George Washington Papers. US Library of Congress. https://www.loc.gov/rr/program/bib/presidents/washington /memory.html.

————. 1781. "From George Washington to Marie-Joseph-Paul-Yves-Roch-Gilbert du Motier, Marquis de Lafayette, 4 June 1781." US National Archives. https://founders.archives.gov/documents/Washington/99-01-02-05956.

Weigley, Russell F. 1977. *The American Way of War: A History of United States Military Strategy and Policy.* Indiana University Press.

Weiland, Noah, and David E. Sanger. 2020. "Trump Administration Selects Five Coronavirus Vaccine Candidates as Finalists." *New York Times*, June 9, 2020. www.nytimes.com/2020/06/03/us/politics/coronavirus-vaccine-trump-moderna.html?searchResultPosition=1.

Welch, Jack, with John A. Byrne. 2003. *Jack: Straight from the Gut.* Grand Central Publishing.

Wells Fargo & Company. 2018. "Proxy Statement, Annual Meeting of Shareholders." https://www08.wellsfargomedia.com/assets/pdf/about/investor-relations/annual-reports/2018-proxy-statement.pdf.

Wharton School, University of Pennsylvania. 2017. "Leadership Conference 2017: Leading in an Era of Rising Uncertainty and Greater Complexity." https://event.wharton.upenn.edu/wp-content/uploads/2018/07/Leadership-Conference-Summary-with-Pictures.pdf.

————. 2020. "Leadership Ventures." https://leadership.wharton.upenn.edu/leadership-ventures-2.

Williams, Ron. 2019. "Why Most Leadership Skills Are Learned." *Knowledge@Wharton*, September 11, 2019. https://knowledge.wharton.upenn.edu/article/most-leadership-skills-are-learned-start-with-lead-yourself.

Winoker, Steve. 2019. "One Year in with GE CEO Larry Culp." GE Reports. October 1, 2019. www.ge.com/reports/1-year-in-with-ge-ceo-larry-culp.

Wong, Grace. 2007. "Tyco: Wait for the Breakup." *CNNMoney*, May 4, 2007. https://money.cnn.com/2007/05/03/markets/spotlight_tyco.

Wood, Gordon S. 2002. *The American Revolution: A History.* Random House.

World Health Organization. 2020. "WHO Coronavirus Disease (COVID-19) Dashboard." Last modified December 12–13, 2020. https://covid19.who.int.

Worldometer. 2020. "Covid-19 Coronavirus Pandemic." Last modified December 14, 2020. www.worldometers.info/coronavirus.

Xie, Stella Yifan, and David Lim. 2019. "Vanguard Taps into Small Investors in China." *Wall Street Journal*, December 28–29, 2019.

Zemmel, Rodney, Matt Cuddihy, and Dennis Carey. 2018. "How Successful CEOs Manage Their Middle Act." *Harvard Business Review*

96 (May–June): 98–105. https://hbr.org/2018/05/how-successful-ceos-manage-their-middle-act.

Zemsky, Robert, Susan Shaman, and Susan Campbell Baldridge. 2020. *The College Stress Test: Tracking Institutional Futures Across a Crowded Market.* Johns Hopkins University Press.

Zieminski, Nick. 2012. "Tyco's Latest Breakup Could Feed Shareholder Activism." Reuters, September 17, 2012. https://uk.reuters.com/article/uk-tyco-breakup/analysis-tycos-latest-breakup-could-feed-shareholder-activism-idUKBRE88G13X20120917.

Zuckerman, Ezra. 2000. "Focusing the Corporate Product: Securities Analysts and De-diversification." *Administrative Science Quarterly* 45, no. 3: 519–619.

INDEX

Michael Useem is the William and Jacalyn Egan Professor of Management and faculty director of the Leadership Center and the McNulty Leadership Program at the Wharton School of the University of Pennsylvania. He offers courses and programs on governance, leadership, and management for MBA and executive MBA students, and midcareer and senior managers in the private, public, and nonprofit sectors in Brazil, China, India, Japan, the US, and elsewhere. He has authored or co-authored articles and books on business and public leadership in a variety of organizations and countries.

His earlier works include *The Leader's Checklist*, *The Leadership Moment*, *Executive Defense*, *Investor Capitalism*, and *Leading Up*. He co-edited *Learning from Catastrophes* and co-authored *The India Way*; *Leadership Dispatches: Chile's Extraordinary Comeback from Disaster*; *Boards That Lead*; *The Strategic Leader's Roadmap*; *Go Long: Why Long-Term Thinking Is Your Best Short-Term Strategy*; *Fortune Makers: The Leaders Creating China's Great Global Companies*; and *Mastering Catastrophic Risk: How Companies Are Coping with Disruption*. He is also a co-anchor for a weekly program *Leadership in Action* on SiriusXM Radio Channel 132, Wharton Business Radio, and he can be reached at useem@wharton.upenn.edu.